Al Pacino

Second Edition

ALSO BY WILLIAM SCHOELL
AND FROM MCFARLAND

Creature Features: Nature Turned Nasty in the Movies (2008, softcover 2014)

The Horror Comics: Fiends, Freaks and Fantastic Creatures, 1940s–1980s (2014)

The Opera of the Twentieth Century: A Passionate Art in Transition (2006)

Al Pacino

In Films and on Stage

Second Edition

William Schoell

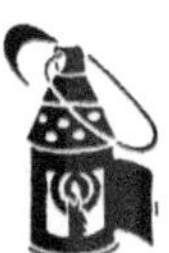

McFarland & Company, Inc., Publishers
Jefferson, North Carolina

Library of Congress Cataloguing-in-Publication Data

Names: Schoell, William author.
Title: Al Pacino : in films and on stage / William Schoell.
Description: Second edition. | Jefferson, North Carolina :
McFarland & Company, Inc., Publishers, 2016. |
Includes bibliographical references and index.
Identifiers: LCCN 2016010989 | ISBN 9780786471966
(softcover : alk. paper) ♾
Subjects: LCSH: Pacino, Al, 1940– —Criticism
and interpretation.
Classification: LCC PN2287.P18 S34 2016 |
DDC 791.4302/8092 [B]—dc23
LC record available at https://lccn.loc.gov/2016010989

British Library cataloguing data are available

ISBN (print) 978-0-7864-7196-6
ISBN (ebook) 978-1-4766-2285-9

Front cover: Al Pacino in the 1983 film *Scarface*
(Universal Pictures/Photofest)

Printed in the United States of America

McFarland & Company, Inc., Publishers
Box 611, Jefferson, North Carolina 28640
www.mcfarlandpub.com

In loving memory of my partner,
Lawrence J. Quirk (1923–2014),
who was a big Al Pacino fan.

Table of Contents

Acknowledgments

The author tenders his appreciation to: the late Lawrence J. Quirk, Gene Massimo, John Cocchi, Billy Otis, Caroline Schoell, the staff of the Billy Rose Theatre Collection at Lincoln Center, Frank Lavena, and Margaret Wolf. And to: Dunne-Didion-Dunne Productions, 20th Century–Fox, Paramount, Warner Bros., Dino De Laurentiis Productions, Columbia Pictures, Lorimar, Universal, Goldcrest Pictures, Viking Pictures, Touchstone, Silver Screen Partners IV, New Line Cinema, City Light Films, Epic Productions, Showtime, Albert S. Ruddy Productions, Francis Ford Coppola Productions, NBC-TV, Artists Entertainment Complex, Inc., United Artists, Jerry Weintraub Productions, Martin Bregman Productions, USA Network, Buena Vista Productions, Fox Searchlight, and Tristar.

All of the stills in this book are from private collections and are reproduced strictly for historical purposes.

Preface

This is an updated and greatly expanded version of my book *The Films of Al Pacino*, published in 1995. As with the original version, this book is not a biography, although it does have a biographical section. Instead, this is a study of Al Pacino's career, with essays on each of his movies and his performances, and a section on his appearances in plays both on and off Broadway.

I chose to write this book on Al Pacino not just because I admired his work, but because he is unique for a movie star. First of all, Pacino has an abundance of talent, which is not always true of many actors whose names light up a marquee and who seem to simply exude personality and little else. Second, unlike many other film actors whose careers began upon the stage, Pacino returns to his roots time and again. There are very few movie stars who not only do theater on a regular basis but have dared to tackle roles by the likes of Shakespeare and Oscar Wilde. Pacino is also unique in that he is a documentarian, making non-fiction films focusing on those two aforementioned great writers (as well as two stage adaptations in which he also appeared); indeed, Pacino has a love affair with Shakespeare just as he does with opera. Unlike most movie stars, Pacino is a cultured man who is knowledgeable and appreciative of arts other than film.

Most importantly, Pacino is not afraid to be passionate on stage or on camera. This is sometimes a risky proposition, as there are those among the critical establishment who prefer their actors to be cool and unemotional—the less charitable might say wooden or stiff—more along the lines of, say, Robert Redford. Pacino has been described more than once as being "over the top" or lacking subtlety, but one must argue that it is these very intense and dramatic qualities that make Pacino so riveting and have garnered him millions of fans. In truth, Pacino's decision to eschew subtlety in many of his portrayals is the absolutely correct choice.

There have been too many actors who have been so afraid to be emotional—they seem to find it "unmanly"—that their portrayals seem perfunctory and half-formed. Pacino has no such fears, and his work is all the better, all the more dynamic because of it—Pacino does not hold back. Here is an actor who can be grandiose and larger than life one moment, and touching and persuasively gentle in the next. In other words, Pacino can "rein himself in" when required, but, thankfully, in most cases it isn't required. Pacino has appeared in dull movies, but he has never given a dull performance. There are people who are embarrassed by the expression of emotion—be it in music, in real life, or in performances—and these people will never be counted among Al Pacino's fans, more's the pity.

When all is said and done, Al Pacino is an Artist, and this book examines that artist in all of his facets. There is his basic life story; a section on his many romantic relationships over the years; and a reevaluation of his career and talent as seen through the eyes of certain critics. As Pacino aged, there were attacks made upon him, suggestions that he "phoned it in" or made very bad picture choices, or was only in it for the money. On occasion, these attacks were warranted, although not their nasty tone. Often this nastiness could be attributed to plain and simple age discrimination. Younger (and not so young) critics couldn't deal with a man in his seventies who was still a movie star. And who says that an actor—especially a serious actor who never gave up the stage—hasn't got the right to occasionally pick a movie for a hefty paycheck and hope that it will at least turn out to be fun for himself and the audience?

It's worth repeating. Whatever his flaws, whatever the problems with his choices, Al Pacino is an artist—an artist who has every right to try different things, new approaches, as he explores his career and his life to its fullest potential.

* * *

A note about the film credits: I list major cast members only, and whichever executive producer or producer is the most important to each project, along with the screenwriter, cinematographer, composer, and editor. Others, such as the production designer and art director, are listed only if their work on the picture is especially noteworthy or elaborate.

A warning: the synopses of the films sometimes contain spoilers.

Part One

Pacino's Life

Al Pacino may have "gone Hollywood," but he's a New York actor in every sense of the expression. First, he was born in New York City. Second, he got his early training in small theater companies in Manhattan and continues to tread the boards of both Broadway and Off Broadway theaters to this day. Third, fully half of his motion pictures take place almost entirely in New York City, and several others contain key sequences or large sections that take place in the area. Finally, there's something about the man—on the screen and off—that *screams* New York. You can see it in his performances (except when he's playing Cubans, maybe). Pacino has confessed that he loves the city; in many ways he *is* New York. He even played the mayor in *City Hall.*

Pacino's early life was not exactly a New York success story, however. He was born Alfredo James Pacino on April 25, 1940, in East Harlem, to Rose and Salvatore Pacino. When Alfred was two, his father walked out on his mother, leaving Rose to fend for both herself and a young boy. Since she was unable to look after Al while she was working, she thought it would be best if he lived with her parents, James and Kate Gerard. Rose eventually moved in with them herself, only adding to the overcrowding in the Bronx tenement. Pacino spent his formative years living in cramped poverty.

Pacino's mother and grandparents were overprotective, so that the boy was rarely allowed outside until it was time for him to start school. For a time he found himself unable to cope and was victimized by both male and female bullies. He later learned to disarm them by telling them elaborate, made-up stories or enacting scenes from the many motion pictures his mother had taken him to see. He also delighted in acting out scenes for members of his family, who were charmed but who had no idea where this talent would lead.

Becoming a class cutup did much for his popularity at school but little for his grades. The only activity he excelled at was performing in the student plays. By the time he was in the eighth grade he was showing such promise that his drama teacher made note of it in a letter to his mother. Rose saw this as a way for her "Sonny" to be somebody, and she echoed the teacher's suggestion that Al apply for admission to Manhattan's famous High School of Performing Arts.

Al's bid was successful, and he stayed at the school for two years. But several factors led to his becoming a dropout at age sixteen. To him, the whole Stanislavsky Method taught in the acting classes took all the fun out of acting, and he was failing in virtually every other subject. It was also a question of necessity. "My grandfather had retired, we had no money, and I was the sole support of my mother, who became ill," he told *New York Daily News* writer Glenn Plaskin. "She was a very high-strung and sensitive woman, an emotional person.... That's where I think I get some of my emotions."

His mother's "emotions" eventually drove him to move to his own apartment; she had initially encouraged Sonny in his acting aspirations, but now she didn't think people from his lowly background could ever make it in show business. Hoping to prove her wrong, Al got a series of jobs to pay his rent (he would also send money home to his mother) and saved up for acting classes. He ushered at the Paris movie theater, delivered mail to the editorial staff of *Commentary*, and fixed leaky faucets as an apartment-house super.

At nineteen, Pacino moved to Greenwich Village, and it was there that his life as an artist truly began. A bright spot was his taking classes at the Herbert Berghof Studio, where he met twenty-nine-year-old acting coach Charlie Laughton and Laughton's actress-wife, Penny Allen, becoming close friends with both. Laughton was not only Pacino's coach but his confidant and older brother. The couple even fed Pacino on occasion, in addition to giving him tips on part-time jobs and acting auditions.

The next few years were creatively interesting but extremely difficult for Pacino. A big blow came when Al was twenty-two and his mother passed away unexpectedly. To this day he has trouble talking about it, some say because he was so immersed in his own problems at the time of her illness that he couldn't worry or even think about what she was going through. And, of course, there's the pain of knowing that his mother never lived to see what a success he would become. To make things worse, his grandfather died of cancer a year later.

"For me, losing them was devastating ... a disaster that floored me," he said years later.[1] "It was hard for me.... I always remember ... and I miss, I miss my mother. They were the closest people to me, and I was not functioning very well. Later, I did therapy, but it was my friends in the theater that saved me." On the professional front, Pacino tried to become a comedian, understudied for onetime roommate Martin Sheen in a "back alley" production, and worked as a stagehand for Julian Beck's Living Theater. On the personal front, he sank deeper and deeper into depression not only because of the deaths of mother and grandfather but because of what little headway he was making as an actor.

He had to cadge money from friends, sneak meals where he could, find a bed to sleep in. Temporary jobs, such as moving furniture and passing out fliers on street corners, could only provide so much. Things got so bad emotionally that he was counseled by one person to have himself committed![2]

Instead, he hung in there, eventually joining up with Joe Cino's Caffe Cino on Cornelia Street, which was also a hangout for such theatrical types as playwrights Sam Shepard, Lanford Wilson, and Robert Heide. Says Heide,[3] "Pacino would do Shakespearean monologues. Joe Cino fed him—provolone and cappuccino." Cino, who later committed suicide, was a figurative godfather to many starving actors and writers. Cino did more than feed Pacino; he put on a production of William Saroyan's *Hello, Out There,* which was an outgrowth of one of Pacino's acting classes with Charlie Laughton. This led to other Off Broadway roles, an Obie nomination, and admission to the prestigious Actors Studio, run by famed acting coach Lee Strasberg.

Pacino was initially intimidated by the high-powered atmosphere at the Studio. "He was always in the shadows, sitting by himself," says Robert Heide,[4] "with this kind of surly attitude." Later, Pacino became friends with—and won the respect of—Strasberg. Like Laughton and Allen, Strasberg gave Pacino lots of encouragement, along with the occasional handout. Pacino never forgot his early roots or the small kindnesses. Says Billy Otis, an actor who studied with Pacino and Laughton, "Al is a very loyal friend; his relationship with Charlie Laughton proves that."[5] Pacino paid tribute to Laughton when he won his Oscar for *Scent of a Woman.* And he remains "very supportive of small theater," says Otis. Pacino doesn't forget the people who've helped him.

In the late '60s things started coming together for Pacino. First, he won an Obie for Best Actor in the 1967–68 production of *The Indian Wants the Bronx* by Israel Horovitz. Then he debuted on Broadway in Don Petersen's *Does a Tiger Wear a Necktie?* and won a Tony for Best Supporting Actor. His film debut came in 1969, when he had a bit—but a memorable one—in the Patty Duke starrer *Me, Natalie.* From the very first he exuded potent authority and charisma.

At the age of twenty-nine Pacino stood five feet seven inches tall and weighed approximately 165 pounds, a figure that might fluctuate now and then but which remained pretty constant over the years. Pacino kept himself in good shape. Some people thought that his comparative shortness might prevent him from making it to the top, but they couldn't have been more wrong. Another person who had faith in him was Martin Bregman, an entertainment manager who signed him after seeing him in *The Indian Wants the Bronx.*

Bregman's clients included Faye Dunaway and her boyfriend Jerry Schatzberg, who was about to direct his second picture, *The Panic in Needle*

Park (1971). Through these connections, Pacino found himself in the lead, with Kitty Winn as his costar. The film was a very graphic, frank study of degenerating heroin addicts, and both actors threw themselves into their research. Preparing for their roles, they could often be found talking to addicts and dealers who hung out in "Needle Park" on Manhattan's West Seventy-second Street. Pacino already had firsthand knowledge of the negative, indeed disastrous, effects of drug addiction: two of his friends had overdosed and died. On another occasion he almost tripped over the body of a young actor he knew who had "OD'd" in an alleyway.

Pacino's performance in *The Panic in Needle Park* did not make him a star, but it did get him some serious attention from filmmakers. It also was the first time he unleashed his trademark "Pacino blast." An intense, moody, passionate actor—and person—to begin with, Pacino always pulls out all the stops in scenes when the character he's playing is supposed to get *mad*. Like a thespian equivalent of a fire-breathing dragon, Pacino uses voice, limbs, every part of him, to create a savage portrait of someone who is temporarily *out of control*, unstoppable, brutally larger than life, maniacally physical. This may or may not be "showy" acting, but it is *not* "overacting." Pacino's blasts always fit the character and the moment, and he uses them sparingly. Most (but not all) of his pictures have one, which Pacino's fans really look forward to.

Pacino got right into the big leagues with his next picture, *The Godfather* (1972), at thirty-two years of age. He received only $35,000 for several months of work and nearly didn't get the part; the studio was more interested in casting Warren Beatty, Robert Redford, Jack Nicholson, or even Frank Langella as Michael Corleone. Pacino didn't help matters by coming unprepared to his audition, doing ill-advised ad-libs, and moaning that he'd rather play the more violent, temperamental Sonny (James Caan). His behavior led initial booster Mario Puzo (who wrote the novel and co-wrote the screenplay) to turn against him, with only director Francis Ford Coppola still in his corner. There were more auditions, more delays. Pacino wondered if a big-time Hollywood adaptation of a best-selling novel was the right project for a "serious" actor, but he *wanted* the part. When he was finally offered the role for real, M-G-M promptly sued him because of a verbal agreement to appear in *The Gang That Couldn't Shoot Straight*. Bregman engineered a settlement.

Pacino was delighted to be working with his idol, Marlon Brando; old theatrical pal and former costar John Cazale (who was cast as Fredo Corleone); and Diane Keaton, with whom he entered into a long-term relationship, but otherwise he felt much like an outsider on *The Godfather* set. Although Pacino was really the main character and true star of the film, Brando received a Best Actor Oscar nomination and Pacino only a Best Supporting Actor nomination. Matters weren't helped when Bregman, his manager, issued the statement that "people may have come to see Brando, but they'll go away talking about Pacino." The statement was wrongly attributed to an "immodest" Pacino by the press, inciting Brando's ire: "I should have crushed the prick like a fly!" the "godfather" ranted, in character no doubt.[6]

Despite his newfound fame, Pacino had no intention of forsaking the stage; he appeared in David Rabe's *Basic Training of Pavlo Hummel* as well as a risky production of Shakespeare's *Richard III*. His film career continued with *Scarecrow* (1973), helmed by *Panic in Needle Park*'s Jerry Schatzberg. Good friend Penny Allen was given a small part, and Gene Hackman was signed as costar. Hackman and Pacino had absolutely no rapport, and there were numerous off-screen altercations. The two would never work with each other again, not enemies but hardly friends.

Pacino's first big *solo* starring part was in *Serpico* (1973), playing a real-life cop who exposed corruption in the department and nearly paid for it with his life. Al and Frank Serpico, who had certain interests, such as opera, in common, got along famously, but such was not the case with producer Dino De Laurentiis and the film's original director John G. Avildsen. The two had such operatic quarrels that they nearly tore the wallpaper off the boardroom in De Laurentiis's offices.[7] Sidney Lumet was brought in as Avildsen's replacement, with felicitous results. Pacino's performance garnered a Best Actor nomination from the Academy, as did his next two pictures; alas, he was a three-time "loser." The consolation prize? *Serpico* turned Pacino into a major star. *The Godfather Part II* (1974) and *Dog Day Afternoon* (1975) only entrenched him further in the firmament.

Proof of his stardom was his fee for *The Godfather Part II*: $600,000, almost *twenty* times as much as he received for appearing in *The Godfather*. (He also got 10 percent of the sequel's profits.) Furthermore, he had enough clout to get friend and teacher Lee Strasberg his *very first* role in a motion picture, and for a better price than first offered. Lastly, he had developed that certain movie star "attitude."

Robert Heide, who had rented a 1954 Packard he co-owned with John Gilman to the producers of *The Godfather Part II*, attended a boat party hosted by an Actors Studio associate around the time of the filming. According to Heide, who was also there, Pacino "had an attitude. He wanted to be treated like a regular guy; on the other hand, if you didn't treat him like 'Al Pacino'—*fuck you*. It was clear that he had conflicted feelings."[8] To Pacino, all the attention and adulation were overwhelming; worse so if he had, as some have suggested, a shy streak. His way of dealing with it was to drink even more than usual. After a while it became a problem.

Pacino was no stranger to alcohol. He had begun to enjoy liquor and its uplifting properties in his early teens. In later years, alcohol would help him deal with his grief over family deaths and his career disappointments. Occasionally, he'd go on binges that would last for several days (although such self-destructive behavior was not a frequent occurrence). Alcohol would help him through difficult moments, such as watching himself for the first time in *The Panic in Needle Park* during its premiere public screening or attending a meeting with Bregman in which his manager extricated him from M-G-M's lawsuit over *The Gang That Couldn't Shoot Straight.* Liquor helped him relax; he could talk to people more easily with a few drinks in his system. Also, there was the simple fact that he *enjoyed*—as millions do—sitting in a barroom with friends and getting pleasantly looped.

But his good friend Charlie Laughton argued that Pacino was overdoing it; Pacino was drinking heavily night after night after night. Laughton felt that Pacino was an alcoholic and if he didn't stop drinking he would destroy everything it had taken him so long to achieve. It was quite some time before Pacino came to share this point of view. He attended a couple of AA meetings, which he found helpful, but basically cut out the drinking on his own. Whether Pacino was ever a bona fide *addict* of alcohol or just an immoderate partyer is debatable; in either case, the excessive consumption of alcohol would have played havoc with his health.[9]

Pacino followed *The Godfather Part II* with *Dog Day Afternoon,* in which he essayed a nebbish bank robber who has two wives, one of whom is a man. Pacino was the first major star to play "gay" in a popular film. Penny Allen appeared with him. Pacino was also instrumental in getting Julian Beck's (of the Living Theater) wife, Judith Molina, cast as his mother—Pacino never forgot those who were kind to him in the past. He got another Oscar nomination for his performance.

On-set battles between Pacino and director Sydney Pollack didn't help *Bobby Deerfield* (1977), his next film, one bit. Not only was Pacino not in tune with what Pollack was aiming for, Pollack lost patience with Pacino's deliberate acting style. The picture had to do with a racing driver's romance with a woman (played by Marthe Keller), who was terminally ill. Ironically, Pacino's close friend John Cazale, with whom he had appeared onstage and in the *Godfather* films and *Dog Day Afternoon,* was diagnosed with incurable bone cancer the year of *Bobby Deerfield*'s release; he died the following March.

It was through costar Marthe Keller that Pacino finally got to meet his chief acting rival, Dustin Hoffman. The two had been carrying on a kind of mock press-fueled "feud" for years. Pacino and Hoffman had been aware of each other since their early days in the Actors Studio, where each was serenaded with lavish descriptions of the other's brilliance. In 1966, Pacino was nominated for an Obie, but Hoffman walked off with the prize. After Hoffman's *The Graduate* opened in 1967 (four whole years before Pacino's first *starring* film role in *The Panic in Needle Park*), Pacino not only had to put up with tales of Hoffman's big success, he even found himself being confused with his fellow actor on certain occasions. Since Pacino is a much sexier and better-looking man—and a very different type of actor—than the rather rodent-like (if talented) Hoffman, these occasions could not have much endeared his rival to him. Their compact figures are about all they have in common.

Yet reviewers continued to make comparisons. Pacino was accused of doing a takeoff on Hoffman's "Ratso Rizzo" of *Midnight Cowboy* in his own *The Panic in Needle Park,* even though the films were made concurrently. *New Yorker* critic Pauline Kael[10]—in one phase of her campaign to seemingly discredit herself with ill-conceived opinions—declared that Hoffman and Pacino were "indistinguishable" from one another. Now and then the two actors were up for the same roles, although this happened far less often than one would imagine. They are simply not the same type at all. According to Pacino's biographer Andrew Yule, Hoffman, for his part, jokingly referred to Pacino as his "nemesis." Nowadays the "feud" is completely forgotten and Pacino seems to have out-stripped Hoffman as a major player.

Keller, who had worked with Hoffman in *Marathon Man,* brought him along for her first meeting with Pacino (on the eve of filming *Bobby Deerfield*) at Hoffman's request. Reports vary, with some saying it was hate at first sight between the two men and others insisting that it was a perfectly cordial meeting but that Pacino and Hoffman would never be good friends; they were different kinds of people as well as actors. One thing is for certain: It was not "hate at first sight" as far as Pacino and Keller were concerned; the two became lovers.

For a while there was little love lost between Pacino and one of his prime patrons, manager Martin Bregman. Bregman was tired of the managerial game and the pressures and demands of clients and decided to turn producer, with his top choice the story of Vietnam vet Ron Kovic, *Born on the Fourth of July.* Pacino was strongly interested in the role and got to know Kovic very well in preparation but bailed out when there was trouble with financing and in determining the right director. Everyone has a different story about who was ultimately to blame for the Pacino version's not getting made (it was later filmed with Tom Cruise in the lead), but the upshot was that Bregman produced no Pacino films for several years and for some time Oliver Stone bad-mouthed Pacino all over town. Some feel that without Bregman's guidance, Pacino made a couple of bad choices when it came to future film projects.[11]

Although its box office may not have been "boffo," *...And Justice for All* (1979) could not have been called a "bad choice"; Pacino was again nominated for a Best Actor Oscar for his performance as a Baltimore lawyer. His next picture, however, was another matter: *Cruising* (1980) may have been an entertaining thriller, but it did little business despite all the press it got due to its controversial nature. Director William Friedkin and company felt that a series of recent real-life murders in Greenwich Village's gay community (which was what the film was about) meant that their movie was too topical to be ignored; they were wrong. Everyone ignored it except for extremely vocal gay-activist protesters, who picketed the location filming. *Cruising* came out years too early to take advantage of the current "serial killer" craze.

As the film was being made, Pacino had this to say to interviewer Laurence Grobel: "If the gay community feels the film shows them in a bad light, then it is good they are protesting, because anything that raises consciousness in this area is all right. But I hope that's not the case."[12] Director Friedkin, who had previously helmed the now-dated gay-themed movie *The Boys in the Band* (1970), originally wanted Richard Gere for the role. "Having seen the film at special screenings," Friedkin said, "I've come to realize [Pacino] is still pretty damn effective in it, but he gave me a rough time for reasons other than the normal actor-director relationship. He wasn't on time and often didn't know what we were doing on a particular day."[13]

Pacino also made an unfortunate choice with *Author! Author!* (1982), in which he played a playwright with a runaway wife, a son, and several stepchildren. He presumably took the part because the screenplay was written by Israel Horovitz; Pacino had appeared in his stage work *The Indian Wants the Bronx* some years before. Director Arthur Hiller had several on-set blowups with Pacino, and most agree the film did little to take advantage of Pacino's particular abilities.

Pacino continued to "tread the boards," appearing in such plays as *American Buffalo* by David Mamet, *The Resistible Rise of Arturo Ui* by Bertolt Brecht, and a new production of *The Basic Training of Pavlo Hummel*, for which he won a Tony, among other awards. By 1983 he was back with Martin Bregman and appearing in more appropriate film fare, *Scarface*, essaying a Cuban drug dealer on his way to the top in Miami. To many fans, Pacino's "Tony Montana" is his most flamboyant role and zestily sensational performance. He and the film got mixed notices, however. Again, one of his films was steeped in controversy, with Cuban-American protesters complaining that *Scarface* did for them what *Cruising* did for gays; that is, nothing except stereotype them. Fear of militant activity led the production to move from Miami to a less volatile (at that time) Los Angeles.

Al Pacino is rare for a movie star. Instead of sticking to safe commercial ventures, he also needs to do the occasional work of art. This is proven not only by his continued interest in the theater (including Shakespeare!) but his willingness to do projects like the long-shot production of Hugh Hudson's *Revo-*

lution (1985) and his own film version of Heathcote Williams's *The Local Stigmatic*. The latter was originally staged at the Actors Playhouse in 1969 (see play section). Intrigued by the storyline, Pacino spent hundreds of thousands of dollars of his own money shooting the film (it was directed by David Wheeler) and perpetually reediting it until a fifty-minute rough cut was available for limited screenings. Pacino deems it "the most important, powerful thing I've done in my life."[14]

"I only made it because I wasn't finished with my character," Pacino told one interviewer. "Maybe that's why I'm still working. You have no way of getting to know a character immediately. He'll pop up, but it takes time. You've got to get a sense of the ambience."[15] In any case, *The Local Stigmatic* was never released theatrically or shown at anything but special screenings until it was released on DVD. As for *Revolution*, the ambitious and interesting film was deemed a financial and critical failure despite all the hard work and good intentions and its noble attempt to do something "different" (by 1985 standards, at least). Undoubtedly, its failure was a major disappointment to Pacino and Hudson both. Pacino did not make another movie for four years and later claimed that he went broke during this period. His last *solid* hit had been *Dog Day Afternoon* ten years before.

Pacino's "comeback" film was *Sea of Love* (1989), coproduced by Martin Bregman, which made money and garnered raves for Pacino. He was back on top again, and a variety of interesting offers came his way. He was nominated (again!) for Best Supporting Actor for his exemplary work in Warren Beatty's *Dick Tracy* (1990). The charming film got mixed reviews from the critics; Hollywood insiders were more interested in which swinging bachelor would get to first base with costar Madonna.

Pacino's screen assignments continued to garner attention—a return to his signature role in *The Godfather Part III*; a fine performance in *Glengarry Glen Ross* (in which he appeared on Broadway many years later, essaying a different role)—culminating in his Oscar for *Scent of a Woman* (1992), although there were many who felt he deserved a much better vehicle. Three years later he joined forces with Robert De Niro for the exciting crime drama, *Heat*. Pacino was now firmly ensconced in middle-age—he was fifty-five—and often found himself teamed with younger actors: John Cusack in *City Hall* (1996); Johnny Depp in *Donnie Brasco* (1997); Keanu Reeves in *The Devil's Advocate* (1997), Pacino's only horror film; Russell Crowe in *The Insider* (1999)—these were essentially supporting roles. Pacino was in the midst of a mob of actors in the football drama *Any Given Sunday* (1999) but still managed to make the best impression of the lot. The "mentoring" or older male–type roles continued with Matthew McConaughey in *Two for the Money* (2005); Brad Pitt in *The Recruit*

(2003)—"it was a movie that I personally couldn't follow," said Pacino[16]—and Channing Tatum in *The Son of No One* (2011).

Eschewing the mentoring roles, Pacino also shared the spotlight with Robin Williams in *Insomnia* (2002); Jerry Orbach in *Chinese Coffee* (2000), a play adaptation directed by Pacino, who had also been cast in the stage version; and Robert De Niro, again, in the excoriated *Righteous Kill* (2008). Pacino signed for *Insomnia* despite his problems with the script because he had liked director Christopher Nolan's work on *Memento*, and felt sure Nolan would become a major player.

But as he got older, Pacino still continued to have solo starring roles in a wide variety of motion pictures. Pacino was excellent in the underrated *People I Know* (2002), but for some reason the film's premiere was on an airplane flight between London and New York.[17] Then there were the bizarre black comedy *S1m0ne* (2002); Shylock in the adaptation of Shakespeare's *The Merchant of Venice* (2004); the creditable thriller *88 Minutes* (2007); King Herod in his adaptation of Oscar Wilde's *Salome* (2013), which Pacino also directed; and big roles in *The Humbling* (2014) and *Danny Collins* (2014). While these last two films received mixed reviews—*Danny Collins* was better received than *The Humbling*—Pacino's personal notices were excellent, with many opining that Pacino deserved another Oscar for his work in either film. Two telefilms also garnered Pacino much attention and praise: as Dr. Jack Kevorkian in *You Don't Know Jack* (2010) and the indicted record producer, *Phil Spector* (2013).

Of the former telefilm, Alessandra Stanley wrote in the *New York Times*: "Mr. Pacino is almost unrecognizable in a shock of puffy white hair and oversize glasses ... the actor manages to convey Dr. Kevorkian's placid tone and occasional flecks of dry humor without masking his reckless indifference to public sentiment and professional caution. His anger is chilling...."

Pacino also gets across the fact the Kevorkian seems to have "virtually no authentic human warmth."[18] Completing a trio of real-life portrayals for television, Pacino also garnered excellent reviews for his performance as the complicated Roy Cohn in the mini-series adaptation of *Angels in America*.

As noted, Pacino turned director with his adaptations of *Chinese Coffee* and *Salome*. He also directed two documentaries, *Looking for Richard* (1996) and *Wilde Salomé* (2011). The former was a look at Shakespeare in general and *Richard III* in particular; the latter examined the life of Oscar Wilde as well as his most controversial play. Pacino played both Richard and King Herod on the stage. "Shakespeare is the writer most likely to touch us," said Pacino, "because he speaks to the emotions and feelings that are in all of us, and he speaks to them in the grandest way." Of *Looking for Richard*, Pacino noted that "the person who sees this picture and enjoys it the most is the person who has a respect for

Shakespeare but is afraid of Shakespeare."[19] *Looking for Richard* won the Director's Guild award, but in spite of this Pacino has never felt that he was a good director, and has criticized his own work with actors. When it comes to actors who also make good directors, Pacino thinks that Warren Beatty and Robert Redford fill the bill much more than he.

As for *The Merchant of Venice*, Pacino hoped the film version, which he did not direct, would seem less anti–Semitic than Shakespeare's play because it could be made more clear on film the motivations of Shylock, the Jewish money lender. Pacino does not think his Shylock is an "overwhelming" performance any more than Laurence Olivier's, Dustin Hoffman's or George C. Scott's. His key to doing the "pound of flesh" scene, which he had trouble with, was "sobriety, no malice just a clear and sober approach."[20]

In both stage and screen versions, Pacino got varying reactions to his portrayal of King Herod. According to Deborah Young in the *Hollywood Reporter* reviewing *Wilde Salomé*: "Why, in the role of King Herod, [Pacino] felt compelled to adopt a whiny, high-pitched voice with gay inflections is a question posed by a journalist in the film, to which Pacino has no answer. Estelle Parsons, the play's director, doesn't weigh in on the matter, which remains a puzzling and uncomfortable choice...."[21] Estelle Parsons directed the stage version of *Salome* even as Pacino used the same cast and sets to direct the film adaptation. "I'm not in charge," Parsons told Patrick Goldstein of the *Los Angeles Times*. "I work *with* Al. He has wonderful ideas. Well, sometimes they're terrible."[22]

Pacino and the Ladies

By 1990 and the time of *The Godfather Part III*, friends and associates of Pacino were wondering if he would finally marry Diane Keaton, with whom he had had a relationship as on-again, off-again as Michael Corleone's with wife Kay. But by 1990, Pacino had formed relationships with *many* women, including some of his costars. Pacino has never lacked for female companionship and has had innumerable long-term relationships that never quite made it to the altar.

Reportedly, Pacino had his first girlfriend at age sixteen when he dropped out of the High School of Performing Arts in order to make money for his family. He moved into his own apartment and moved his girlfriend in, too. If he had to give up some dreams and toil at tedious employment so early in life, at least he had the compensations of his own place and a gal to go with it. There have also been many rumors about how Pacino managed to get by between acting gigs and part-time employment in the days before stardom. On at least one occasion, he went home with an older lady who offered him bed and board in exchange for sex.[23]

Actress Susan Tyrrell (*Fat City*), a buxom, blowsy brunette who appeared in some plays with Pacino, was one of his earlier theatrical conquests. Another was Jill Clayburgh (*An Unmarried Woman*), whom he met while appearing at the Charles Playhouse in Boston. Pacino was Clayburgh's first-ever boyfriend, and her womanly instincts were aroused enough for her to follow him back to New York and move into a fifth-floor walk-up with him. Clayburgh stayed with Pacino during his worst periods of heavy drinking and, on top of that, had to watch him become a star in *The Godfather* in 1972 while her career limped along until *An Unmarried Woman* in 1978. Clayburgh definitely drew on much of her five-year experience with Pacino for her performance in the picture, but she would have remained an "unmarried woman" had she stayed with him. The two broke up in 1972. Years later, Clayburgh married playwright David Rabe, in whose work Pacino appeared. Pacino reportedly loved Clayburgh but wasn't ready for marriage.[24]

Next came a brief dalliance with Tuesday Weld (*Pretty Poison*), who had been considered "wild" in her teens.[25] By 1972 she was coming out of a failed marriage to a writer. The equally wild Pacino was more Weld's speed, but only until she could land the diminutive comedian Dudley Moore, whom she married. This union didn't last very long, either. Ten years later, Pacino found himself *playing* Tuesday's husband in *Author! Author!*; although Weld was cast, amusingly enough, as a "wild" wife, her appearance had become comparatively matronly by then.

Diane Keaton's relationship with Pacino—she met him on the set of *The Godfather*—spanned all three Mafia mini-epics and nearly two decades. For a long time she was the lady love of fellow Hollywood cocksman Warren Beatty, and she also dallied with Woody Allen in his pre–Mia Farrow days. By the late 1980s Keaton was back with Pacino. The two shared a villa in Rome during the filming of *The Godfather Part III*, but as the weeks progressed, things became strained. Reportedly, Keaton had already miscarried Pacino's baby; she not only wanted another child but marriage and stability. Pacino could offer neither, and the relationship was over.[26]

One of Pacino's most serious involvements was Marthe Keller, with whom he costarred in *Bobby Deerfield*. Their relationship, oddly, somewhat mirrored the one in the film, with Keller more free-spirited and demonstrative and Pacino more cautious and laid back. After filming, Keller moved into his apartment and got him to change his style of dress. A minor health problem of Keller's, before diagnosis, made them wonder if life was going to imitate art (Keller dies in *Bobby Deerfield*) and spell *finis* to their relationship. Instead, it died of natural causes. Pacino was in love with Keller, but not quite ready to commit himself fully to her.[27]

This was evidenced by the presence of young actress Maureen Springer in his life, both personally and professionally. Springer was given the part of his girlfriend in *Cruising*, but she was hastily replaced by Karen Allen when her affair with Pacino ended. *She* was replaced in his affections by Kathleen Quinlan (*I Never Promised You a Rose Garden*), with whom he was heavily and very romantically involved in the early to mid–'80s. Although both spoke to friends in glowing terms of their love and high regard for each other, things had petered out by 1985, when Pacino would give a blast to anyone who even spoke of her.[28]

After Quinlan, Pacino had a brief interlude with Jan Tarrant, who had been an acting teacher at the Strasberg Institute. He segued from Tarrant to her friend Annie Praeger. The relationship with Ms. Praeger was quite intense for a while, until she found out that Pacino had had a child with Tarrant. When news of the child leaked out, Pacino's publicist, Pat Kingsley, did her best to downplay it, issuing a terse statement that Pacino "does have a daughter. I won't go further than that."[29]

Later on, Pacino was only too happy to acknowledge his daughter by Tarrant, Julie Marie. "I love being a father, and I'm actively involved," he told Glenn Paskin. "What a *relief* to see that life is not about me; it's about *her*. I can be away from Julie for a certain time, but then I have a real *need* to see her that's beyond my control. Fatherhood has changed me in a big way—and in lots of little ways." One friend agreed: "It's a totally different Al."[30]

Since Pacino was not romantically involved with Julie Marie's mother or with her friend Praeger, he was open to a new relationship with Lyndall Hobbs, at the time a forty-one-year-old Australian director. Things did not always go smoothly in the relationship between Pacino and Hobbs. Reportedly, Hobbs was not well liked by many of Pacino's friends and associates, especially because she was perceived as being too "controlling." In particular, tension existed between Hobbs and producer Martin Bregman, Pacino's former manager, because Bregman felt Pacino should have stayed with Hobbs's predecessor, Annie Praeger. Parts of an angry letter Hobbs sent Bregman surfaced on page 6 of the *New York Post*, but Bregman denied ever receiving it.[31]

Of more immediate concern to Hobbs were reports that Pacino was seeing Praeger again, not to mention his relationship with *Carlito's Way* costar Penelope Ann Miller. Pacino kept mum about the affair, which lasted for several months, but Ms. Miller was not so reticent, ensuring several inches of press clippings.[32] To her it was no "fling"; she was really in love. For his part, Pacino stated on the subject of affairs with costars: "A lot of people think that it allows you to bring personal things to the work, but it isn't true.... It's an interference."[33] Miller took up with musician Gary Allegretto, while Pacino went back to Hobbs. Pacino's attitude toward Hobbs: "They say whatever works for you, and she works for me."[34]

Whatever chemistry existed between Pacino and Hobbs didn't work for too long because Pacino next had a long-term relationship with Beverly D'Angelo, with whom he had twins, Anton and Olivia, in 2001. Pacino was sixty and D'Angelo forty-six when she conceived the twins through in vitro fertilization. The relationship ended two years later and a bitter custody battle began for the children. Pacino's lawyer Martin Wasser charged that Beverly "continues to use the kids in a way that almost makes them hostages. We sometimes joke that we are dealing with a baby rental company. For every extra hour Al wants to spend with the children, she wants to be paid more money."[35]

D'Angelo's lawyer Dan Klores counter-charged that "the conduct of Al Pacino's attorney has been reprehensible. There should not be a mother in America who isn't appalled by his language, deceptions and untruths. He's trying to make a name for himself by attacking the mother of two children."[36] Months later Pacino was told that he could enjoy sleepovers with the two-year-old twins one night per week. But this victory was short-lived when D'Angelo petitioned the court to move to Los Angeles where she could try to jump-start her film career. A hearing was canceled and it was said that an out-of-court settlement was reached in addition to the $93,000 that D'Angelo receives from the star each month. Pacino structures his work schedule so that he can spend as much time with his children as possible.[37]

The next woman in Pacino's life was Lucila Sola, a beautiful Argentine model and actress with career ambitions, who was first revealed to the public during the premiere of *You Don't Know Jack*. Sola, thirty-one at the time, was forty years younger than Pacino, and a photo surfaced that some said almost made the couple resemble Snow White and one of the Seven Dwarfs. It was not helped by the fact that Sola looked casually glamorous and Pacino grubby and unshaven. The two were together for three years before Sola left Pacino to take up with the handsome Mexican singer Luis Miguel, who was only nine years older than she.[38]

Pacino may never get married—he feels he doesn't need that piece of paper—but whenever a relationship fails, he always has one faithful "spouse" waiting in the wings, the only love that truly matters: his work. As for his personal life and romantic pursuits, Pacino does not welcome news reports or questions about them, saying he is concerned about anonymity as an actor because once an actor's private life becomes known to an audience, they watch the movie thinking about the actor instead of the performance.

Reassessing Pacino

As Pacino entered the 21st century, there were charges from many that he was selling out his talent. Francis Ford Coppola told GQ magazine[39] that stars such as Pacino and Robert De Niro were taking too many parts just for the money and had lost their passion for their art. "Now Pacino is very rich, maybe because he never spends any money; he just puts it in his mattress," claimed Coppola. "They all live off the fat of the land." (With alimony and child support, it's unlikely that Pacino doesn't "spend any money," regardless of what Coppola says.) Taking a cue from Coppola, Patrick Goldstein of the *Los Angeles Times* charged in 2008 that "the two icons of '70s New Hollywood [Pacino and De Niro], heroes to a generation of young actors and filmmakers, have become parodies of themselves, making payday movies and turning in performances that are hollow echoes of the electrically charged work they did in such films as *Serpico*, *Dog Day Afternoon*, *Mean Streets*, and *Taxi Driver*."[40]

Jessica Winter of *Slate* headlined her 2007 article on the actor: "Ham of the People: How Al Pacino got typecast as Al Pacino."[41] Winter wrote: "Pacino saw his fortunes flag in the '80s ... [he] increasingly sought out big, shouty parts and then inflated them past their already outsized proportions." Winter felt that in certain roles Pacino's large-than-life quality was more appropriate, such as when he essayed Roy Cohn in *Angels in America* (2003). "It's a stroke of genius to ask Al Pacino, of all people, to listen, to react, to efface himself. If only it could strike more often."

Pacino has indeed made his share of bad movies and occasionally given an indifferent performance, but Pacino's fans hardly object when he's being dramatic and explosive—it's not only that that often works for the character, but it's what his fans have come to expect. Does any Pacino fan really want a demure and self-effacing Al Pacino? It also must be said that Pacino clearly did not do every project just for the money, and that he did some superlative work in the years since these attacks were posted.

For creative sustenance, Pacino has his theatrical assignments. If he were only after money, he could certainly get it: Pacino was paid $6 million for *Frankie and Johnny* (1991), $1.5 million for a smaller role in *Glengarry Glen Ross* (1992) and another $6 million for *Carlito's Way* (1993). After *finally* winning an Oscar for his performance in *Scent of a Woman* (1992), his asking price went way up. He still commands star salaries and often gets more money for a smaller role than the stars do.

Honors

In February 1993, Pacino was honored with a tribute at the Waldorf-Astoria, hosted by the American Museum of the Moving Image (AMMI), partly because he had just been nominated for two Oscars in the same year (for *Glengarry* and *Scent of a Woman*). In her witty write-up in the *New York Post*, Jami

Bernard said that the crowd at the event "was about as electrified as a beached whale."[42] Bernard blamed neither Pacino nor the AMMI but all of the "listless" presenters. Bernard spoke for many when she wrote that his "is a rare talent. Pacino is so good he can now unbalance movies that aren't up to his speed." For a retrospective of his films at the AMMI's Astoria, Queens, headquarters, Pacino supervised the reediting of the master-piece-that-wasn't, *Revolution.* (This new version was released on DVD and retitled *Revolution: Revisited,* adding narration and making some cuts and changes.) Then on October 21, 2005, there was an American Cinematheque tribute to Pacino at the Beverly Hilton Hotel with comments and tributes from the likes of James Caan, Andy Garcia, John Goodman, Colin Farrell and many others.

In 2001 there was "An Evening with Al Pacino" at the Fowler Museum auditorium at UCLA. Pacino answered questions from the audience and talked about his career. From time to time he would do these evenings in other venues, calling them "Al Pacino: One Night Only." In 2015 he appeared in Atlantic City, where reporter Scott Cronick described the scene: "Atlantic City has seen its share of one-man shows and celebrities pass through its gambling halls ... but never—perhaps in the city's 35-plus-year casino history—has anyone with such star power as Al Pacino performed a one-man show in Atlantic City."[43] Pacino received a standing ovation when he came out on the stage of Caesars Atlantic City Circus Maximus Theater. The show, entitled *Al Pacino: One Night Only,* began with a video retrospective of his career, and then had hostess Joy Behar asking questions that had been carefully selected beforehand. There was a question and answer period afterward. The cost was $135 per ticket and some brokers were getting twice that much.

In May 2015 Pacino planned to do one of these special programs, retitled "An Evening with Al Pacino," with the usual clips and questions, in Glasgow, Scotland. Pacino offered fans the opportunity to have lunch with him at a cost of $12,000 per person. Members of the audience could spend twenty minutes with Pacino in his dressing room for the mere price of $4,000 each. A tour company in the United Kingdom offered fans the equivalent of $36,587 for the opportunity to fly along with Pacino in a private jet. "An incredible opportunity to experience a unique Meet & Greet with one of Hollywood's greatest actors; the legendary Al Pacino," read the brochure. The package also included "3 nights in London at a 5 star Hotel, transfers, VIP event hosts, and 24/7 Customer Support."

Over the decades, some of Pacino's potentially interesting film projects never materialized. These include a film version of David Mamet's *American Buffalo,* costarring Robert De Niro and Leonardo Di Caprio, directed by John McNaughton; and a remake of *Love Me or Leave Me* with Winona Ryder as singer Ruth Etting (originally played by Doris Day in the 1955 version) and Pacino stepping into Jimmy Cagney's shoes as the gangster she's involved with, "Gimp" Snyder, directed by Harold (*Sea of Love*) Becker. Pacino had planned to do a bio of Manuel Noriega for Oliver Stone, but Stone canceled the production in early 1994. His film *Manglehorn,* is already completed. Pacino turned down roles in *Kramer vs. Kramer, Absence of Malice* and *Prince of the City,* among others; he wanted to appear in *Johnny Handsome* and *Slapshot,* but the parts went to other actors.

Future projects for Pacino include *Beyond Deceit,* a first-time teaming with Anthony Hopkins of *Silence of the Lambs.* In this thriller Pacino plays yet another mentor role as the head of a law firm who advises an employee, played by Josh Duhamel, in his battle against a huge pharmaceutical firm, run by Hopkins. Duhamel's lawyer winds up being accused of murder. The film will be directed by Shintaro Shimosawa. As of this writing Al Pacino is rumored to be cast in director Harmony Korine's *The Trap,* exposing the members of a crime family down south.

Whatever Pacino decides upon, there is no doubt that he will be riveting audiences for years to come.

Part Two

Pacino's Films

Me, Natalie

A National General Pictures release;
a Cinema Center Films presentation, 1969

Producer, Stanley Shapiro; director, Fred Coe; director of photography, Arthur J. Ornitz; editor, Sheila Bakerman; screenplay, A. Martin Zweiback; based on a story by Stanley Shapiro; associate producer, Kurt Newmann; music, Henry Mancini (with lyrics by Rod McKuen); art director, George Jenkins. Running time: 111 minutes.

Cast

Patty Duke (*Natalie Miller*); James Farentino (*David*); Nancy Marchand (*Mrs. Miller*); Martin Balsam (*Uncle Harold*); Elsa Lanchester (*Miss Dennison*); Salome Jens (*Shirley Norton*); Philip Sterling (*Mr. Miller*); Deborah Winters (*Betty Simon*); Ron Hale (*Stanley Dexter*); Bob Balaban (*Morris*); Al Pacino (*Tony*).

Al Pacino's screen debut was not especially auspicious, but he proved that he had *presence* right from the very start.

Me, Natalie was a Patty Duke project from the word go. The director, Fred Coe, had produced both the play and film versions of Duke's triumph *The Miracle Worker*, and this whole project was built around the talents of the former Helen Keller. Pacino had only a bit part, as a tough guy named Tony.

Natalie Miller (Patty Duke) is a plain girl from Brooklyn who is tormented by her lack of beauty and the terrible blind dates that her well-meaning parents are always planning for her. She goes so far as to pretend that she has a date for the prom just so they won't set her up with anyone. Her uncle Harold (Martin Balsam), who always calls her his "little princess," assures her that substance is more important than beauty, but Natalie is completely disillusioned when she meets the woman he has chosen to marry: a blonde go-go dancer and bimbo (Salome Jens). When Harry dies, she refuses to go to his funeral.

Eventually, Natalie winds up in the East Village, where she interacts with a kooky landlady (Elsa Lanchester), and a neighbor, David Harris (James Farentino), who was a successful architect now planning to become an artist. He asks Natalie to pose for him, and the two soon fall in love. When she learns that David is married, Natalie botches a suicide attempt by jumping in the East River during low tide! David assures her that he will divorce his wife and convinces her to move in with him. But while he's in Connecticut finalizing his affairs, Natalie changes her mind and realizes that she can't be responsible for the breakup of his marriage. Their affair has given her the confidence to go on alone. (Inexplicably, she moves back in with her parents!)

Pacino shows up about halfway through the picture, during a dance sequence that he spent a whole day shooting. He asks his partner if she "puts out." When she replies indignantly in the negative, he snaps, "Listen! Somebody like you oughta be asking *me*!" In his minute or so of screen time he gets across that prickly insolence and charisma that would become his trademark.

The film was shot all over New York City, which delighted producer Stanley Shapiro. "Every single foot of this film is being made in New York," he told reporters, "and the whole process has been a happy one. It's the most professional crew I have ever seen. The police have been fantastic. Even the people have been great. We had two thousand people standing there out in Brooklyn, and we told them to be quiet, and they were quiet."

The gritty *Me, Natalie* seemed a change of pace for Shapiro, who had formerly produced glossy Doris Day films like *Pillow Talk* and *Move Over, Darling*. Some critics quipped that with this picture he was still working with a "virgin."

Me, Natalie got very mixed reviews, with many critics suggesting that it was corny, sitcomish, contrived, and much too "cute" by far. Fred Coe's "mod" direction also came under attack. However, *Saturday Review* opined, "Natalie is ... a creature of delightful wit and warmth—and so is the film which tells her story."

Donald J. Mayerson, in the *Villager*, felt just the opposite: "[Natalie] moves to Greenwich Village, meets two homosexuals, freaks out on LSD, falls in love with a married artist who deflowers her and finally discovers her identity, which is, by the way, hardly worth writing home about ... the worst piece of publicity about Greenwich Village to come along since that psychotic Nazi in *The Producers*."

Mayerson did add, however, that "Al Pacino, in a bit part as an aggressive hood, is funny." Praising the performances (if not the picture) in *New York*, Judith Crist listed Al Pacino before the other supporting players (who had much bigger parts) and purred that they all "matched the perfection" of Duke and Balsam in the leads.

Bob Balaban, who played the nervous character who gives John Voight a blow job in a movie theater that same year in *Midnight Cowboy*, also got good notices in *Me, Natalie* as nerdy Morris, an acne-ridden optometrist who is rebuffed when Natalie tells him she's a call girl. (He later calls her later to say he's raised the money.)

Outfitted with a fake putty nose and large buck teeth to make her homely, Patty Duke received generally good notices, although not everyone was taken by her performance, with one critic suggesting she was just walking through it.

One of the most admirable things about *Me, Natalie*—which is an uneven, often exasperating picture—is that it resists making Natalie herself too sweet or entirely likable, realizing that her torment would realistically turn her into someone who was not always pleasant or reasonable. The trouble with the movie is that it becomes pure Hollywood (despite those New York locations) wish fulfillment when the handsome artist "falls in love" with the abrasive, unattractive title character. (We're never shown what it is he sees in her.) Worse, Natalie dumps the artist for unselfish motives that are somewhat contrary to her character.

Despite excellent performances and some fine scenes, *Me, Natalie* smacks of compromise; a noble, ambitious attempt is muffed.

Pacino, at least, would go on to better things.

The Panic in Needle Park

20TH CENTURY-FOX;
A DUNNE DIDION DUNNE PRODUCTION, 1971

Producer, Dominick Dunne; director, Jerry Schatzberg; director of photography, Adam Holender; editor, Evan Lottman; screenplay, Joan Didion and John Gregory Dunne; based on the book by James Mills; associate producer, Roger M. Rothstein; costume design, Jo Ynocencio; art director, Murray P. Stern. Running time: 110 minutes.

CAST

Al Pacino (*Bobby*); Kitty Winn (*Helen*); Richard Bright (*Hanky*); Alan Vint (*Hotch*); Warren Finnerty (*Sammy*); Kiel Martin (*Chico*); Raul Julia (*Marco*); Paul Sorvino (*Samuels*); Dora Weissman (*Pawnshop Lady*); Bryant Fraser (*Prep-School Boy*).

Hangout of heroin addicts and dealers, Manhattan's Sherman Square (located at West Seventy-second Street where Broadway and Amsterdam

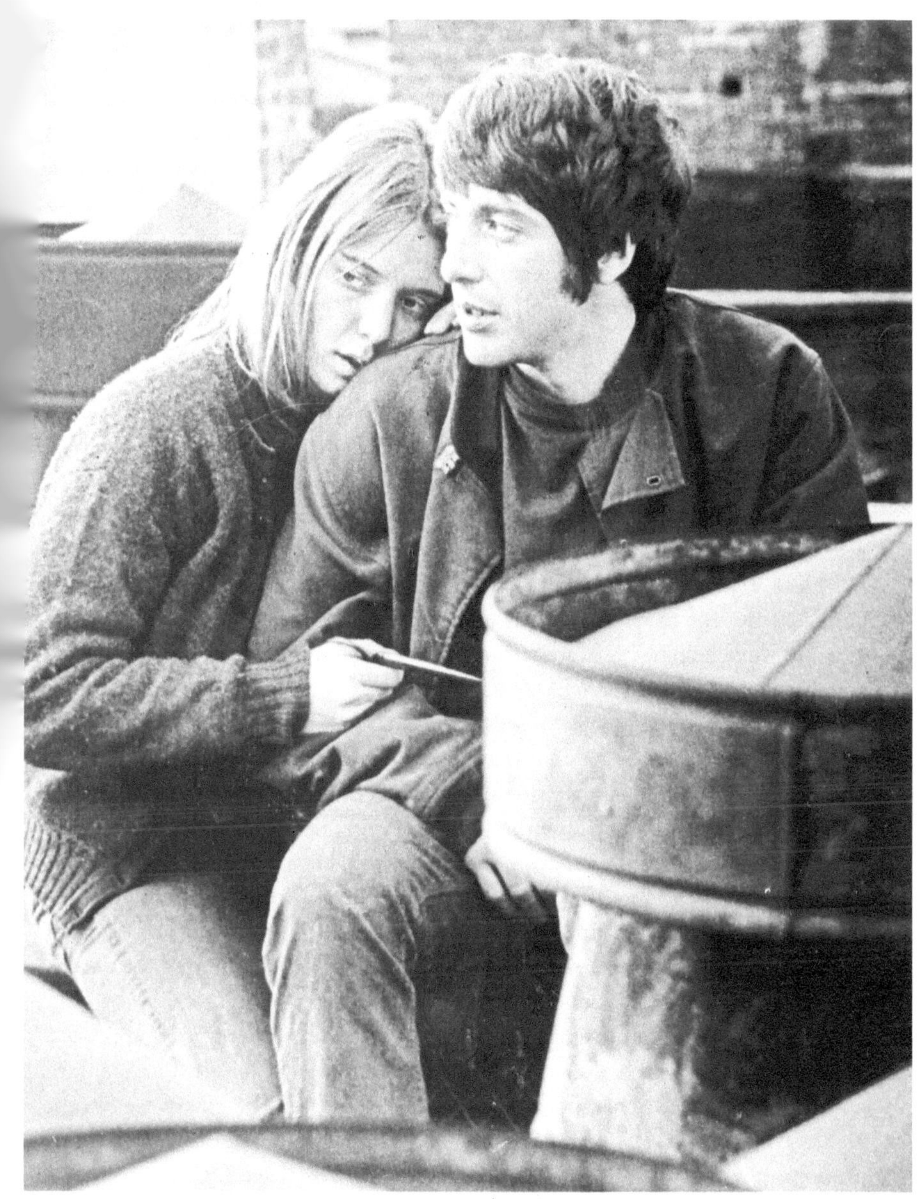

Bobby (Pacino) and Helen (Kitty Winn), the desperate drug addicts in *The Panic in Needle Park* (1971).

Avenue intersect) had become known as "Needle Park" by the 1960s. The "panic" of the title refers to what drug addicts feel when their supply has run out.

The Panic in Needle Park is a gritty study of the kind of people who have contributed more than their share to the then-decline of New York and all great cities in the United States: drug dealers and users. Made at the height of the hippie/love/drugs-are-great period in America, *Panic* deserves high marks for having the courage to present the downside of indiscriminate drug use during a time when no one wanted to hear it. Admittedly, the characters in this movie are heavy into hard drugs, heroin—they are not casual joint smokers—but the movie had important points to make during a period when popular culture was doing its best to make drugs seem like a magic panacea. This is not to say it was necessarily intended to be a "message" film; it gets its point across with a proliferation of documentary-like detail.

Bobby (Pacino) and Helen (Kitty Winn) eke out a pathetic existence on the Upper West Side of Manhattan. Bobby is a small-time drug dealer and occasional user; Helen wants to get a real job but quits as a waitress in a Broadway coffee shop when she can't put up with the demanding customers. When the two are locked out of their residential hotel room for nonpayment of rent, they sleep wherever they can. Helen eventually succumbs to trying heroin to temporarily escape her bleak existence and becomes hooked on it. From then on things get worse and worse for the couple: she turns to prostitution to support her habit; he gets arrested while helping his brother during a robbery. Months later, Helen "rats" on Bobby to a sympathetic narc (Alan Vint) in order to avoid imprisonment. Bobby is put back in the joint ("Cunt! I was gonna marry you!" he screams at her, as if he were some prize), but Helen is waiting for him when he is released. They walk off together, companions in nightmare till death do they part.

All of this is played out with often unnerving realism, particularly scenes showing assorted junkies shooting themselves up (both in long shot and close-up; no cutaways saying, "It's only actors") and immediately zonking out into whatever dreamland awaits them; or a long sequence in which Bobby watches as the heroin is cut, carefully measured, and rapidly packaged behind the deceptively prosaic wooden doors of a Harlem apartment.

Although the picture employs a shapeless, formless cinéma vérité approach (which doesn't always work), the filmmakers were hardly hippie documentarians. Director Jerry Schatzberg had previously directed the glossy study of a fashion model, *Puzzle of a Downfall Child*, the year before. (A former fashion photographer, Schatzberg starred his then-girlfriend Faye Dunaway in that film.) Producer Dominick Dunne would come to write glitzy tales of the rich and powerful in *Vanity Fair* and in such novels as *The Two Mrs. Grenvilles*. These were odd choices to put together a film about such drab, outré, disreputable New York denizens; it is to their credit that they avoided any and all sentimentalization or glamorization of the downbeat, lurid subject matter.

Although the picture begins slowly, it soon rivets the viewer with some excellent sequences and telling details. When Helen gets a letter from her mother, Bobby's first response is to open the envelope to see inside. "Any bread?"

he asks hopefully. Playing stickball with Helen and some neighborhood youngsters, Bobby grabs her in an exuberant hug and then notices that look in her eyes that indicates she's crossed over the fatal line into addiction. "When did that happen?" he asks.

A particularly lively and funny-ugly scene has Pacino passing out in a woman's apartment. The woman, who, like Helen, turns tricks to support her habit, is expecting a John any minute and is panicking that he'll be frightened away by the other people, not to mention Pacino's body. "He can't die here!" she screams as her baby wails in the background and Helen and a pal try desperately to revive Bobby. An even more grotesque scene has Bobby and Helen shooting up in the men's room of the Staten Island Ferry as the little dog they just got runs off by itself to explore the boat. They come out of the men's room just in time to witness the dog jumping off the back of the ferry and drowning. (The trouble is that the sequence borders on black comedy, and Helen's reaction, her hitting Bobby and crying hysterically, should have been strengthened and expanded.)

Pacino's performance in his first starring role is excellent, exhibiting the ability and charisma that would carry him to even greater heights in years to come. Clearly, he put much of himself, his early struggle to survive, into the role of Bobby (although Bobby, unlike Pacino, is essentially a loser). Pacino looks oddly "geeky" in the opening scenes but is still attractive, masculine and "lethal" to the ladies; one can see why his Bobby exudes a fatal attraction over poor Helen, whose attachment to him is her downfall.

The Pacino charm is also in evidence, such as when he sneaks into the hospital against nurses' orders to see Helen and makes her smile; or when he gets extra money from an old lady pawnbroker. "I'm dying of dope," he tells her. "I'm dying of hunger," she replies. Although Pacino is a bit too intelligent and "cultured" a person to be 100 percent convincing as a hopeless lowlife, he does register at an admirable 98 percent, and his performance betrays no *controllable* false notes at all.

The Panic in Needle Park is the first film in which Pacino unleashes his patented Pacino blast, the one moment when he really hauls off, busts ass, and *explodes*. This occurs when he learns that Helen has been selling her body to support her eighty-dollar-a-day drug habit. Running from his blows, Helen bolts into the bathroom and locks the door. Hollering and cursing, Pacino pounds the door and threatens to break it down.

Kitty Winn is also admirable as poor Helen. She had won raves playing *Saint Joan* in San Francisco at the American Conservatory Theater, and her performance in *The Panic in Needle Park* garnered her a Best Actress prize at the 1971 Cannes Film Festival. It's a shame that we never learn more of her character's motives for leaving home. "I was born and went to school," she says of her former life. "I had a mother and a father and a little brother and a lawn. I was always going to art classes, and my mother was always going to the doctor. It was all right."

All right, maybe, but not enough. Helen is one of those girls who leaves home to seek adventure excitement, something different, but hasn't the determination or drive or wherewithal to have a goal or any kind of realistic game plan. Too many wind up lost or dead or buried in unmarked graves or, like Helen, enthralled by a man who is no good.

Richard Bright also scores as Bobby's burglarizing brother, Hank, who looks so respectable in suit and tie when we first see him but who reveals his true nature when we hear his low-class accent (more common than Pacino's) and see the missing teeth when he smiles. Hank is just as much on the outside as his brother is.

Smaller roles are played by Raul Julia as an artist-friend of Bobby's and Paul Sorvino as a John who is robbed of twenty-five dollars by Helen. Alan Vint is fine as a police officer, Hotch, who tries to pry Helen away from Bobby for her own sake and his; Dora Weissman and Bryant Fraser also make their mark in the film as, respectively, the likable old lady in the pawnshop and a young preppie who buys Helen's body but winds up giving a threatening Bobby all of his money.

Adam Holender's cinematography—atmospheric shots of Seventy-second Street and Broadway and its environs, lots of close-ups of needles and other drug paraphernalia—is appropriately murky. Never has Manhattan looked so drab and ugly. There is no musical score—music would have helped create some pathos—but lots of background noise, which adds to the veracity of the picture but occasionally almost drowns out the dialogue.

The Panic in Needle Park is an absorbing but ultimately minor work. Great stories can be told about strugglers and losers in New York City, but this lacks sympathetic characters who have a purpose and (thwarted) goals. Bobby and Helen are primarily responsible for their own problems; there is nothing remotely "heroic" about either of them, which is perhaps the point. *The Panic in Needle Park* also lacks that certain *depth* which distinguishes other (often foreign) studies of losers, misfits, and lowlifes, such as Britain's 1963 film *The Leather Boys.*

The Godfather

PARAMOUNT, 1972

Producer, Albert S. Ruddy; director, Francis Ford Coppola; director of photography, Gordon Willis; editors, William Reynolds and Peter Zinner;

screenplay, Coppola and Mario Puzo; based on the novel by Mario Puzo; associate producer, Gray Frederickson; music, Nino Rota; production designer, Dean Tavoularis; costume designer, Anna Hill Johnstone; hairstylist, Phil Leto. Running time: 171 minutes.

Cast

Marlon Brando (*Don Corleone*); Al Pacino (*Michael Corleone*); Diane Keaton (*Kay Adams*); Robert Duvall (*Tom Hagen*); James Caan (*Sonny Corleone*); John Cazale (*Fredo Corleone*); Talia Shire (*Connie*); Gianni Russo (*Carlo*); Lenny Montana (*Luca Brasi*); John Marley (*Jack Woltz*); Alex Rocco (*Moe Green*); Richard Conte (*Barzini*); Simonetta Stefanelli (*Appollonia*); Abe Vigoda (*Tessio*); Sterling Hayden (*Captain McCluskey*); Al Martino (*Johnny Fontaine*); Al Lettieri (*Solfozzo*); Tony Giorgio (*Bruno Tattaglia*); Richard Castellano (*Clemenza*).

After a lot of hassle—somebody made Pacino "an offer he couldn't refuse" (the picture made that phrase part of our national lexicon)—Pacino took the part of Michael Corleone in the film version of Mario Puzo's best seller, and the rest is history. This was the film that catapulted Pacino into stardom.

In post–World War II New York, Don Vito Corleone (Marlon Brando) is the godfather of the Italian mob. His two sons Sonny (James Caan) and Fredo (John Cazale) are part and parcel of the family business. His adopted son, Tom Hagan (Robert Duvall), acts as the family lawyer but is generally kept outside of the dirtier parts of the business. Corleone's third son, Michael, who enlisted in the service, has an independent mind and at first wants nothing to do with the family trade.

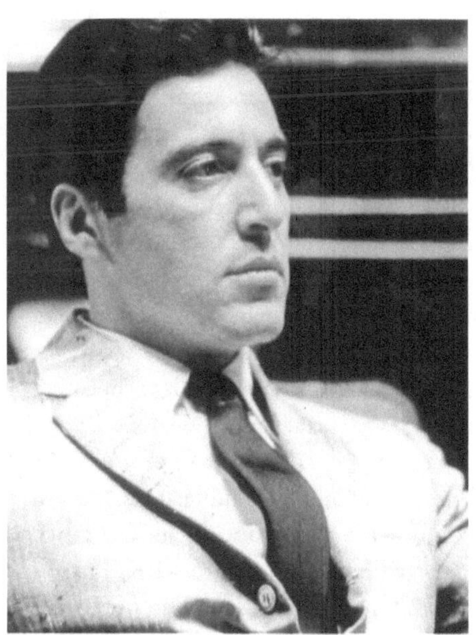

Pacino as Michael Corleone in Francis Ford Coppola's 1972 film adaptation of Mario Puzo's novel *The Godfather*, the role that propelled Pacino to stardom.

The Corleones are, if possible, "good"—and self-justifying—mobsters. They only traffic in the "harmless" vices of gambling and prostitution. When someone points out that "senators and presidents don't have men killed," they accuse the speaker of naiveté. Don Corleone doesn't want to get into the "dirty business" of drug dealing not because of the innocents who will be corrupted but because his "friends in high places" won't be able to look the other way, as they do with his less controversial (if equally illegal) activities.

Don Corleone's not-so-noble-minded refusal to traffic in narcotics leads to a war between crime families, with the don himself nearly the first casualty. Seeing his family under attack, Michael develops a new attitude: he himself will assassinate two of their enemies, who will be taken completely by surprise. This sets him down a completely different road from the one he had intended to travel, and before long his corruption is complete. He takes over the family and is soon eliminating all enemies just as ruthlessly as his father before him. The new godfather, it seems, has grown quite comfortable in his role.

Completely absorbing during its nearly three-hour running time, *The Godfather* has plenty of colorfully gruesome and flavorful highlights to punctuate the many scenes of mafioso talking and planning and vowing vengeance and havoc. One of the first murders is of Corleone henchman Luca (Lenny Montana), who has a quiet drink with members of the drug cartel in a deserted bar. Suddenly, one of the men plunges a knife through his hand and into the bar counter below it, pinning his hand to the bar, while another strangles him from behind. A more low-key murder has another Corleone henchman, Paulie (John Martino), shot in the back of the head by an associate (in the distant background) as family friend Clemenza (Richard Castellano), who ordered the hit, urinates into some bushes at the side of the road in the foreground. Not only do these mobsters talk about murder casually, they even *enact* it that way.

Sonny's murder at the tollbooth on the causeway is also exciting, as are the events leading up to it. First, Sonny's sister Connie (Talia Shire) has a plate-smashing free-for-all with her slick, no-good husband, Carlo (Gianni Russo), who has sold out to the Corleones' enemies. Carlo takes a belt to Connie, knowing that when news of his actions reach Sonny's ears, he'll jump into his car and head straight for him to avenge his sister. However, the rival faction has set up an ambush at the tollbooth, and Sonny is riddled with so many bullets that it's a miracle (and a bit implausible) that he manages to last as long as he does. Before he expires, defiant to the last, Sonny manages to get a few licks in himself.

The most suspenseful passage in the film details the double assassination that sends Michael spiraling downward into a life of corruption and brutality. Michael insists that he be allowed to meet with the head of the drug faction and a sinister police captain who has been bought by the Mob. The site of the meeting is a down-market Italian restaurant where a gun has been hidden in one of the stalls in the men's room. Michael excuses himself from the table, gets the gun, and after a few moments of trepidation, steps out to blast away at both completely surprised adversaries.

Pacino's acting certainly helps maintain the high degree of tension in this scene. When first we see him, during his sister's wedding at the opening of the film, he displays a kind of scrubbed innocence, a healthy attention to grooming, and a basic decency that is in sharp contrast to his character in *The Panic in Needle Park*. As the picture progresses, however, he slowly becomes more authoritative and menacing. Driving to the restaurant with the police captain and his druggie chum, his face betrays a growing amorality, hardened determination, and seeping viciousness that has wiped out all traces of innocence. Pacino looks convincingly tense and nervous before committing the double hit—but not guilt-wracked. Michael Corleone has crossed over, and there's no turning back.

Although Marlon Brando probably got more press (and certainly more money), Pacino is clearly the film's true protagonist and has the pivotal role; it's a charismatic, star-making performance. Oddly enough considering the subject matter, there is no Pacino blast in the film. Instead of screeching and kicking the furniture (that Pacino leaves to James Caan's Sonny), Pacino underplays his scenes, whether making a casino owner an offer he can't refuse (he wants to buy him out and *that's that*) or questioning his terrified quisling brother-in-law Carlo, Pacino is the essence of menacing cool.

Interspersed with the bloody action, the picture has a lot of *talk*. In these quieter moments Pacino shows what a good listener he can be, such as when he talks patiently to an increasingly confused Don Corleone in the garden. (Brando himself is charming as he clowns with his grandson in the garden moments before suffering a fatal heart attack.)

Speaking of Brando, *The Godfather* was his big comeback film, and he shocked everyone by consenting to audition for the role. Opinion was sharply divided as to the veracity of his performance. He does play Don Corleone with appropriate toughness and virility—he retains his great presence—but that voice! His cheeks stuffed with jowl-creating cotton or the like, Brando sometimes sounds like Daffy Duck and is often nearly unintelligible. (That didn't stop him from winning an Academy Award as Best Actor!)

Pacino had to settle for a nomination as Best Supporting Actor (as did Duvall and Caan)—a dubious honor at best. Pacino was far more than "support" for Brando. His, in fact, was the lead role, the "Godfather" of the title. For the record, Coppola was nominated for his direction but won for his screenplay (co-written with Mario Puzo). *The Godfather* earned an Oscar for Best Picture.

But the sum of *The Godfather*'s parts don't really add up to a whole. Audiences and critics were so entertained by the fast-paced, larger-than-life story and film that it escaped many that *The Godfather* is an "amusing" potboiler but hardly a work of art. Francis Ford Coppola is no William Wyler; there isn't the care in each shot and setup that would indicate truly *great* filmmaking. *The Godfather* plays like a parody at times—the severed horse's head found in the uncooperative director's bed, for instance—but it lacks a subtext of *humanity*, people that we could root for and care about.

Still, a great many talented people made significant contributions to *The Godfather*'s success. In addition to the aforementioned fine actors, Diane Keaton, as Michael's wife, is expressive and generally believable. Although his Tom Hagen isn't personally involved in any killings, Robert Duvall hints at the sociopathology hiding just beneath the surface. Al Lettieri really scores as the sleazy drug kingpin Sollozzo, and Richard Castellano hits the mark as the "lovable" Clemenza, who talks about killing people as he stirs his spaghetti sauce. All the supporting roles—from John Cazale's Fredo and Talia Shire's Connie down to Al Martino's Johnny Fontaine (said to be inspired by Frank Sinatra) and Sterling Hayden's Captain McCluskey—have been cast with great care and felicitous results. Production designer Dean Tavoularis and costume designer Anna Hill Johnstone conspired to re-create a believable New York—and Nevada (where the family relocates)—of the 1940s. But hairstylist Phil Leto should have been run out of town; most of the boys' haircuts would have been more appropriate to the 1950s or 1960s than the postwar period! They are much too long and shaggy. Why did director Coppola let Leto get away with such an anachronism?

Gordon Willis's cinematography is mostly first-rate; there are particularly beautiful shots of Sicily and the town of Corleone, where Michael goes to hide after the double assassination. Nino Rota has written a good, effective score for the picture; it has a sinister quality that adds to the tension and functions as a "storm warning." His famous theme music for the film is also quite memorable. However, some of the best music comes from other sources. The "Brindisi" (or drinking song) from Verdi's *La Traviata* plays during the second wedding sequence, and the music of J. S. Bach does the same during the film's climactic baptism.

The Godfather elicited some criticism as to the possibility that it romanticized the Mafia. To a certain extent this is true—the movie is a somewhat cosmeticized study of lowlifes, making these sordid people seem like characters in an opera (not that every character in an opera is *nice*)—but essentially the film resists making true heroes out of these scumbags. Case in point? The aforementioned baptism of Michael's nephew in a bucolic church, which is splendidly intercut with scenes of hit men putting paid to various enemies of the Corleone family in several well-orchestrated strokes. As we see murder after murder occurring in quick spurts, the camera always returns us to that church, where the new godfather swears to forgo all sin and evil even as dozens of assassinations he ordered are being carried out. (Only a short while later Michael even orders the murder of the baptized child's *father*!) This important sequence, the best in the movie, seems to say: these people, *heroes*? Forget it!

But for Al Pacino, it was only the beginning.

Scarecrow

WARNER BROS., 1973

Producer, Robert M. Sherman; director, Jerry Schatzberg; director of photography, Vilmos Zsigmond; editor, Evan Lottman; screenplay, Garry Michael White; music, Fred Myrow; assistant director, Tom Shaw; production designer, Al Brenner; costume designer, Jo Ynocencio. Running time: 115 minutes.

CAST

Al Pacino (*Francis "Lion"*); Gene Hackman (*Max*); Dorothy Tristan (*Coley*); Ann Wedgeworth (*Frenchy*); Richard Lynch (*Riley*); Penny Allen (*Annie*); Eileen Brennan (*Darlene*); Richard Hackman (*Mickey*); Al Cingolani (*Skipper*); Rutanya Alda (*Woman in Camper*).

Pacino was back working with director Jerry (*The Panic in Needle Park*) Schatzberg in *Scarecrow*, in which he was teamed with a post–*French Connection* Gene Hackman for this *Midnight Cowboy*–influenced American Odyssey. Max (Hackman) has just come out of San Quentin and is heading for Pittsburgh, where he plans to open a car wash. Another hitchhiker, Francis (Al Pacino), whom he meets on the road, is heading to Detroit after a stint in the navy. Francis, whom Max insists on calling "Lion" (short for his middle name, Lionel), is naively hoping for a happy reunion with the woman he ran out on as well as getting his first glance of their child, whose gender he does not know. After a stopover in Denver to spend time with Max's cousin—and a few weeks of incarceration due to a bar fight—the buddies arrive in Detroit, where Francis's ex-girlfriend, Annie (Penny Allen), tells him that their son died before he could be born or baptized. (She's lying; the six-year-old boy is actually playing beside her.) Suffering a delayed reaction to this devastating news, Francis has a nervous breakdown while playing with some small children at a public fountain. Francis is institutionalized. Max buys a round-trip ticket to Pittsburgh. He has come to care deeply for "Lion" and will use the money with which he planned to finance his car wash to make sure Francis gets proper treatment.

Pacino's Lion is a lovable schnook and borderline simpleton. His philosophy toward life (and the meaning of the title) is: "You don't have to fight people if you make 'em laugh." In his view crows aren't scared of scarecrows. "They

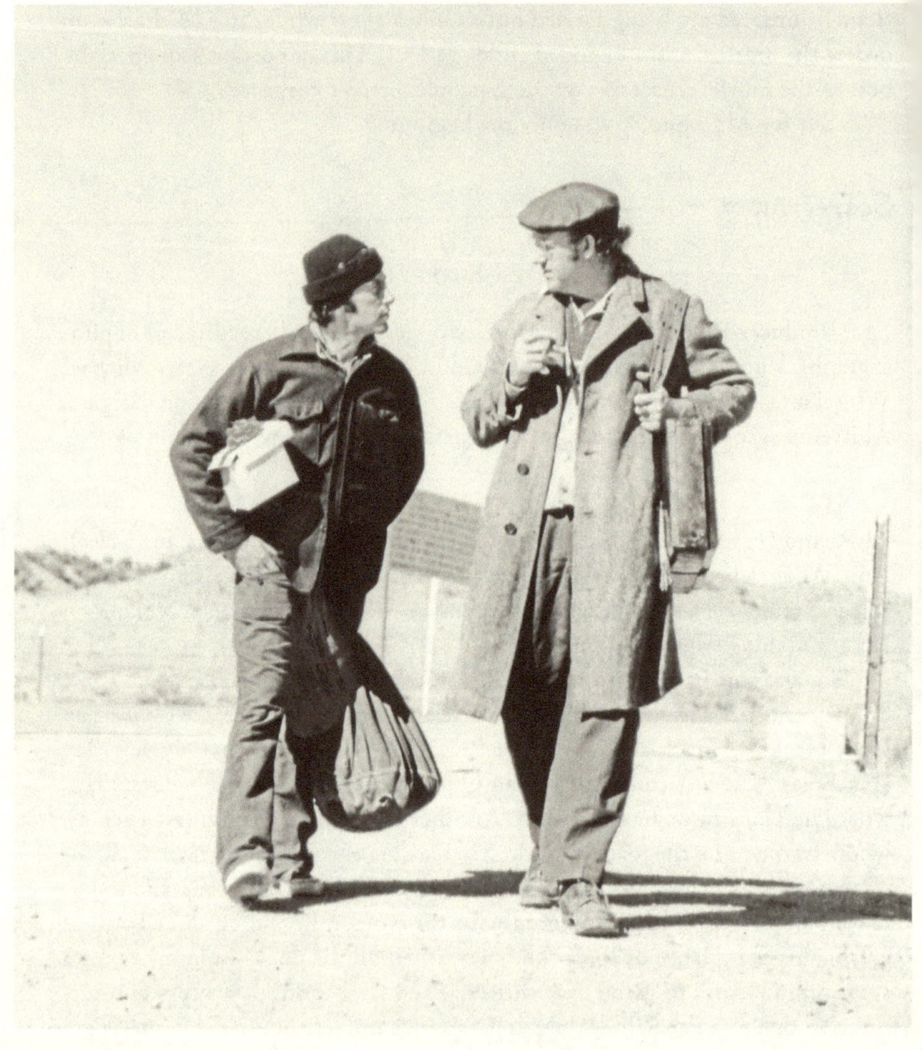

Two drifters (Pacino, left, Gene Hackman, right) team up in the road movie *Scarecrow* (1973).

make 'em laugh. They think the farmer's a good guy and fly on by." Max admits that he finally warmed up to him on the highway (Francis tried all sorts of tricks to ingratiate himself with the taciturn Max) not only because Lion gave him his last match but because "you made me laugh."

Pacino is terrific in *Scarecrow*; he almost makes it all seem effortless. His Francis is irresistible; his need to be liked and his irrepressible good humor in the face of adversity, admirable. In the prison-camp sequences, Max seems to blame Lion for their incarceration, although it was quick-with-his-fists Maxie who started the fight. Driving past a pigpen with a smitten trustee (who wants Francis to help him put on a prison show), Lion sees Max feeding slop to the pigs and quips, "Us show people sure do envy yo' simple folk of de land," giving the line an almost campy insouciance. Speaking of the trustee, Riley (Richard Lynch), Lion's later encounter with him shows that he can't always count on his sense of humor to get him out of tight places. While sharing a quiet drink with Francis, Riley tries to kiss him and, when rebuffed, gets angry. Doing an on-the-nose imitation of Boris Karloff ("Go back, Igor! Go back!"), Lion tries to make light of the whole incident, sparing Riley's feelings, but Riley is too determined to get what he wants. When Lion refuses to go down on him, Riley beats him within an inch of his life. Throughout this long sequence Pacino plays with absolute conviction: a nice guy faced with an impossible situation, not wanting to hurt or offend but completely unable to comply with an unfair demand and suffering because of it.

Although he avoids being raped, this is the first time Lion is unable to get out of a scrap with his sense of humor, and it sobers him. Later on, Maxie uses this method to avoid a fight with a bar punk—he does an impromptu striptease that has the joint in an uproar and leaves the punk nonplussed—but Francis's face, watching, betrays only world-weariness and a fatigue of the spirit that hints at the breakdown to come. This occurs when he's doing a spirited pirate imitation for some kids at a water fountain. Suddenly, he walks into the fountain carrying a young boy—to the child's delight and his mother's consternation—and completely loses it. (Pacino seems a little self-conscious in this scene but is effective.)

The opening highway scene shows Pacino at his most charming. Standing across the road from Maxie, Francis is determined to make the fellow respond to him. He jumps up and down like a monkey, digs in his ear with a thumb and pretends his hand is a telephone, screams obscenities at the cars that pass them by. Francis is a sweet person who only wants to be liked. Although he behaved irresponsibly with his pregnant girlfriend (one can't see Francis being very successful at the husband-and-daddy bit), he was thoughtful enough to send money home on a regular basis. But while Francis may think he's ready for an instant family, Annie—who was married in the interim—is too bitter to play along.

Scarecrow is saved from complete depression by several infusions of comic relief. One has Maxie hollering at barfly Darlene (Eileen Brennan) as she sits in a seedy dive but winding up dragging her home while Lion follows with a department-store dummy in tow. Trying to get work in a restaurant, the two buddies are bodily thrown out of the kitchen by chattering, furious Hispanics. The funniest sequence has Maxie requesting that Lion provide a distraction so he can shoplift a couple of purses in a department store. Lion's distraction—he runs all over the store like a maniac or a gridiron hero on uppers—is so distracting that Maxie forgets to hide the purses under his jacket. After the breakup of one of several bar fights in the picture, Lion and Maxie wind up dancing together. (Despite this, the picture seems devoid of genuinely homoerotic overtones.)

Gene Hackman's performance is almost as good as Pacino's. To his credit, he never overplays or sentimentalizes his character. Some critics complained that Hackman's Maxie remained too cold and aloof, too distant from Pacino's Lion, but Hackman was probably aware that the paranoid, prickly Maxie was not exactly a likable person or one who warmed up to people very easily. The picture's final sequence, with Maxie buying a round-trip instead of one-way ticket, is supposed to show how he has *changed*.

Eileen Brennan is as much fun as ever, and Richard Lynch—one of our most reliable character actors—makes the most of the horny trustee bent on having his way with Pacino. Ann Wedgeworth, as Frenchy, who has a yen herself for Hackman's (rather hidden) charms, does the same sexy, vague "bimbo" routine that she's done from this picture up until the TV show *Evening Shade* nearly twenty years later. Wedgeworth is good—but talk about being typecast!

After Pacino and Hackman, the acting honors have to go to Penny Allen, who has the small bit as Lion's girlfriend, Annie. When Lion calls her on the phone after a several-year absence and she recognizes his voice, she puts more into the word "Francis?" than lesser actresses have done with entire monologues. Her superb reaction is sustained throughout the conversation, in which she reveals that she got married to a man known in town as the Banana King. "Am I happy?" she says to Francis with exquisite bitterness. "I'm Mrs. Joey Banana King, and I look like an old lady!" Allen makes her character instantly sympathetic, but we can also see why Francis left her.

The extras and bit players in *Scarecrow*—those haunted midnight denizens of bars soaking up alcohol to ease their disappointment—capture the drunken good times of losers very vividly. (If movie extras don't know about disappointment, who does?)

Fred Myrow has written some nice jazz rifts for the picture—his horns and drums matching the beat of the window wipers in the police car as our heroes are taken to jail is an inspired touch—but it is Vilmos Zsigmond's superb cinematography that really helps put *Scarecrow* over. From picture-postcard country lanes to rat-infested auto junkyards, from sunny, flat highways to smoky, crowded gin joints, Zsigmond provides atmospheric vistas of an America both pretty and *grim*.

Garry Michael White's screenplay was attacked for its obvious symbolism and pretentious aspects—and the risqué humor seems more the stuff of sitcoms with each passing year—but it is a more than workable script. With its screwed-up people, wasted lives, and embittered characters hurting each other in both a casual and deliberate manner, *Scarecrow* works up some evocative pathos and hints at things perhaps better left unspoken.

Pacino won the Best Actor prize at Cannes for his work in *Scarecrow*, which he fully deserved.

Serpico

PARAMOUNT; A DINO DE LAURENTIIS PRESENTATION, 1973

Producer, Martin Bregman; director, Sidney Lumet; director of photography, Arthur J. Ornitz; editor, Dede Allen; screenplay, Waldo Salt and Norman Wexler; based on the book by Peter Maas; associate producer, Roger M. Rothstein; music, Mikis Theodorakis. Running time: 130 minutes.

CAST

Al Pacino (*Frank Serpico*); John Randolph (*Sidney Green*); Cornelia Sharpe (*Leslie*); Biff McGuire (*Captain McClain*); Barbara Eda-Young (*Laurie*); Jack Kehoe (*Tom Keough*); Tony Roberts (*Bob Blair*); Norman Ornellas (*Rubella*); Ed Grover (*Inspector Lombardo*); Richard Foronjy (*Corsaro*); Mildred Clinton (*Mrs. Serpico*).

Frank Serpico is essentially a synthesis of Pacino's Lionel in *Scarecrow* and Michael Corleone in *The Godfather*. Like the former, he was a decent, if imperfect, human being. Like the latter, he has definite goals and a certain amount of "seedy" polish. Otherwise, he is nothing like Michael Corleone. Frank Serpico was a real-life cop who blew the whistle on corruption in a police department and nearly paid for it with his life. He is a man of principle and initiative. Pacino was attracted to his story and wanted to play the part, particularly after meeting the man himself, who impressed him mightily.

Frank Serpico, as portrayed by Pacino, is a fresh-faced kid straight out of the police academy with a naive attitude toward law enforcement. Gradually, he develops a grungy sophistication and becomes a maverick on the force. He wears his hair too long and grows a mustache. He listens to opera and demonstrates ballet steps in the precinct. He carries a small white mouse around with him wherever he goes. When some of his more macho colleagues in the B.C.I. (Bureau of Criminal Investigation) assume he's gay, he winds up transferred to the plainclothes division, where his hair and mustache will be more appropriate.

One day he is handed an envelope with money in it, but Serpico wants no part of payoffs. "Who can trust a cop who don't take money?" someone tells him. Frank is appalled to learn that one precinct alone is collecting $250,000 a year in payola. He is a rare bird, a cop who thinks the police should spend their energy fighting crime and not collecting payoffs. Informed of the situation, the mayor is afraid to alienate the police force because he anticipates a summer of riots. Serpico takes out his frustration on his girlfriend.

A special commission is set up to investigate the problem, but Serpico is afraid it will go after the small fries but ignore the big guns, like the commissioner, who "knew about it for years and did *nothing*." Serpico tells his story to the *New York Times* and is promptly switched to narcotics, where he is set up during a drug bust and shot. He survives but loses hearing in one ear. Offered a gold shield, he turns it down and resigns from the force, moving to Switzerland. Serpico was eventually awarded a "medal of honor for conspicuous bravery in action."

Serpico takes a while to pick up under Sidney Lumet's styleless direction but eventually becomes grittily absorbing. Pacino, at the height of his appeal and attractiveness, looks suitably fresh-scrubbed and innocent as a young cadet and convincingly grungy and disgusted as the story proceeds; it is a notable performance. The picture gives Pacino plenty of opportunities to display the Pacino blast. Threatening to implode under all the pressure and going crazy from frustration, he hollers at his girlfriend: "Clean this place up! I don't want to pick up shit!" When Captain McClain (Biff McGuire) goes ballistic when he learns that Serpico is going to an outside agency with what he knows—"We wash our own laundry!" McClain screams—Pacino blasts back: "*We don't*!"

By far the most impressive blast—and the best scene in the picture—occurs when Serpico arrests Corsaro (Richard Foronjy) and brings him back to the precinct for processing. As Serpico runs around with the paperwork, Corsaro sits and jokes with the other cops behind his back. (The acting of Richard Foronjy, quite cocky and vivid in mustache and panama hat, adds immeasurably to the success of the sequence.) When Serpico sees what is happening, he is infuriated. "This man did fifteen years for killing a cop," he hollers (or words to that effect), "and you assholes are palling around with him!" First he picks up Corsaro and slams him into the holding cage. Then he steps back into the room and literally starts throwing chairs around, a frightening spectacle in his completely justified outrage. No one can hold a candle to Pacino when he is throwing the furniture (and maybe chewing the scenery, some might suggest).

Pacino is surrounded by other fine actors in *Serpico*. Ed Grover gives a good account of himself as Inspector Lombardo, a tough, tired but honest cop and the only guy at the Sixth Precinct who will work with Serpico. John Randolph is excellent, as usual, as the head of the task force gathered to investigate Serpico's claims. Jack Kehoe, Norman Ornellas, and Biff McGuire all register as some of Serpico's associates. Tony Roberts seems a bit out of place as a friend who tries to help Serpico get justice. Barbara Eda-Young is a bit too low-key as Serpico's second girlfriend, failing to make the most of their confrontation, although Cornelia Sharpe is fine as the first girlfriend, Leslie. Mildred Clinton, who plays Serpico's mother with warmth and humanity, was to really click four years later as the deranged "Mrs. Tredoni" in Alfred Sole's shocker *Communion*.

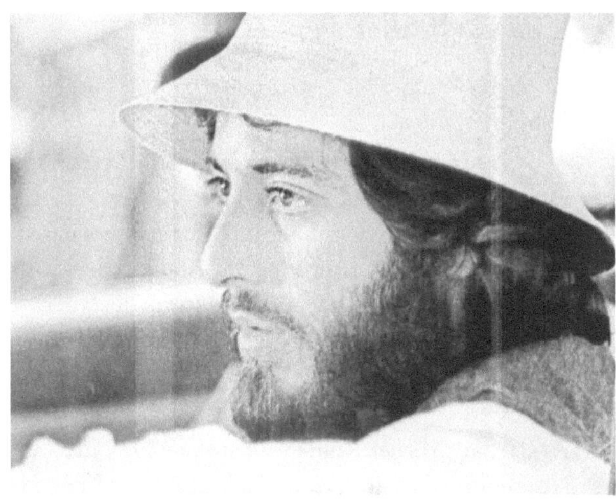

A character study of Pacino as New York City undercover cop Frank Serpico, one of many real-life people the actor would portray on film. *Serpico* (1973).

Despite the intense tone and grim subject matter, *Serpico* does have its lighter moments, such as when Serpico sings (?) an aria from Puccini's *Gianni Schicchi* as he drives to work. (Placido Domingo has nothing to fear from Al Pacino.) And a scene when Serpico and other cops are told to light up some joints so they can "learn" about grass is hilarious because it is obvious that most of them have already been stoned on marijuana many times!

Arthur J. Ornitz's cinematography of various New York City locations, from Gay Street in Greenwich Village (where Serpico lives) to the meat-market district at Ninth Avenue, are more than adequate, but Mikis Theodorakis's brassy score does absolutely nothing for the picture.

Pacino received an Academy Award nomination as Best Actor; he copped the Golden Globe Award, however. This time there was no Brando or Hackman with whom to share the spotlight. Pacino was a star—the sole star—in his own right.

The Godfather Part II

PARAMOUNT, 1974

Producer, Francis Ford Coppola; director, Coppola; director of photography, Gordon Willis; editors, Peter Zinner, A.C.E., Barry Malkin, and Richard Marks; screenplay, Coppola and Mario Puzo; based on *The Godfather* by Puzo; music, Nino Rota; coproducers, Gray Frederickson and Fred Roos; associate producer, Mona Skager; production designer, Dean Tavoularis; costume designer, Theodora Van Runkle. Running time: 200 minutes.

CAST

Al Pacino (*Michael Corleone*); Robert De Niro (*Vito Corleone*), Diane Keaton (*Kay*); John Cazale (*Fredo*); Robert Duvall (*Tom Hagen*); Talia Shire (*Connie*); G. D. Spradlin (*Pat Geary*); Mariana Hill (*Deanna*); Michael V. Gazzo (*Frankie*); Lee Strasberg (*Hyman Roth*); Dominic Chianese (*Johnny Old*); B. Kirby Jr. (*Young Clemenzo*); Gaston Moschin (*Don Fanucci*); Troy Donahue (*Merle Johnson*); Joe Spinell (*Cicci*); Leopoldo Trieste (*Don Roberto*); Roger Corman (*Senator Number* 2).

How to continue the saga of the Corleone family? wondered producer-director-cowriter Francis Ford Coppola. The future? The past? Why not both? It was decided that *The Godfather Part II* would be a two-part film: One would be a prequel showing how the original godfather, Vito Corleone (played in the original film by Marlon Brando), came to power; the second would be a sequel continuing the adventures of new godfather Michael Corleone (Al Pacino).

For the plum role of Vito Corleone as a young man, a relative unknown named Robert De Niro was chosen. There was no thought of replacing Al Pacino with anyone else in the role of Vito's son Michael. Rather than show an hour and a half of the prequel and then an hour and a half of the sequel, the two story lines were intercut, moving back and forth through time at significant moments in the lives of the characters. It was an effective way of linking father and son, showing how each dealt with problems and did away with adversaries in similarly ruthless fashion.

In the prequel, Vito Andolini is born in the Sicilian town of Corleone in 1901. By his ninth birthday, Vito's brother, father, and mother have all been murdered by the local don. Vito escapes to America, where an immigration official mistakes the name of the town he comes from for his surname. Years later, Vito is married and living in Little Italy in New York, a neighborhood controlled by Don Fanucci (Gaston Moschin) of the Black Hand. Fanucci has a stranglehold on the local merchants with his protection racket. When Fanucci insists that the owner of the store where Vito works replace Vito with his nephew, Vito turns to house robbing with a friend. When the don asks for a cut, Vito murders him and takes over his activities. He returns briefly to Sicily to kill the godfather who wiped out the rest of his family.

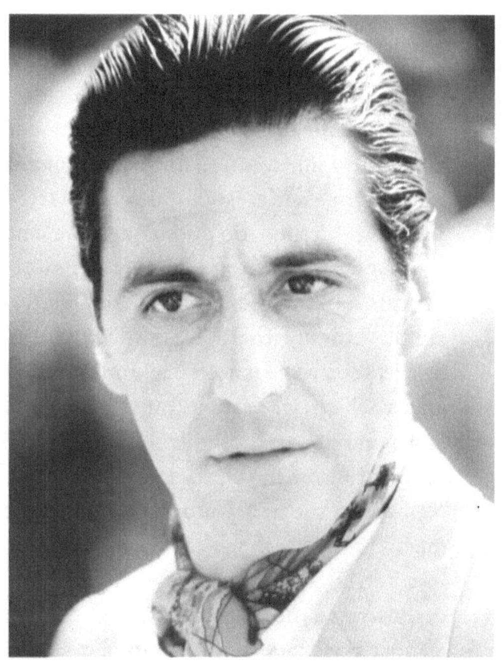

The melancholy "don," Michael Corleone (Pacino) in the highly successful *The Godfather Part II* (1974).

The sequel takes place mostly in Lake Tahoe in 1958, where Michael masquerades as a successful hotel owner. His promise to his wife, Kay (Diane Keaton), to get out of the family business within five years has not been kept. Attacked in his own bedroom by gunmen, who nearly kill his wife and child, Michael vows to destroy those both inside and outside his operation who put his family in danger. More ruthless than his father ever was, Michael wipes out rival factions and even orders a hit on his own brother, Fredo (John Cazale), who has "innocently" given potent information to their enemies. A disgusted Kay walks out on Michael, leaving him a godfather alone except for adopted brother, Tom Hagen (Robert Duvall), and his sister, Connie (Talia Shire), who has forgiven him for murdering her husband.

Some sections of *The Godfather Part II* have an undeniable sheen of class and artistry, an unmistakably polished craftsmanship, that is all the more ironic, since it is several cuts below the original. Considering that two years had gone by since they saw the first film, most audiences didn't notice. Besides, they were riveted by several top-notch sequences, most dealing with the gruesome dispatching of several individuals no one would miss.

For instance, there's Vito Corleone's murder of Don Fanucci, with the former waiting beside the stairs as the latter slowly and confidently ascends to his apartment. Fanucci thinks himself master of all he surveys and has no inkling that the arrogant Vito is waiting in the shadows. With a towel over his hand to hide the gun, Vito walks into the don's apartment, shoots him, then calmly goes home to his wife and babies as if nothing had ever happened. While

Fanucci is hardly an innocent victim, it is also clear that there is something of the sociopath in Vito Corleone's makeup. Another "fun" scene has loudmouth Frankie (Michael V. Gazzo), a renegade member of the family, being garroted in the back of a bar just as a policeman decides to step into the place for a drink. The timely intervention of the flatfoot saves Frankie's life (for the moment) but leads to an exciting shootout on the street.

One victim who doesn't deserve what she gets is Vito's mother, who early in the picture confronts the Sicilian don who has murdered one son and husband for an alleged insult to his family. She begs him to spare her youngest child, Vito, but the don is unmoved. He knows young Vito will want to kill him as soon as he is able. Right in front of the boy the mother's throat is slashed, an act which, we assume, must have a traumatic impact on the lad. (The *Godfather* movies are potboilers which rarely, if ever, delve into the psychological motivations of the characters.)

As in the first picture, perhaps the best sequence in the sequel is the climactic montage in which all of the godfather's prime enemies are taken care of in a series of vignettes: Jewish gangster Hyman Roth (Lee Strasberg), who orchestrated the unsuccessful hit on Michael at Lake Tahoe, is murdered at the airport as he talks to reporters; Frankie slashes his wrists in the bathtub while in protective custody; and—best of all—Fredo is shot in a rowboat on the quiet lake while Pacino watches sorrowfully but determinedly from the shore.

Clad in ascot and with slicked-back hair, Pacino plays with restraint and ever-present menace, icy, smooth, with a poker-player, butter-wouldn't-melt-in-his-mouth expression. The trouble is, Pacino isn't really given a *character* to play, as Michael Corleone is more of an icon in *The Godfather Part II* than a fully realized human being. Worse, Pacino at times underplays too much and talks too low and in an enervated fashion that borders on somnambulism. Perhaps he felt that the once-decent Michael Corleone would be suffering a deep depression because of all the vile actions he must undertake, with those enervating results. If so, Pacino was giving the material too much credit and subjecting it to too much analysis. Besides, one suspects that Michael Corleone, like his father before him, was never *that* bothered by anything he did.

Still, Pacino has more than his share of impressive sequences, such as when he confronts his brother Fredo over his betrayal, kisses him full on the lips, and says, "I know it was you, Fredo. You broke my heart. *You broke my heart.*" He registers a quivering, quiet intensity during a confrontation with Kay, when she tells him she had an abortion without his knowledge. One of Pacino's best scenes is an ironic 1941 flashback that shows him and the other members of the Corleone family at the dinner table. While his slimeball relatives talk about avoiding the post–Pearl Harbor draft, Michael calmly announces that he has enlisted in the marines. What a tragedy that the only heroic individual in the Corleone family should ultimately choose a path so corrupt and debasing.

As for the famous Pacino blasts? Well, Pacino's underplaying in this, as in the original *Godfather*, keeps the blasts to a minimum and reduces their intensity, but he does explode more than once, screaming at Kay (after hitting her), "*You won't take my children!*" He also gives Robert Duvall a miniblast when the latter tries to tell him the news of Kay's so-called miscarriage. "Can't you give me a straight answer? *Was it a boy?*" The best blast occurs when Michael confronts turncoat Frankie after being nearly riddled with bullets in his own bedroom. He dances about the man very quietly, deceptively, then bursts out with, "*In my home!*" (Only a murderous mafioso could be so filled with righteous indignation.)

The Godfather Part II is packed with talented supporting players, but three deserve special mention. Talia Shire (Coppola's sister) proves that it wasn't mere nepotism that got her the coveted role of sister Connie. Whether flaunting her gigolo boyfriend (Troy Donahue) and dissipated lifestyle in Michael's face or telling him she forgives him for the murder of her husband ("You were being strong for the family like Papa was"), she gets across her rather desperate, pathetic character very tellingly. Celebrated acting coach Lee Strasberg had never appeared in a film before being cast as the genteel (but not Gentile) gangster Hyman Roth; quietly telling lies to Michael as he watches TV or chairing a meeting of mobsters in Havana, he proves that during all those years of teaching he knew what he was talking about. John Cazale, as Fredo, gives a very strong performance and etches a memorable portrait of the screw-up Corleone brother who has been passed over as Michael makes it to the top. "I want *respect*," he tells Pacino. Any actor who can make a loser like Fredo seem sympathetic deserves respect, all right. Unfortunately, Shire and Strasberg were nominated for supporting Oscars, while Cazale—like Fredo—was overlooked.

Michael V. Gazzo also got a supporting Oscar nomination for playing the gravel-voiced, whining turncoat Frankie. Gazzo is good, but one suspects this is an actor of decidedly limited range whose whole career has been playing one variation of Frankie after another. (He was also a playwright, responsible for *A Hatful of Rain*.) The role of Kay has practically been reduced to a walk-on, and this time Diane Keaton isn't very good. During the Senate hearings on the Mafia, one of the senators is played (adequately) by Roger Corman, who produced some of Coppola's earliest features and gave him a start in the business.

Pacino was nominated for Best Actor and De Niro for Best Supporting Actor; this time the screen father won out over his "son." Although De Niro became a star with *The Godfather Part II* and is fine in the role, his performance is hardly Oscar-worthy. (Neither is Pacino's, for that matter.) But it was a "big" picture, and the academy loves big pictures and the actors in them. The movie also won Oscars for Best Picture, Best Screenplay, Best Score, and Best Director. Practically a solid sweep.

Not even nominated were production designer Dean Tavoularis, who provided an excellent re-creation of 1917 Little Italy, teeming with merchants, wagons, and children, and cinematographer Gordon Willis, who contributed some sumptuous shots of beautiful Sicilian settings, not to mention New York and Lake Tahoe.

Despite the accolades, there are problems with *The Godfather Part II*. The script for the 1950s story line is too diffuse, moving in too many directions, and hasn't a strong enough plot. The whole mid-film business with the gangsters and unstable political situation in Cuba is convoluted and tiresome and belongs in a different picture. Running over three hours, the movie is often quite slow-paced. It is not as strong or as entertaining as the original film.

There is no question that the Mafia is romanticized a bit too much in *The Godfather Part II*. Virtually all of the adversaries of the Corleone family are reptiles. (But surely the Mafia kills innocents once in a while?) Young Vito Corleone's victims are two slimy dons, one who rides herd over Little Italy and another who kills women and children with hardly a backward glance. Once Vito is set up as the new don in New York, his first act is to keep a poor, helpless widow from being thrown out onto the street! Decades later, the murder of Connie's husband is minimized because he was a creep and a wife beater. It's as if the film were saying: "These guys are good guys. They were victims, too. They only kill people who deserve it." The real-life Mafia is hardly so benign.

The question persists: Why do so many talented Italian-American filmmakers and actors—the best of their community—insist on making motion pictures that celebrate the activities of the *worst* of their community?

The saga of the Corleone family wasn't over, but Al Pacino had many other projects before it was through.

Dog Day Afternoon

WARNER BROS., 1975

Producers, Martin Bregman and Martin Elfand; director, Sidney Lumet; director of photography, Victor J. Kemper; editor, Dede Allen; screenplay, Frank Pierson; associate producer, Robert Greenhut; art director, Burtt Harris; production designer, Charles Bailey; costume designer, Anna Hill Johnstone. Running time: 130 minutes.

Cast

Al Pacino (*Sonny Wortzik*); John Cazale (*Sal*); Chris Sarandon (*Leon*); Susan Peretz (*Angie*); Judith Malina (*Mother*); Charles Durning (*Detective Moretti*); Penelope Allen (*Sylvia*); Sully Boyar (*Mulvaney*); James Broderick (*Sheldon*); Lance Henriksen (*Murphy*); Dick Anthony Williams (*Limo Driver*); Carol Kane (*Jenny*); John Marriot (*Howard*); Sandra Kazan (*Deborah*); Gary Springer (*Stevie*); Beulah Garrick (*Margaret*); Marcia Jean Kurtz (*Miriam*); Amy Levitt (*Maria*).

One of the zaniest—and most pathetic—bank-robbery attempts of all time took place on August 22, 1972, in Brooklyn, New York. So bizarre were aspects of this real-life occurrence that it is easy to see why the subject matter proved irresistible to filmmakers. The result was *Dog Day Afternoon*, which takes place on a hot August afternoon and part of the evening. The "dog" was Sonny Wortzik (Al Pacino)—a variation of the man's real name—and a bigger loser it would be hard to find. The bank holdup he plans with two colleagues goes awry right from the start. First, one of the robbers chickens out immediately after Sonny makes his move and has to be let out of the bank.

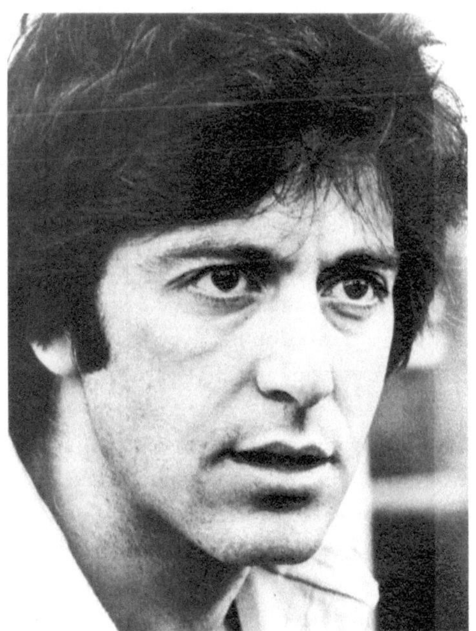

Pacino is electrifying in his performance as an incompetent bank robber in Sidney Lumet's *Dog Day Afternoon* (1975).

"Don't take the car!" Sonny tells him, knowing he'll need it for a getaway.

"How'll I get home?" whines the boy, Stevie (Gary Springer).

"Take the subway," Sonny tells him.

Then it turns out that most of the money in the bank was picked up earlier in the day and only $1,100 is left in the vault. Sonny lights a fire in a garbage can, and the smoke attracts the attention of a shopkeeper and then the police. Before Sonny and his remaining colleague, Sal (John Cazale), can make their getaway, they are surrounded by 250 cops. Drawn into hostage negotiations with a detective, Moretti (Charles Durning), Sonny says he wants to talk to his wife, but the wife they bring is not his spouse, Angie (Susan Peretz), but a male lover whom Sonny married in a special gay ceremony. Leon (Chris Sarandon), fresh from Bellevue, needs a sex-change operation, which Sonny apparently was planning to finance with the proceeds from the robbery.

Sonny, Sal, and their comparatively friendly hostages set off in a limo to the airport, where the police supposedly have a plane ready to take the two desperadoes to Algeria. "There's a Howard Johnson's there," Sonny explains. But before they can board the plane, Sal is shot in the forehead by a Federal Bureau of Investigations (FBI) man, and Sonny is taken into custody. His sentence: twenty years in a federal penitentiary.

At first, Pacino, who is not a nerd as Sonny is, seems miscast. But he manages to play a dork dynamically without making the character seem *less* of one. Although far more attractive than the real Sonny, Pacino does an excellent imitation of him, getting across his essential *schlumpiness*, the puppylike, shuffling manner, and the incipient craziness lying just below the surface. The voice is also perfect, reeking of Brooklyn and hinting of vulnerabilities that Sonny tries to disguise with nervous, angry chatter and vocal outbursts, such as when he yells at Durning—whom he feels is trying to put one over on him—"Kiss me! When I'm being fucked, I like to be kissed!" He delivers a mini-Pacino blast to his chatterbox wife. "Will you shut up and *just listen to me*!"

Pacino had mixed emotions about playing a major gay (or bisexual) lead in a popular (as opposed to "art") film, which had really not been done before. To his credit, he resists camping it up or stereotyping the character. In real life, Sonny may have been a nerd, but he was not a lisping, limp-wristed "queen," and Pacino was right not to play him that way.

Pacino is matched in brilliance by Chris Sarandon as his lover, who really doesn't want any part of him. Leon, who *is* a queen, holds one hand perpetually up to his neck as if to register his disbelief that any of this can be happening. Leon likes how he's treated in Bellevue but has some doubts. "They say you're crazy, and right away they stick somethin' in ya arm, and pretty soon you're sleepin.' How can you get uncrazy when ya' sleepin' all the time?" Leon's sense of humor is his saving grace. "[Sonny's] mother and father together are like a bad car wreck," he says. The highlight of the picture is Sonny's phone conversation with Leon; the two principal actors improvised much of their dialogue, according to Sidney Lumet. When Sonny asks Leon to accompany him on his flight out of the country, Leon snaps: "I've been tryin' to get away from you for six months, and I'm gonna go with you on a *plane trip*?" Then he asks, "Where are ya goin'?" Sonny is unmoved by Leon's whining. "Sal thinks Wyoming is a country. He doesn't know where it is. You think you got problems? I'm with a guy who doesn't know where Wyoming is!"

Speaking of Sal, he's very well played by John Cazale, who had also supported Pacino in the *Godfather* films. The role of Sal is not as showy as that of Fredo Corleone—Cazale actually hasn't much to do and is saddled with an impossible, ambiguous part—but he plays it with quiet effectiveness and restrained intensity. The look on Cazale's face as he sits in the backseat of the limo at the airport seems to suggest that Sal senses the approach of his own death moments later. (Sadly, Cazale himself would be dead of bone cancer within three years.)

Cazale also has a few good moments when Sal hears a news report claiming that "two homosexuals" have robbed the First Brooklyn Savings Bank. "But *I'm* not a homosexual" he says in distress. When an FBI agent comes into the bank to check on the hostages, Sal says to him, "Tell the TV to stop sayin' there's two homosexuals in here." Sal doesn't care if people know he's a bank robber, but he doesn't want anyone to think he's gay.

Another highlight is Sonny's phone conversation with spouse Angie, who is convinced she is the cause of Sonny's falling for Leon. "I know I let myself get fat," she says. Susan Peretz manages to make Angie touching beneath the farcical exterior. For her part, Sonny's mother (Judith Malina) agrees with her daughter-in-law: "You wouldn't need Leon if Angie were treating you right," she avers in a hilarious encounter with her nebbish son on the sidewalk outside the bank as hundreds of cops, spectators, and media people watch Sonny trying to deal with his well-meaning, if kvetching, mother. Malina makes the most of her brief bit, as does Gary Springer, as Stevie, the friend who bolts from the bank at the beginning of the picture. Also in the cast was Pacino's old friend Penny (now billed "Penelope") Allen, as the chief teller Sylvia. Allen, who was wonderful in *Scarecrow*, has more to do in *Dog Day Afternoon* but fewer *dramatic* scenes (nothing along the lines of her phone conversation with Lion in *Scarecrow*). Still, Allen has a breezy way with the material. Witness her evocative delivery of "So you rob a bank, but you keep your body pure" to health advocate Sal, who has chided her for lighting a cigarette. Charles Durning's contribution as Moretti cannot be underestimated, and James Broderick and Lance Henriksen are also fine as FBI agents who finally put a stop to the nonsense. Dick Anthony Williams as the limo driver (who is also a cop) is also fun as he chortles to Sonny, "You gonna shoot, aim for white meat."

Although talky, the film has a few spurts of excitement, such as when Sonny nearly causes a riot by throwing money into the crowd outside the bank. The excellent opening montage of New Yorkers at work and play, its beaches, sidewalks, bridges, and traffic, winds up with a striking, ominous—and prescient—shot of a cemetery with the New York skyline in the background. Editor Dede Allen really shows her stuff with a cinematic sequence showing cops trying to enter the bank through the back of the building. Bits with the security guard being mistaken for one of the bank robbers, a pizza delivery boy who carries on like a star when he hands the pizzas to Sonny, and a hostage's Italian boyfriend who pounces on Sonny and is carted away by the cops for his trouble (*he's* treated far more roughly than Sonny is!) also compensate for the film's slower stretches. The climactic motorcade to the airport is also well handled, with crowds alternately rooting for the robbers or trying to smash the windows of the limo with bottles.

Dog Day Afternoon was made at a time when the country was more naive about the crime situation, when it was still possible to laugh at bungling bank robbers. Sonny tells Sal that he doesn't mean it when he threatens to "throw out the bodies of the hostages," but early in the picture he tells Stevie, the recalcitrant robber, to "take his head off!" if the security guard makes a move (which prompts Stevie to bolt from the bank). Whatever Sonny's nature, Sal seems more than capable of killing someone. If no one but Sal died, it may have been due more to luck than Sonny's alleged compassion. When Sonny expresses concern over the bank manager's diabetes, the manager says: "I wish you had never come into this bank. Don't try to act like you're some angel of human kindness!"

There was a predominance of antiauthority feeling in the seventies, and this was carried over to the police, who are booed by the crowds outside the bank when Sonny screams, "Attica! Attica!" When it is discovered that Sonny has a male lover, the "lunatic fringe" of the gay community (hardly its more sensible, mainstream members) also show up to cheer Sonny on. (None of these nitwits, however—gay or straight—offers to take the place of one of the hostages in the bank!) But Sonny isn't an anti–Establishment hero; he's a loser with a wife and kids on welfare who seeks money not to help his family but his lover, who wants no part of him.

To their credit, the filmmakers *aren't* saying that Sonny is a hero; they are only documenting the moronic reactions of the crowd. But the comic aspects of his actions serve to minimize the actuality of what he's doing, as well as the sheer *terror* that must have been felt by the bank tellers. We're even manipulated into feeling bad for the creepy Sal when he's killed by the FBI. (Moral: if you don't want to get shot by the cops, don't commit crimes.)

Dog Day Afternoon was probably as upsetting to the Polish-American Anti-Defamation League as it was to some gays, but it is memorable as a generally funny burlesque show and slice of outré New York life—and for Pacino's excellent performance. Pacino, Sarandon and Dede Allen were all nominated for Oscars, as were the picture and Lumet (who turned in one of his better directorial efforts). Only screenwriter Frank Pierson brought home the coveted statue, however.

After his sex-change operation ("Leon Schermer is now a woman and living in New York" reads an end-credit title), the real Leon changed his name to Liz Eden. Liz danced topless at the Hungry Hilda on Eighth Avenue for a while, then tried to become one of the endless New Yorkers famous for being famous, but nobody cared. She, like Sonny, has faded into well-deserved obscurity.

Bobby Deerfield

WARNER BROS./COLUMBIA PICTURES, 1977

Executive producer, John Foreman; producer, Sydney Pollack; director, Pollack; director of photography, Henri Decae; editor, Fredric Steinkamp; screenplay, Alvin Sargent; based on *Heaven Has No Favorites* by Erich Maria Remarque; music, Dave Grusin; production designer, Stephen Grimes. Running time: 123 minutes.

CAST

Al Pacino (*Bobby Deerfield*); Marthe Keller (*Lillian*); Walter McGinn (*Leonard*); Stephan Meldegg (*Karl Holzman*); Anny Duperey (*Lydia*); Romolo Valli (*Uncle Luigi*); Norm Nielsen (*the Magician*); Jaime Sanchez (*Delvecchio*); Mickey Knox, Dorothy James (*Tourists*).

Bobby Deerfield was Al Pacino's eighth picture and the first of his that wasn't a particularly good movie. The movie's intentions may have been admirable, but its execution faltered. Some critics felt *Bobby Deerfield* was Pacino's certified turkey; it is actually only one of half a dozen or so really disappointing films in a career of mostly hits. *Bobby Deerfield* isn't a complete stinker—but it's close.

Pacino plays a racing driver, Bobby Deerfield, whose friend has just died in an accident. Bobby wonders what caused the accident—something on the track, perhaps?—and heads for a clinic where Karl Holzman, another racer-friend, is recuperating. In the dining room an enigmatic young lady at the next table asks to borrow the butter and begins a conversation with Bobby. She is another patient, named Lillian (Marthe Keller). Lillian is insolent and presumptuous, borderline rude and insulting, yet oddly engaging. Bobby agrees to give her a ride home from the clinic. The two begin an affair, and Bobby learns that Lillian is dying of an unspecified illness. After a few days together, Lillian asks Bobby to take her back to the clinic. ("I was thinking about your friend Holzman. I think I would like to go back—to see how he is.") Lillian dies while at the clinic, and Bobby goes on with his life.

Bobby Deerfield presents a kinder, gentler Al Pacino than had been seen in previous pictures, Lion in *Scarecrow* notwithstanding. Alvin Sargent's screenplay doesn't tell us much about Bobby—or Lillian, for that matter—but Pacino does the best he can with the material. Pacino is never somnambulistic, as he sometimes is in *The Godfather Part II*, just more subdued. Even the sweet character of Lion had a little more of an edge to him (with a nervous breakdown to boot). Deerfield may have come from Newark, New Jersey, but he's as suave and polished as the European surroundings.

Pacino's acting cannot be faulted. He has an expert, natural reaction when he learns from his French girlfriend, Lydia, what she already heard through the grapevine, that Lillian is dying. Later on, as Lillian lies in her bed in the clinic singing, her death is mirrored only in Pacino's eyes as her singing stops, the camera fixed on Bobby's face. Pacino underplays the scene beautifully. At one point, Pacino is allowed to work up some fire (if not quite a blast) as he confronts Keller in a big field where she is waiting to take off in a hot-air balloon. Deerfield is exasperated at Lillian's attitude and at the way she left him in the morning without saying where she was going. But Lillian refuses to behave like a typical dying person. When she leaves the clinic early, the nurse says, "Madame—the rules?" to which Lillian replies, "No rules. I come to death on my own terms." Trying to make Lillian laugh at one point, Bobby/Pacino launches into one of the most godawful impersonations of Mae West ever recorded on camera. (Pacino should stick to Boris Karloff, whom he did pretty well in *Scarecrow*.) Of course, Bobby's impression isn't supposed to be very good.

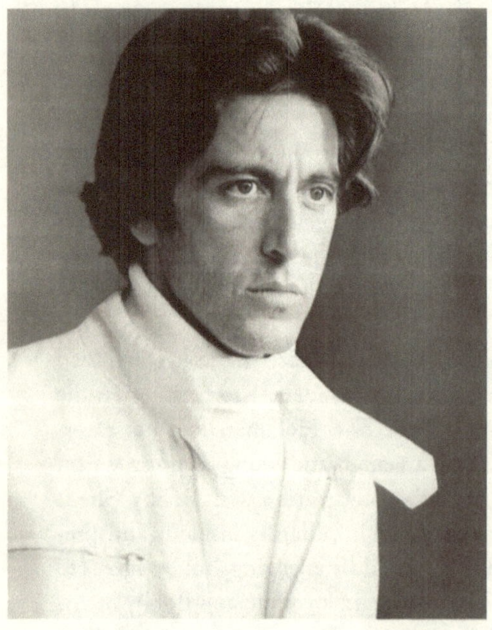

As fictional Grand Prix race-car driver *Bobby Deerfield* (1977), Pacino lacks his usual sparkle. The film was, according to the select few who saw it, a car wreck.

Marthe Keller makes a very chic—if, at times, tacky—Camilla. Lillian tells Bobby that she thinks racing is boring and that a racing car "is only an extension of a man's penis." She asks Bobby, "Are you a homo?" and wonders if there are any "homos" in New Jersey. Passing through a tunnel in Bobby's car, she screams out loud. She is a scared, defiant woman-child saying whatever comes into her mind, regardless of its effect. It's as if she feels that the fact that she's dying gives her the right to say or do anything. Marthe Keller is adept at revealing the surface of her character but, in this film at least, lacks the virtuosity to show us the vulnerability underneath. (In a previous decade Margaret Sullavan, who did appear in two adaptations of Erich Maria Remarque novels, would have been cast in the role and would have been much better, delineating both Lillian's desperate obnoxiousness and the sad, frightened, lonely quality beneath.)

While Keller may not have overly impressed the critics, she did make an impression on Pacino, who took her for his lover and moved her into his apartment back in New York City. Keller's American film career never really took off, however (the disappointing grosses of *Bobby Deerfield*, after appearances in such blockbusters as *Marathon Man* and *Black Sunday*, couldn't have helped); she was a limited performer and perhaps too Germanic to appeal to American audiences, the more talented Marlene Dietrich notwithstanding.

One actor in *Bobby Deerfield* who was closer to the mark was Walter McGinn, who does a nice job as Bobby's brother Leonard. Pacino and McGinn help sustain the tension in a restaurant encounter between brothers in which Leonard—who has a safer, if less glamorous, job in the printing business—chastises Bobby for not taking time to see their mother, an alcoholic. McGinn gets across the brother's bitterness; Leonard is saddled with a wife, three kids, and a mother-in-law and, in addition, has to attend to the family responsibilities all by himself, while footloose Bobby indulges in an irresponsible lifestyle. Yet Leonard has made his choices and must live with them. (Ironically, McGinn was killed in an automobile accident only a few months after the film was released.) Anny Duperey and Romolo Valli are also notable as, respectively, Bobby's appealing French girlfriend, Lydia, and Lillian's Uncle Luigi, with whom Lillian lives.

The picture is not without its worthwhile moments, such as a charming scene in a nightspot when Bobby and Lillian ask the magician who has just performed to give away his secrets. "It's magic," he insists. An oddly touching moment (one that some viewers giggle at) occurs when Bobby takes pieces of Lily's hair that have fallen out onto the pillow and pointlessly tries to place them back on her head. Yet it bespeaks tenderness and confusion and somehow works. By far the best scene is a poignant bit when a couple of middle-aged tourists, a husband and wife, ask Bobby to take their picture and then snap one of Bobby and Lillian. They ask for an address where they can send it. All the while it is apparent to us and to the young lovers that Lillian will probably be dead before they ever receive it. (We see a shot of the snapshot at the end of the film.) For a few moments you're almost fooled into thinking you're seeing a better picture than *Bobby Deerfield* really is.

What went wrong with *Bobby Deerfield?* Sydney Pollack's direction is perfectly fluid; the acting is acceptable (and in the case of Pacino and some others even better than that); Henri Decae's cinematography, with its striking shots of Paris and Florence and, in particular, a flight of hot-air balloons (the balloons look like mammoth, bloated sailboats in the sky), is excellent; and Dave Grusin's music, with its Spanish guitars and European flavor, is often lovely.

The trouble is that the source material, Erich Maria Remarque's novel *Heaven Has No Favorites,* is essentially a European product, and a period piece at that. Updated and made by (mostly) Americans, with an insufficient script (the novel may not have been a good bet for film adaptation), the results were less than felicitous. *Bobby Deerfield* was an attempt to make an *English-language* European film, but Sydney Pollack is no Fellini. The movie is an odd, moody hybrid that never quite soars. The enigmatic main characters are of no help. The picture should have been a powerful study of loneliness, but it isn't. Still, it has its evocative moments, such as when Lillian tells Bobby the story of her father's death, how he keeled over suddenly on the beach and fell on top of a child. "It was like, in dying, he gave birth to the child, like an egg."

But all the (at times) heavy-handed death symbolism isn't enough to save *Bobby Deerfield,* which had many Pacino fans wishing it had been an offer Pacino could have refused.

...And Justice for All

COLUMBIA PICTURES, 1979

Executive producer, Joe Wizen; producers, Norman Jewison and Patrick Palmer; director, Norman Jewison; director of photography, Victor J. Kemper; aerial photography, Frank Holgate; editor, John F. Burnett, A.C.E.; screenplay, Valerie Curtin and Barry Levinson; music, Dave Grusin; production designer, Richard MacDonald; costume designer, Ruth Myers. Running time: 117 minutes.

CAST

Al Pacino (*Arthur Kirkland*); Jack Warden (*Judge Rayford*); John Forsythe (*Judge Fleming*); Lee Strasberg (*Grandpa Sam*); Jeffrey Tambor (*Jay Porter*); Christine Lahti (*Gail Packer*); Dominic Chianese (*Carl Trovers*); Thomas Waites (*Jeff McCullough*); Robert Christian (*Ralph Agee*); Craig T. Nelson (*Frank Bowers*); Stephen Blackmore (*Robert Winkle*); Charles Siebert (*Kane*); Keith Andes

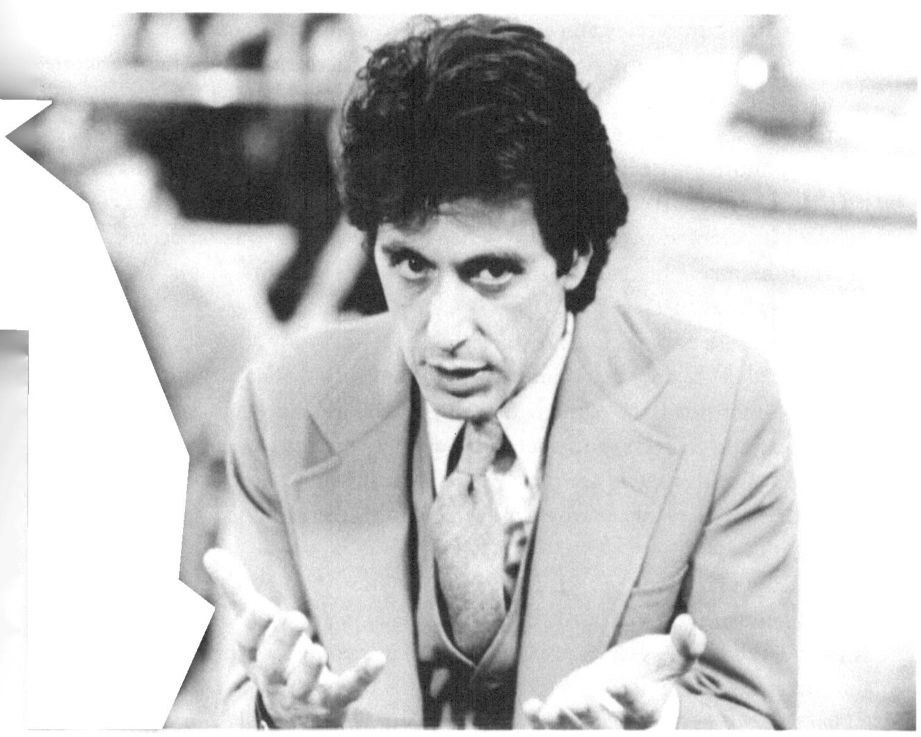

Pacino is back in form as passionate lawyer Arthur Kirkland in the judicial system satire *...And Justice for All* (1979).

(*Marvin Bates*); Sam Levene (*Arnie*); Teri Wootten (*Leah Shephard*); Larry Bryggman (*Warren Fresnelf*).

Baltimore lawyer Arthur Kirkland (Al Pacino) is being kept very busy. His nemesis, Judge Henry Fleming (John Forsythe), has had him thrown in jail for contempt of court. A wealthy client is trapped in his car with a hooker after an accident. Another client—whose arrest was due to mistaken identity—must remain in jail because the statute of limitations has run out on presenting new evidence. Kirkland's partner suffers a breakdown and must be carted away, with Kirkland at his side, meaning a disinterested associate has to stand in for the sentencing of a transvestite. When the associate muffs the whole thing, the client commits suicide when he learns he has to go to jail. To cap it all, Judge Fleming is accused of raping, beating, and sodomizing a young lady and chooses Arthur for his lawyer. Arthur knows this is a case that can make or break a reputation, but when he learns Judge Fleming is guilty, he goes berserk in the courtroom and delivers a speech condemning the hypocritical Fleming, to all intents and purposes destroying his own career in the process.

Pacino again received an Academy Award nomination for Best Actor for *...And Justice for All*; it is one of his most winning performances, with the actor at his most assured, confident, and charismatic. Arthur Kirkland is one of Pacino's most likable creations. Whether he is quietly but firmly telling off an ethics committee or telling a recalcitrant client not to "bullshit" him, you're with him all the way *...And Justice for All* gives Pacino plenty of opportunities to deliver his patented blasts, but he is also excellent in the quieter scenes, such as when he meets his grandfather's elderly lady friend and displays a polite, realistic awkwardness.

Humor isn't always Pacino's forte, but he's very funny when Judge Rayford (Jack Warden), a certified eccentric, takes him for a helicopter ride and tells him he might not have enough fuel to get back. Pacino evinces convincing queasiness and distress, and then hilarious hysteria, as the copter plummets into the bay and the two are nearly killed. Sitting in a coffee shop later, chattering, and with a blanket thrown over him, his barely restrained fury at Warden is delightful.

Pacino's climactic speech to the jury is "showy" in the best sense of the word, filled with riveting pyrotechnics, as if Pacino knew the only way to make the contrived scene work was to play it for all it was worth. He builds up slowly but forcefully to the Pacino blast, then points to Judge Fleming and screams: "*That man should go right to fuckin' jail*!" But Pacino's finest moment occurs after his associate, Warren (Larry Bryggman), blows it in court and their transvestite client kills himself rather than go to jail, which Pacino had promised him would not happen. First, Pacino smashes the windows of Warren's car as it halts on its way out of the parking garage. He continues battering the automobile as Warren does his best to calm him down. Finally, Warren gets out of the car to talk to him after making Pacino promise to rein himself in. Pacino plays the scene with heart-breaking sincerity, going from fury, righteous anger, and passion to grief and simple compassion: "Don't you *care?*" he says to Warren. "They're just people—*don't you care?*" It is one of the strongest scenes Pacino has ever played and proof positive that he is one of our most passionate and poignant actors.

Others in the cast also give fine performances, such as John Forsythe as the reptilian Judge Fleming, who sits in court with a smug, calm demeanor as if only he is allowed to be above the law regardless of what atrocities he has committed. Jack Warden scores, as expected, as the unconventional judge who eats his lunch on a ledge outside his window several stories up, attempts suicide every so often for the hell of it, and bets his (and his passengers') lives on whether or not his copter can make it back on however little fuel remains. Lee Strasberg essays a very different part from his mobster in *The Godfather*

Part II as Pacino's wise, warm, but hopelessly senile grandfather, but is just as strong and convincing. Talented actress Christine Lahti (in her feature debut) however, is pretty much wasted as Gail Packer, with whom Kirkland has a relationship of sorts.

The usually reliable Jeffrey Tambor, as Kirkland's partner, Jay Porter, seems a bit off in *...And Justice for All,* possibly because of the way his role is written. Porter's problems begin when a murderer whom he has gotten off murders again. We're asked to believe that a slick lawyer who would have no problem defending someone he knows to be guilty of a heinous murder would suffer a nervous breakdown because his client has murdered again. But if the lawyer didn't care about the first victim, why the second? While it might be believable that Porter would feel some slight guilt, it isn't believable that he would shave his head as a reaction to his internal distress or grab stacks of plates from the cafeteria and fling them at all and sundry who walk down the hall toward his office in the courthouse. At least this situation makes for a lively sequence, with Warden running interference as he and Pacino hurl themselves down the corridor dodging missiles as Tambor screams, plates smash on walls and floor, and Pacino makes a desperate bid to stop and control his partner before the police can make their move. Like a lot of scenes in this picture, it *plays* without ever being convincing.

The casting of some of the smaller parts is particularly good, such as Robert Christian as the pathetic drag queen who has been arrested for participating in a holdup of a taxi driver, and Thomas Waites, who makes the most of the kid incarcerated simply because he was mistaken for somebody else. Dominic Chianese is fun as Pacino's big-bucks, womanizing client who says to a rescue worker trying to cut him out of a smashed-up automobile: "Can't you see I'm on the [car] phone?" Sam Levene as Grandpa's buddy, and Keith Andes as Bates, Judge Fleming's colleague, are also notable.

But as entertaining and well acted as *...And Justice for All* may be, it almost sinks under its contrivances. And the script has too many melodramatic scenes in a row: Tambor goes berserk, the transvestite commits suicide, the wrong-identity client also loses it, ties up two guards, and winds up shot to death by the police—all of this happens within half an hour, it seems. Worse still, much of the screenplay asks us to accept too much. Forsythe *admits* his guilt to Pacino, which he *would never* have done. Pacino (earlier) assumes that Forsythe is guilty simply because someone gives him sleazy pictures showing Fleming with a hooker. Kirkland is mad at Fleming because the judge refuses to look at new evidence which might free the wrong-identity client, but it takes weeks for him to say to the judge that he'll represent him *if* he agrees to look at the new evidence. Why didn't Kirkland make this point the *first* time Fleming asks him to be his lawyer?

The whole business with Tambor's guilt and breakdown might have been believable if it had been developed properly. And while Kirkland's telling the jury in righteous outrage that his client Fleming is guilty and should go to jail is a hell of a lot of fun, it doesn't make a lick of sense. Pacino is throwing his career away (what client, guilty or innocent, would want this loon for a lawyer?), and Fleming will simply be given a new trial and a more amenable solicitor. For all Kirkland's indignation and integrity, *nothing has been gained*. Everyone knows that Fleming and Kirkland hate each other, so the latter's outburst won't even be taken that seriously (and it certainly doesn't mean that Fleming will be convicted). In its effort to be a "feel good" movie, *...And Justice for All* sacrifices veracity.

"*Let* criminals create their own hellhole," says Judge Fleming. "What we need is unjust punishment. Is bringing Johnny Cash into prison to sing songs going to rehabilitate anyone?" The judge actually makes some excellent points, but the script's somewhat "bleeding heart" slant ensures that the audience won't take them seriously because Fleming is a hypocrite, a ranter, and never listens to what is actually being said by Kirkland (for instance, that his wrong-identity client is innocent). We're asked to cry for the drag queen who kills himself but not to feel anything for the hardworking cabdriver he helped rob.

Still, *...And Justice for All* tries to be fair and does get across the insanity of the so-called justice system. One scene has a public defender pleading with an assistant D.A. to reduce his client's sentence because he's *afraid* to tell him he'll have to spend a year in jail. A criminal who grabbed an elderly woman's purse and *beat her* in all sincerity blames the victim because he "meant no harm ... she shoulda let go." The picture is consistently flavorful and colorful and fast-paced, even if Norman Jewison's unobtrusive direction doesn't really do much for the film.

Al Pacino deserves high marks for triumphing over an impossible script and coming out on top, after all.

Cruising

LORIMAR, 1980

Producer, Jerry Weintraub; director, William Friedkin; director of photography, James Contner; editor, Bud Smith; screenplay, Friedkin; based on the novel by Gerald Walker; music, Jack Nitzsche; art director, Edward Pisoni; production designer, Bruce Weintraub; costume designer, Robert de Mora. Running time: 106 minutes.

Cast

Al Pacino (*Steve Burns*); Paul Sorvino (*Captain Edelson*); Karen Allen (*Nancy*); Don Scardino (*Ted Bailey*); Allan Miller (*Chief of Detectives*); Jay Acovone (*Skip Lee*); Richard Cox (*Stuart Richards*); Arnaldo Santana (*Loren Luka*); James Remar (*Greg*); Joe Spinell (*DeSimone*); Edward O'Neil (*Detective Schreiber*); Powers Boothe (*Hanky Salesman*); James Sutorius (*Voice of Jack*).

Why did Al Pacino want to do *Cruising*? Regardless of its controversial aspects, the script offered Pacino very few dramatic possibilities and not even a great deal of dialogue. His role is primarily a passive one: he goes from place to place studying, watching, occasionally reacting. The true mystery of the film is why he thought it would be a good project for him.

Cruising began life as a penny-dreadful thriller by former *New York Times* editor Gerald Walker. The novel deals with a cop who goes undercover to catch a serial killer of gay men. The killer, a college student, goes berserk in a bathhouse,

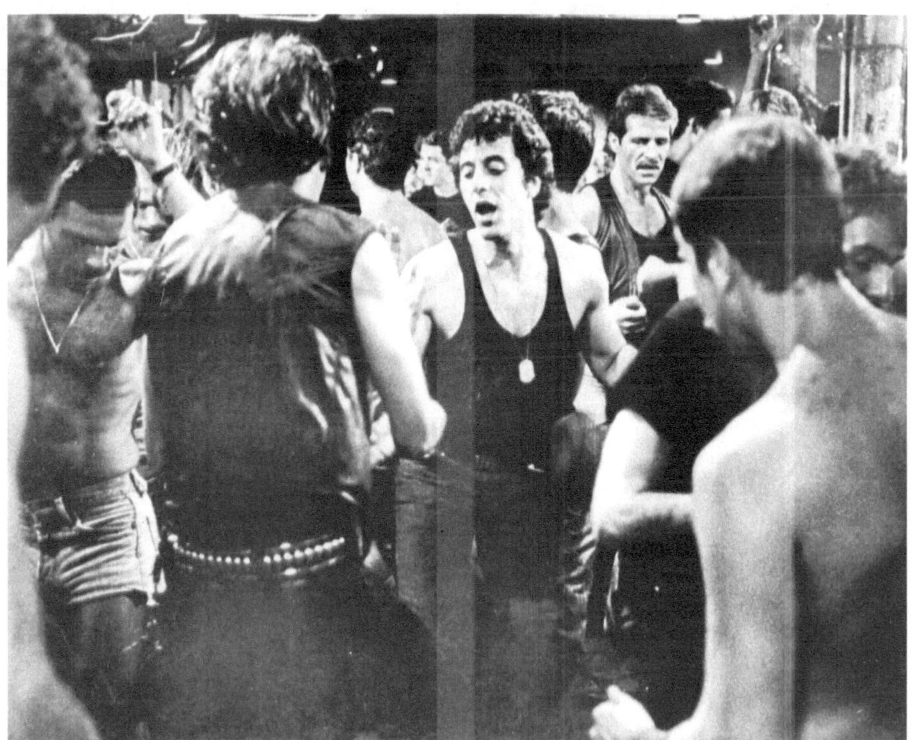

In one of his most ill-advised career moves, Pacino essayed the role of Steve Burns, an undercover cop attempting to ferret out a vicious serial killer in Greenwich Village's leather bar scene. *Cruising* (1980).

severing men's penises and placing them in their mouths. The student's spree of violence is ended, but it is suggested that the whole business will start all over again when the cop kills a man with whom he has his first homosexual experience.

Walker felt that he had exposed the roots of homophobia: his killers are murdering their repressed homosexual natures. But homophobia, like all prejudice, has a variety of causes, from inferiority complexes to ignorance to societal and religious pressures. Walker compared his novel to Martin Sherman's 1979 play *Bent*—which detailed the persecution of homosexuals during the Nazi regime—ignoring the fact that the play was a serious work of theater and of artistic merit, while his novel was an indifferently written potboiler devoid of much depth or characterization. (This same problem was carried over to the film.)

Brian De Palma, with whom Pacino would work on *Scarface* and *Carlito's Way*, was first interested in filming *Cruising*, but his script was very different from the one penned by eventual director William Friedkin. De Palma's killer is not a repressed homosexual but a failed actor who videotapes his murders (as does the killer in Michael Powell's 1960 film *Peeping Tom*) and kills a woman at one point just to throw the police off his track. (This particular murder became the elevator razor-slashing of Angie Dickinson's character in De Palma's *Dressed to Kill*.)

Director William Friedkin, famous for *The Exorcist* (1973), *The French Connection* (1971) and the gay-oriented stage adaptation *The Boys in the Band* (1970), hadn't had a hit in years—and needed one. For his part, Pacino had only made two pictures in the five years since *Dog Day Afternoon*, and neither of them had done that well at the box office. Both men undoubtedly felt that an unusual, graphic shocker like *Cruising* would stir up a lot of controversy, get plenty of advance press, and emerge a hit. They were mistaken.

The police find a human arm in the river and assume it's from the latest victim of a killer who preys on homosexuals. Steven Burns (Al Pacino), a young police officer, is chosen to go undercover in the gay community because of his strong resemblance to the other victims. Steve finds himself somewhat mesmerized by the hedonistic, sensual goings-on in the gay S&M hangouts he must frequent as part of his investigation. He tells his captain that it's too much for him, but the superior officer insists he remain on the case. After a series of killings, the trail leads to Stuart Richards (Richard Cox), a student at Columbia University. Richards and Burns square off in a tense Central Park encounter, with Burns the victor. After Richards's arrest, Burns's gay neighbor Ted Bailey (Don Scardino) is found murdered. When the captain learns that Steve was living just down the hall from the victim, he mutters, "Oh, my God."

Affecting a curlier, fluffier hairstyle than usual, Pacino dresses in leather throughout most of the picture and at one point employs an eyebrow pencil before going out for the evening. (Why he would use makeup before going to a bar frequented by "butch" gay men who disdain stereotypical effeminacy is never explained.) At first, he looks realistically uncomfortable dancing with and among men in the crowded bars, but eventually he loosens up and really works himself into a sweat.

As already noted, Pacino doesn't really have that much to do in *Cruising*—the film consists mostly of wild inside glimpses of the goings-on in gay leather bars, with an occasional murder thrown in for good measure—but he is allowed two good opportunities to emote. The first has him telling his captain, Edelson (Paul Sorvino), that he just can't handle the assignment; it's just too weird, and it's having a bad effect on him. He vividly gets across Burns's fear and stress and near panic without any overacting. Later on, he gives us a bona fide Pacino blast when gay neighbor Ted's bitchy roommate, Greg, calls him "trash." Reacting negatively (to put it mildly) to Greg's insinuation that he's in love with Ted, Burns starts hollering and trying to kick his door down. (This, of course, sets up Ted's murder. Burns—if he *is* the killer—doesn't murder Greg, but the object of his alleged affection, Ted; hence, he's "killing" his homosexual feelings.)

Is Burns Ted's killer? In Walker's novel, he was, and he was supposed to be in the movie, too. (The implication is still very much there.) Responding to gay protesters, who understandably objected to the insinuation that exposure to the gay subculture would turn one into a homicidal maniac (assuming that was ever what Friedkin intended to suggest), Friedkin made the ending more ambiguous.

Another possibility as *Ted's* killer (as opposed to the serial killer who is operating at the beginning of the film) is Patrolman DeSimone (Joe Spinell). We first see DeSimone and a partner in their police car early in the picture. When two gay guys walk by (improbably clad half in drag and half in leather!), DeSimone starts hassling them. Later on, one of the "queens" tells Captain Edelson that DeSimone forced him to give him a blow job. DeSimone is later clearly seen cruising Burns both in a leather bar and in Central Park. At the end of the picture, he is one of the officers in the apartment where Ted's bloody body has been found. Captain Edelson looks suspicious when DiSimone introduces himself and he recognizes the name. Has the closet-queen cop moved a step up from harassment to murder?

Ted's murder after the arrest of the main suspect in the serial killings certainly confuses the issue (not to mention the audience) but ultimately points to the true solution of the mystery. We never actually see Stuart Richards murder anyone. True, he pulls a knife during his park confrontation with Burns, but so does Burns. We do, however, clearly see the face of the killer in the first murder scene early in the picture—*and it isn't Stuart Richards*. To further confound us, this first killer *becomes the victim* when the killer strikes "again" in Central Park (about midway through the film). This time we don't see the killer's face, but he has the same body type as Stuart Richards. (The killer in the third murder sequence, in a porno movie theater, is hardly glimpsed at all.) All three or so killers sing the same childish refrain—"Who's here, I'm here, you're here"—before the murders.

So what's going on here? Who the hell is the killer? The clue lies in writer-director Friedkin's having directed *The Exorcist*, with its theme of the *transference of evil*, a theme which he (mistakenly) uses once again in *Cruising*. The evil force responsible for the murders apparently moves from victim to killer to victim to killer, the killer becoming the victim and so on down the line. If this *is* what Friedkin was aiming for, it was ill advised and poorly executed, only serving to perplex viewers and water down a gruesomely fascinating storyline.

While the picture was being filmed in Greenwich Village, hundreds of gay people and their supporters came out into the streets to protest, the feeling being that *Cruising* would present only the ugly, negative side of gay life and not offer any positive *human* illumination. To a large extent, this is true. Like the novel it was based on, *Cruising* presents no three-dimensional characters at all, gay or straight. Pacino's part is badly underwritten, as is Sorvino's. We barely get to know Burns's pleasant gay neighbor Ted. And as Burns's girlfriend, Nancy, Karen Allen has so little to do that her part amounts to a cameo. The screenplay never rises above its penny-dreadful origins. Had it included *real people* that we could care about, it would only have enhanced the macabre, fascinating aspects of the production. As it is, *Cruising* holds the attention, but on no deeper a level than, say, the average *Friday the 13th* installment.

Still, the picture does have several memorable sequences. The first murder is greatly enhanced by the performance of Pacino look-alike Arnaldo Santana. (In fact, the film is filled with Pacino look-alikes, creating more obfuscation.) Santana is tied up on the bed by the killer, who sadistically teases him, asking if the ropes are too tight when all along he intends to kill him. Santana evokes the terror of the victim so convincingly that the scene is very disturbing and nearly repellent. This is no "fun" cinematic murder you can distance yourself from. Santana not only resembles Pacino, he does an excellent imitation of his acting style. Perhaps in some alternate universe Santana is the star and Pacino the supporting player.

Friedkin used openly gay extras in the gay-bar scenes, which is why they seem so spirited and realistic. And, yes, that *is* sex (real, not simulated) going on in the background, often of a particularly outré variety even by so-called

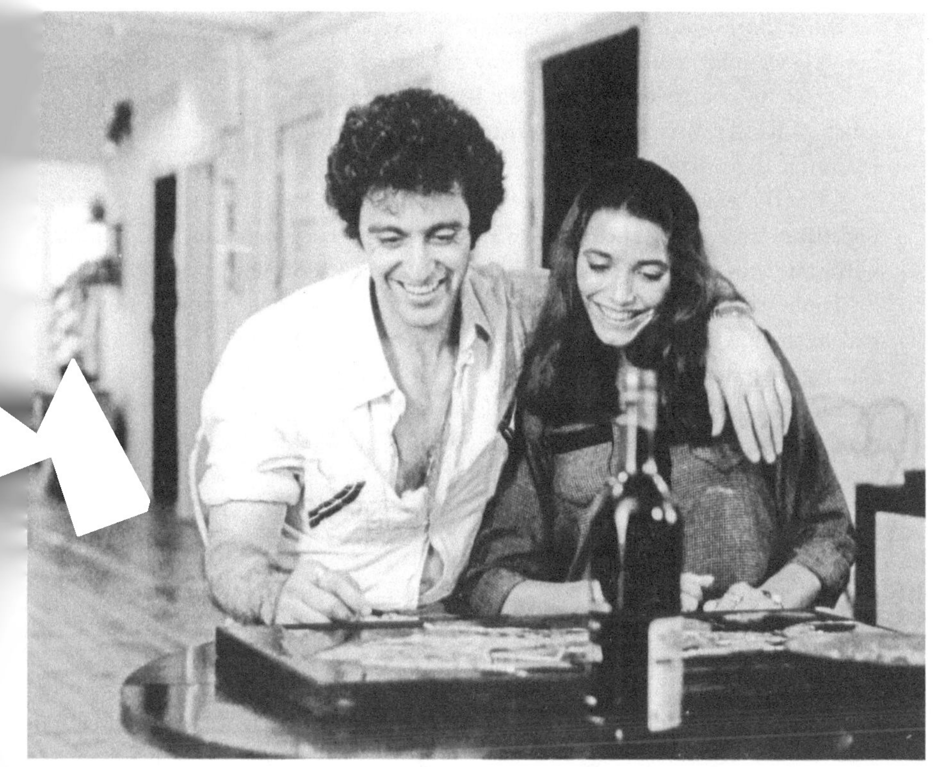

Officer Steve Burns (Pacino) shares an evening at home with his girlfriend, Nancy (Karen Allen), in the unsuccessful crime thriller *Cruising* (1980).

"gay" standards. These scenes, with a pounding rock soundtrack, are filled with energy, but they certainly scared off some of the critics. Although *Cruising* was almost universally excoriated, in some cases it wasn't clear if the reviewer objected to the film's "homophobia" or its homoerotic content, indeed its essentially homophilic nature.

Unlike the source novel, the film set its story amid the sadomasochistic subculture of the gay community. (S&M, or "leather," bars, gay or straight, attract patrons who range from those merely interested in a more masculine atmosphere to those into heavy role-playing.) *Cruising* contains a disclaimer, engendered by activists' protests, stating that the picture deals with only one fragment of the gay community. Others argued that there was nothing wrong with the leather scene or with scenes of gay men enjoying themselves with abandon (in those pre–AIDS days).

Before long, different factions in the community were at each other's throats. Columnist Rex Reed suggested that articles about gay murders written by the *Village Voice*'s Arthur Bell—who was a vociferous opponent of the movie—were far worse than anything in *Cruising*, prompting the vituperative Bell to write an article "Will the Real Rex Reed Stand Up!" which claimed that much of Reed's work was ghostwritten. Bell also got into arguments with Pete Hammill and others.

On the production end, James Contner's cinematography of smoky bars, nighttime streets, and such well-known New York City locations as Columbia University, the Central Park Ramble, the Fourteenth Street meat market, and St. James Hotel is always evocative. Jack Nitzsche's score contains hardly any real music but is filled with atmospheric electronic "sounds." The film is well cast right on down to the smaller roles, which include Ed O'Neil (later known for his roles on TV's *Married with Children* and *Modern Family*) as a homicide detective who tails Burns when he is wearing a wire, and Powers Boothe as a salesman in a gay sex shop.

This was the second time Pacino had played a "gay/bisexual" role—sort of, leading to the usual tiresome speculation: Was *he* a closet case, a "Don Juan homosexual" romancing a series of women to cover up his true nature? What was going on in his mind while he filmed such steamy homoerotic sequences (in which he was always more of an observer than participant)?

Whatever Pacino's reasons for doing the picture, *Cruising* did nothing for his career—or anyone else's. It disappeared from theaters in a matter of days.

Author! Author!

20TH CENTURY–FOX, 1982

Producer, Irwin Winkler; director, Arthur Hiller; director of photography, Victor J. Kemper; editor, William Reynolds; music, Dave Grusin; screenplay, Israel Horovitz; production designer, Gene Rudolph. Running time: 110 minutes.

CAST

Al Pacino (*Ivan Travalian*); Tuesday Weld (*Gloria*); Dyan Cannon (*Alice Detroit*); Alan King (*Kreplich*); Bob Dishy (*Morris Finestein*); Bob Elliott (*Patrick Dicker*); Ray Goulding (*Jackie Dicker*); Eric Gurry (*Igor*); Ari Meyers (*Debbie*); Benjamin H. Carlin (*Geraldo*); B. J. Barie (*Spike*); Frederic Kimball (*Larry Kotzwinkle*); Florence Anglin (*Bag Lady*); James Tolkan (*Lieutenant Glass*); Ken Sylk (*Roger Schlesinger*).

Al Pacino couldn't have chosen a project more different from *Cruising* than *Author! Author!*, a family comedy with him as husband and father to many children, though not always in the biological sense. Unfortunately, *Author! Author!* wasn't exactly a step upward in either screenplay or entertainment value. Perhaps in an effort to erase the "stigma" of *Cruising*, Pacino too readily accepted this project, written by Israel Horovitz, in whose play *The Indian Wants the Bronx* Pacino had appeared some years earlier. Pacino should have thought of a different way to repay a professional favor.

Playwright Ivan Travalian (Pacino) has just turned forty-three. His irresponsible wife, Gloria (Tuesday Weld), goes off with another man, leaving Ivan to care for their son, Igor (Eric Gurry), as well as his many stepchildren from Gloria's previous marriages. Ivan has an affair with Alice Detroit (Dyan Cannon), the star of his new play *English with Tears*, which needs a new second act. Ivan finds it nearly impossible to work on the play; he is too busy trying to keep his stepkids from being sent back to their respective fathers. In desperation he runs up to Massachusetts to get Gloria back from her lover, but discovers that he, Ivan, no longer wants her. Alice and Ivan come to an amicable separation; and Ivan revises his play. The review in the *New York Times* is favorable, Ivan gets to keep all the kids, and all is right with the world.

Frankly, Al Pacino is *miscast* as a devoted family man. Ivan Trevalian is a Jack Lemmon or Woody Allen role, and both would have been better in the part. One senses that Pacino can be very funny personally, but he hasn't that required "light touch" on camera. His Trevalian always seems as if he's on the edge of violence. Pacino can be great at broad comedy (to which *Dick Tracy* would later attest) and be awfully amusing in certain roles (*Scarecrow*; *Dog Day Afternoon*) that have humor written into them, but he's no Cary Grant. Besides, who really wants to see Michael Corleone bouncing little kids on his knee?

This is not to say that Pacino's performance is *bad*; it is just not a real Pacino role. His acting is often first-rate, such as in a scene during opening-night intermission when Ivan confesses his fears about the play, the future, that nobody else may want "Gloria's kids," to his son, Igor. "The only thing I fear," Igor tells him, "is that I inherited your nose." Pacino is very vulnerable—he seems the boy, and wise Igor, the father, soothing the "boy's" fears. It is a warmly human scene in a movie that has too few of them. Young Eric Gurry, as Igor, plays up to Pacino every step of the way.

Understandably, this family comedy is short of Pacino blasts, but our hero does get across a few zingers. "I'm at the goddamn typewriter because I'm a goddamn writer!" he screams at one point. When Gloria finally comes home after a few days' disappearance, he snaps, "Where have you been? *Answer me!*" Viewers cheer when Trevalian finally tells off his wife when he tracks her down in Massachusetts. "1 don't want you back. You are a cold, heartless *bitch!* Don't go in the water—give the sharks a break!" Tuesday Weld, with whom Pacino had had an affair years earlier, is very matronly looking as the supposedly wild Gloria. Weld plays her character too straight for her ever to be likable; but she is the villainess of the piece. Dyan Cannon is just right as the borderline-zany Alice Detroit. When Ivan asks her at their first meeting why she's taking aspirin with her champagne, she replies, "Because champagne gives me a headache."

But the only actor who *really* registers (beside the kids) is Alan King as producer Kreplich. This is King's kind of material, and he plays it for all it is worth, making the often clichéd dialogue and stale old jokes sound fresh and inventive. King has the right touch throughout and is better (as is practically everyone) than the material. In addition to Eric Gurry as Igor, child actors Benjamin H. Carlin (the insolent little Geraldo), B.J. Barie (Spike), and Ari Meyers (Debbie) are excellent. Meyers is given a particularly good scene when she sits sadly listing all her stepsiblings, stepfathers, aunts, uncles, cousins, etc. Florence Anglin and James Tolkan also score in brief bits as, respectively, a bag lady (whom Trevalian asks for an opinion of his tie) and a police officer who comes to return Debbie and her sister to their dad.

The picture sometimes summons up a spirit of fun, but such moments are few and far between. At one point, Pacino comes to the theater with a new hairdo because he got the skinny on his wife's affair from her hairdresser. Trying to talk to his wife for ten minutes at the school where she teaches, he heads off her objections by asking, "What's the class?"

"Conversation," she tells him.

"Well," he says, "can't they just chat?" When the play's director is the only one who doesn't want to hire an actor everyone else likes, Pacino says to King: "Fire *him*."

Author! Author! is an odd mixture of inside theatrical hipness (none of which is very compelling) and contrived sentimentality. The characters never seem like real people, and the complications and conflicts are as stupid and phony as all get-out. One idiotic development has Pacino taking the girls who ran away from their father up to the roof of his apartment house in an attempt to escape the officers sent to escort them home. In the street below more cops arrive, and a crowd gathers while Pacino yells down to the girls' father, Roger (Ken Sylk). None of this is even remotely funny.

Of course, one might ask if the shattered home lives of unwanted (by their mother) children is really a fit subject for a comedy to begin with. Another problem is that Ivan Travalian is an irritating character, a successful playwright who doesn't revel in it but moans about his lot in life and takes his kids with him to show-biz hangouts like Elaine's, where he looks bored and uncomfortable. Who can feel sympathetic toward someone who can't enjoy his—how awful!—success. *Author! Author!* has a Neil Simon plotline but is done mostly without Simon's trademark wit or charm. Arthur Hiller hardly directs at all—the usual case with this impersonal, generally mediocre filmmaker. Composer Dave Grusin's pop tunes on the soundtrack are pleasant but unmemorable. There are some nice shots of New York City locations, such as Sheridan Square, Waverly Place, and other Village spots, as well as Roseland and the theater district.

Author! Author! may not be Pacino's worst film, but it's the one few Pacino fans will want to see again.

Scarface

UNIVERSAL, 1983

Executive producer, Louis A. Stroller; producer, Martin Bregman; director, Brian De Palma; director of photography, John A. Alonzo; editors, Jerry Greenberg and David Ray; screenplay, Oliver Stone; music, Giorgio Moroder; art director, Ed Richardson; visual consultant, Ferdinando Scarfiotti. Running time: 170 minutes.

CAST

Al Pacino (*Tony Montana*); Steven Bauer (*Manny*); Michelle Pfeiffer (*Elvira*); Mary Elizabeth Mastrantonio (*Gina*); Robert Loggia (*Frank Lopez*); Paul Shenar (*Alejandro Sosa*); Arnaldo Santana (*Ernie*); F. Murray Abraham (*Omar*); Miriam Colon (*Mama Montana*); Pepe Serna (*Angel*); Dennis Holahan (*Banker*); Harris Yulin (*Bernstein*); Richard Delmonte (*Fernando*); Richard Belzer (*MC*).

Sidney (*Dog Day Afternoon*) Lumet was the first choice to direct *Scarface*, but he wanted to make changes in the script, add a political subtext, that would make the movie less of a "cartoon" (which is ultimately what *Scarface* is). Brian De Palma, who had nearly directed Pacino in *Cruising*, was called in to helm the feature instead. Since De Palma did not work on the script—as is his usual wont—*Scarface* has few of the director's typical personal flourishes. For that sort of thing, De Palma fans would have to be satisfied with the likes of *Body Double* and *Dressed to Kill*.

Oliver Stone based his screenplay on the original film's, written by Ben Hecht in 1932. (The 1983 version of *Scarface* is dedicated to Hecht and Howard Hawks, who directed the 1932 version with Paul Muni as star.) In the original picture, Scarface was a bootlegger; Stone made him a cocaine dealer. Stone retained the subplot of the gangster's incestuous feelings for his sister but made them much more overt. He later claimed that De Palma's direction so stretched

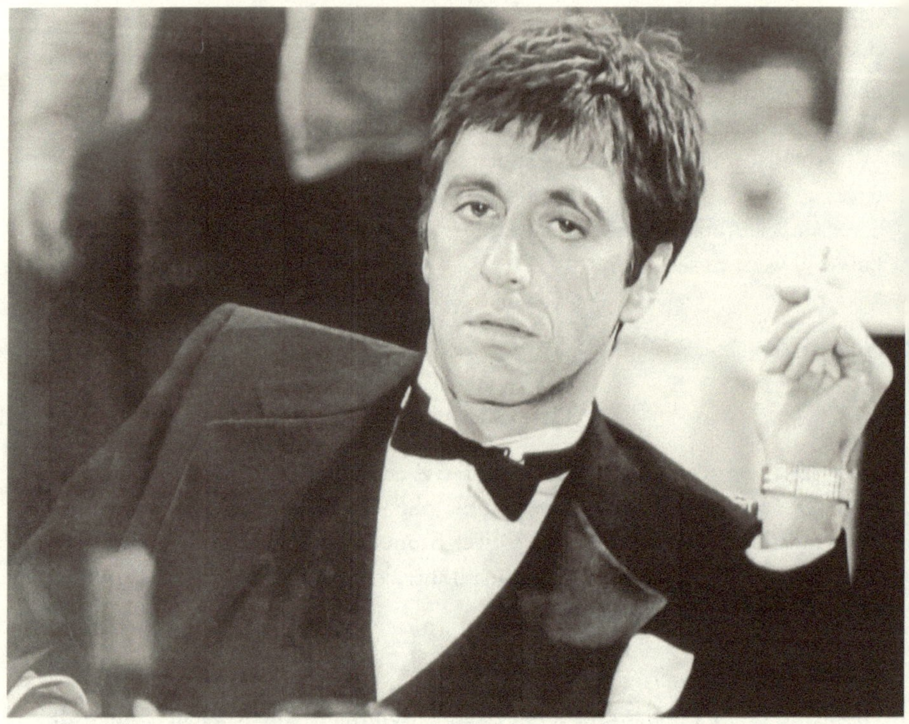

For many Pacino fans, his scenery-chewing performance as Cuban drug lord Tony Montana in *Scarfacce* (1983) is one of his most dynamic and entertaining.

out some scenes that other scenes which helped delineate the characters had to be omitted.

Tony Montana (Pacino) is one of tens of thousands of Cuban refugees (20 percent of whom were from the criminal classes) arriving in Miami in May 1980. His first antisocial action on American soil is to carry out a hit during the turmoil of a riot at Immigration. Later, he's recruited by Frank Lopez (Robert Loggia), a drug kingpin with a haughty girlfriend, Elvira (Michelle Pfeiffer). Determined to make money and thereby have power, as Lopez does, Tony moves onward and upward in the drug trade, eventually replacing Lopez and marrying Elvira.

Tony's mother wants nothing to do with him, but his sister Gina (Mary Elizabeth Mastrantonio), fascinated by his glamorous lifestyle, falls in love with Tony's friend and partner, Manny (Steven Bauer). But Tony has incestuous feelings for Gina and murders Manny when he finds them together, just before Gina screams at him that she and Manny had been married. Elvira walks out on Tony, Gina taunts him and shoots at him, and finally a defiant-to-the-end

Montana succumbs to the bullets of a small army sent to finish him by a rival drug dealer.

With his shaggy dry haircut (as opposed to the slicked-down look of *The Godfather Part II*) and bantamweight, cocky authority, Pacino is in full command of all he surveys in *Scarface*. He is charming, polite, proud, obscene, vulgar, and mesmeric all in a single sequence—and then some. He struts through the picture with intensity, cool aplomb, and total authority. *Scarface* is many fans' favorite Pacino performance. Hard-to-please critic and film historian Lawrence J. Quirk, devotee chiefly of Hollywood's golden age, was so bowled over by Pacino in *Scarface* that he said to me, "Edward G. Robinson, Cagney, Paul Muni—none of them could hold a candle to Pacino when Pacino's playing a gangster. He's like a male Bette Davis on a *rampage*. Al Pacino is a *star!*"

The only negative is that Pacino's diction in this is occasionally horrendous, and the thick accent he affects doesn't help. The Cuban accent is thicker at some times than at others, but this isn't necessarily unrealistic. What *is* unrealistic is that Tony and his buddy Manny would speak English to each other when alone. Subtitles, anyone?

Montana's insolent pride, as displayed by Pacino (who clearly put some of himself in the role, remembering early insults as to his background, height, ability, etc.), is almost admirable. "Don't call me no fuckin' dishwasher," he says to one of Lopez's snotty associates. When bitchy Elvira patronizes him at first meeting, he says with breezy rudeness, "You're good-looking, got a great face, great body, but you got a look in your eye like you haven't been fucked in years." Soaking in a magnificent, round, golden-marble bathtub the size of an automobile, Pacino hurls scatological insults at everything and everyone. "Do you have to say 'fuck' all the time?" Elvira asks him. (The "f" word is Tony's favorite.)

Naturally, *Scarface* allows Pacino to unleash plenty of his blasts, both minor and major. He drunkenly "tells off" some ritzy restaurant patrons: "You need people like me. Somebody to point the finger at and say, 'There's the bad guy.'" Referring to some rivals in the drug trade, he screams, "Fuck the Diaz brothers! I *buried* those cock-a-roaches!" He really lets loose with a blast when he busts in on his beloved kid sister and her date, who are in a stall in the men's room, snorting coke. An animal that can barely be contained, he kicks the door, hollers, lunges at the boy-friend, even hits his sister.

Pacino has a lively supporting cast in *Scarface*. Steven Bauer as handsome buddy Manny wisely underplays, creating contrast with the almost manic Montana. Manny thinks all he has to do is stick out his tongue insinuatingly at the stuck-up rich Miami blondes and they'll fall into his arms, but it doesn't work. "You have to get the money first," says Tony. "The money and the power." Michelle Pfeiffer is properly glacial and contemptuous ("Didja just get off a banana boat?") but not really *common* enough as the sluttish, stupid, and utterly amoral Elvira. Mary Elizabeth Mastrantonio, as Gina, has a very convincing accent but is also saddled with the biggest, bushiest "Afro" in creation. "You have some nerve!" she screams at Tony. "I'll fuck who I want to fuck!" (Fifty percent of Oliver Stone's screenplay is the "f" word.)

Mastrantonio's big scene is a very sleazy but undeniably bravura one at the end of the picture, after Tony has murdered her husband. Clad in a sexy negligee and carrying a handgun, Gina walks toward Tony in his study. "Is this what you want? Why don't you fuck me? Is this what you want, Tony?" *Bang, bang.* She keeps firing at him but fails to kill him. Mastrantonio's performance is good, and both she and Pfeiffer went on to bigger and better vehicles.

Robert Loggia is terrific as drug lord Lopez, with his white suit and the gold chains around his neck. His big scene has him begging for his life after Tony learns that he ordered a hit on him in a nightclub. Tony, of course, blows him away but he does spare Lopez's bodyguard Ernie, played by Arnaldo Santana. Santana was the Pacino look-alike who gets murdered in *Cruising,* but he doesn't look much like Pacino in *Scarface.* Harris Yulin also scores as the corrupt narcotics detective Bernstein; it's a slick, smooth, subtle performance in a film in which subtlety is in scant supply. One of the best performances is by Mariam Colon as Tony's mother. Her haunted expression of disillusionment over her boy, mixed emotions about seeing him, and deep reservations about his being a part of his sister's life is worth a million words. When Tony hands her a thousand dollars, this mother with no illusions instantly snaps, "Who did you kill for this, Antonio?" When her son apologizes for taking so long to get in touch, she sniffs, "No postcards in jail, huh?" Mother Montana provides some balance to the film's depiction of the Cuban-American community. "It's Cubans like you who are giving a bad name to Cubans who come here, who word hard." But the mother is more than just a positive spokesperson; Colon makes her entirely believable and human.

Scarface is quite long—nearly three hours—but is filled with memorably exciting sequences. First there's the drug deal (in the apartment) that goes sour. A woman who sits calmly on the bed watching television as the men talk actually has a shotgun hidden under her newspaper, which she employs when all hell breaks loose a moment later. Montana and an associate are dragged into the bathroom and chained to the shower rod, whereupon one character employs a chainsaw to remove the associate's limbs. (Fortunately, this all occurs mostly off camera. De Palma had to cut shots of limbs being severed to avoid an X rating.) As Pacino waits his turn, there comes an excellent crane shot that goes from the bathroom all the way down to a car on the street, where Manny, unaware of what is happening, chats with a girl, and all the way back up to the bathroom. Eventually, Manny comes to Tony's rescue, resulting in an expertly edited sequence where he bursts in, machine gun blazing, as the chainsaw goes flying, and Pacino pursues the fiend who made chop suey of his friend and shoots him point-blank on the street in front of dozens of horrified spectators.

The attack on Tony in the nightclub is also well handled, though it's hard to believe the would-be assassins hit him only once instead of turning him into a messy wedge of Swiss cheese. (The comic doing Ricky Ricardo imitations—Richard Belzer of *Law and Order: SVU*—isn't so lucky, however.) The climactic assault on Montana's ostentatious estate by the forces of rival Alejandro Sosa (Paul Shenar) is the liveliest scene in the picture (again Pacino seems as invulnerable as Superman against so many bullets), with Montana sticking a kind of mini-grenade launcher between his legs and chortling, "Say hello to my little friend." When Tony goes out, he goes out in style, collapsing off his balcony with his arms spread out defiantly and landing in the pool below with a mighty splash. Tony Montana has finally been brought down in a very "dramatic" larger-than-life exit. Pacino fans could ask for no more.

The "quieter" scenes in the picture (with Pacino as star, there are very few of them) sometimes work and sometimes do not. Pacino kills an assassin sent by the South American drug cartel to silence an antidrug crusader when he learns that the man also plans to blow up the victim's wife and kids. The sequence showing Tony and the hit man in their car trailing the victim and family in *their* car (with a bomb attached to the undercarriage)—Montana registering discomfort but uncertain how to proceed—is suspenseful and compelling. Tony's murder of the assassin (before he can blow up the car) angers the South Americans and leads to his undoing; ironically, it's the only decent thing he's ever done. It is because of this action that the army descends upon his estate. (Of course, Montana never considers how the woman and children would feel about their husband and father being murdered.)

On the other hand, a restaurant confrontation between Pacino and Pfeiffer is less successful. The dialogue in this sequence holds certain truths about these people, about their marriage and Tony's profession, but would these people be able to articulate these truths so well? Would they even *think* such thoughts, let alone verbalize them? Perhaps De Palma had good reason to cut much of Stone's screenplay. These are not exactly people who spend much time analyzing their lives and actions, after all.

This blood-drenched remake for the eighties is energetic, fun, and vivid, but—let's face it—*Scarface* is a real junk movie. If you thought the "heroes" of the *Godfather* films were bad, the main characters of *Scarface* are absolutely on the bottom of the food chain. And yes, they are romanticized a bit, even with that "crime does not pay" finale. This is perhaps the main difference (even with all the graphic language and violence) between the 1983 *Scarface* and the 1932 original. Writing in the September 1932 issue of *Photoplay*, editor James R. Quirk (uncle of the aforementioned Lawrence) claimed that Scarface deglamorized criminality, that the title character was not a "shrewd, exciting personality" but "a criminal moron ... a half-mad killer, a man set apart from other men." Quirk calls Scarface "a coward ... he dies yellow." This is quite different from the way Pacino's Tony Montana goes to his death while fighting back with defiance and courage.

Note also that Montana is not brought down by police or FBI agents but by rival drug dealers. As well, *Scarface* makes the point that the U.S. government spends millions fighting the drug industry, which is in turn supported by other millions from American customers in the United States. The over-the-top 1983 *Scarface* is a product of its time. Nowadays, there are *too many* Tony Montanas.

Revolution

WARNER BROS., GOLDCREST AND VIKING, 1985

Executive producer, Chris Burt; producer, Irwin Winkler; director, Hugh Hudson; director of photography, Bernard Lutic; editor, Stuart Baird; screenplay, Robert Dillon; music, John Corigliano; production designer, Assheton Gorton; costume designer, John Mollo. Running time: 125 min.

CAST

Al Pacino (*Tom Dobb*); Donald Sutherland (*Sgt. Major Peasy*); Nastassja Kinski (*Daisy*); Sid Owen (*Young Ned*); Dexter Fletcher (*Older Ned*); Joan Plowright (*Mrs. McConnahy*); Dave King (*Mr. McConnahy*); Malcolm Terris (*Dr. Sloan*); Annie Lenox (*Liberty Woman*); Eric Milota (*Merle*).

Director Hugh Hudson (*Chariots of Fire*; *Greystoke: The Legend of Tarzan, Lord of the Apes*) had the idea of making a sort of silent-movie epic with sound when he started work on *Revolution*. The Revolutionary War itself was to be the star, with select characters moving in and out of the tapestry in much the way that they did in D. W. Griffith's 1915 silent masterpiece *Birth of a Nation*, about the Civil War. Hudson wished to eschew normal filmic storytelling and let the action speak for itself, at the expense of the narrative. Even nominal "star" Al Pacino, when he found himself getting few close-ups, wondered why Hudson was paying him so much money if he wasn't going to use him to his fullest capacity.

A force of thirty-thousand redcoats is preparing to march on New York City; to head them off, a people's army is rapidly being gathered. Tom Dobb

(Al Pacino), an apolitical fur trader, is forced to give up his boat to "drive the British out of Brooklyn." While Dobb tries to redeem the temporarily worthless note he was given in exchange for the boat, his son Ned signs up as a drummer boy in the army. Dobb objects vociferously but is himself forced to join up for a payment of five shillings.

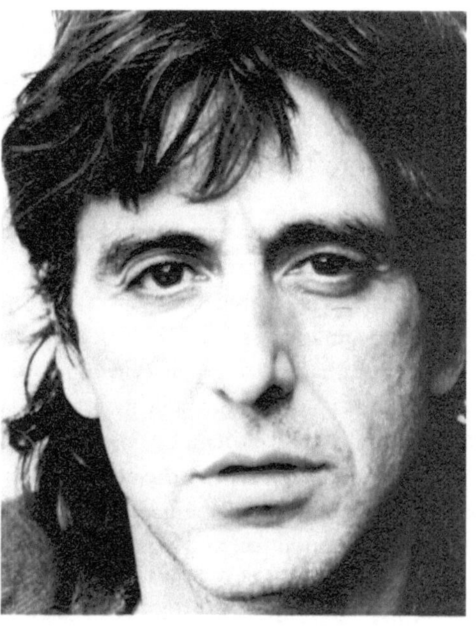

Does Pacino look like a soldier in the Revolutionary War? Critics didn't think so either. Despite the critical drubbing it received, *Revolution* (1985), and Pacino's acting specifically, might be described as interesting failures.

Injured after his first battle, Dobb is given food and succor by Daisy McConnahy (Nastassja Kinski), whose father is collaborating with the British for money. "It doesn't matter who deserves to win; it's who *does* win," he tells his daughter. "Now, you remember that the next time you're out there screaming liberty." Concerned primarily with his son's welfare amid the madness of war, Dobb deserts with the boy and returns to New York, where he earns both Daisy's and young Ned's enmity. When Ned is spirited off by Peasy, the head of the redcoats (Donald Sutherland), Dobb follows him and effects a rescue. Dobb ultimately becomes an army scout at Valley Forge, where Daisy is apparently killed fleeing from Peasy. Three years later, however, she and Dobb are reunited in Yorktown. "Ain't no one ever gonna treat nobody like a dog in the dirt in this country," Dobb intones.

Not since *Cruising* had a Pacino film received such a critical drubbing as *Revolution*. First to enflame the ire of the critics was the casting of the very contemporary Pacino as a Revolutionary War hero (albeit a reluctant one). To hear them tell it, it was another case of Tony Curtis croaking, "Yondah lies da castle of my faddah" in a medieval costume epic. It seems native New Yorkers were not allowed to do period pieces in which traditionally the accents (by way of Hollywood) were upper-crust and European in flavor. But the one critic who liked the picture asked: "Who knows how they talked two hundred years ago?"

True, Pacino takes some getting used to. He has a naturalistic acting style and contemporary accent that is quite different from the usual stylized approach to period dramas; sometimes he seems like an "East Side Kid" or "Bowery Boy" magically transplanted in time to the 1700s. But he is actually quite effective as Tom Dobb, skillfully getting across the character of a man who just wants to protect his son, stay out of trouble, and get on with his interrupted life more than anything. (Pacino's one concession to the period is the small pigtail he wears.)

Pacino is given several powerful scenes, such as when he finds out that his son has been compelled to sign up with the army and is himself forced into conscription by rebels who won't take no for an answer. His rage and frustration at the unfairness of it is almost palpable. He admirably evinces Dobb's fear and determination to stay alive during a grotesque "fox hunt" in which British officers set dogs on Pacino, a colleague, and an effigy of George Washington they must drag along with them. Cornered by a sneering redcoat, Dobb braces himself for the killing stroke, but the officer sticks his sword in the effigy instead.

By far Pacino's greatest scene is when some friendly Indians tend to the badly injured feet and legs of young Ned after Dobb has rescued the boy from the British. Ned is in great pain and near death; as the Indians work on his lower extremities, Dobb holds Ned and comforts him, exhibiting such great intensity, paternal passion, and "hopeful despair" as he begs his son not to die that he seems to be *living* it instead of just acting. It is moments like this that show why Pacino can almost always triumph over "miscasting" with shear acting virtuosity.

Because it is the emotionalism and not the dialogue that carries this scene, its efficacy is not blunted by Pacino's unfortunate mumbling throughout. Pacino is often mush-mouthed in *Revolution*, which was certainly a factor in the bad notices he received. Not only a Bronx accent, the critics thought, but such impenetrable diction! His goodbye speech to his son at the end of the picture is nearly unintelligible. Better, some thought, if Hudson *had* done a "silent movie" with subtitles. Undoubtedly, Hudson was carried away by Pacino's powerhouse emoting, but why didn't he just say: "Al, love, maybe the audience would kind of like to know what you're *saying*." At least Pacino had more of an excuse in *Scarface*, what with his Cuban accent. A minor Pacino blast occurs when Dobb finds out that the U.S. government can't make good on its promise to reimburse veterans with parcels of land. "What happened to the 150 acres I was promised?" he hollers, looking as if he's about to grab somebody and start chewing on them any second.

Compared to poor Donald Sutherland, as Sgt. Major Peasy, Pacino seems like Oscar material. Sutherland *looks* the part, all right, radiating evil authority, but his acting and speech (British accent notwithstanding) leave something to be desired. Somebody should have told him he was not in a Victor Herbert operetta. Warner Bros. wanted the loathsome Peasy to die so that the audience could experience some catharsis, but Hudson saw him as the spirit of England and just lets him wander off at the end after a pallid "confrontation" with Dobb. The "Snidley Whiplash" nature of the British soldiers isn't helped by the fact that they are generally depicted as overaged bullies and borderline pedophiles.

Nastassja Kinski is fine as Daisy McConnahy, who is as patriotic as her father is not. The spirited Daisy wants nothing to do with the British. When her father and mother entertain them in their home, Daisy stabs one would-be lothario with an American flag pin. His wig falls off as he jumps up and screams, "Yankee bitch!" To Daisy's parents he yells, "Your daughters are *whores*!" Kinski also figures in a moving, evocative sequence when she allows a doctor operating on a screaming, frightened boy to use her shawl as a tourniquet. Daisy was supposed to die—and stay dead—in the film, but Warner Bros. insisted she be brought back and reunited with Dobb in an epilogue. Hudson won his point with Peasy/Sutherland but lost with Daisy/Kinski.

The "relationship" between Daisy and Tom Dobb seems to come out of nowhere, however. Dobb spends more time hugging and kissing his son than he does Daisy, and she evokes little emotion in him. Hudson muffs a "romantic" scene in which Dobb runs after Daisy's wagon as she rides away, declaring his love as she does the same—all in long shot. (The bit with the redcoats chasing after the wagon and "killing" Daisy immediately afterward is exciting, however.) Dobb's true love is for his son, expertly played by Sid Owen as a young boy and Dexter Fletcher as a teenager.

The one thing in which *Revolution* excels is in its delineation of *battle*; the redcoats lining up and literally marching off to war, the initially overwhelmed rebel forces running off in panic. The battle scenes are extremely well staged and realistic: these soldiers aren't always supremely cool and confident, they don't always know what they're doing, and there's often a natural *sloppiness* to their actions. Indeed, all the extras milling about messily (which initially seems comical) manage to approximate the confusion of the period. *Revolution* vividly gets across the ugliness, tedium, grimness, boredom, and loneliness of war. Its matter-of-fact approach to sudden death is all the more chilling and poignant.

As well, its production designer, Asheton Gorton, costume designer, John Mollo, and others expertly re-create the period with terrific settings, elaborate outfits, and thousands of teeming extras going in every which direction but up. Bernard Lutic's photography offers some superb shots of a pristine countryside and cluttered cityscape, but the wavering, handheld-camera cinéma vérité approach isn't always efficacious. John Corigliano's musical score is nice and atmospheric.

The tragedy with the ambitious *Revolution* is that it starts off so well and *collapses* so completely in the second half. The many missteps indicate a director who is overwhelmed and not in full command of his production. For every scene that works, there are two that are completely devoid of cinematic authority. Robert Dillon's screenplay sets up some interesting and unpredictable conflicts, but they are all muted by the meandering direction. Directed by William Wyler or even "One Take" Woody Van Dyke in Hollywood's golden age, *Revolution* might have emerged as a classic. Hugh Hudson knew what he wanted, but this time the talented director couldn't quite get his vision on the screen. Which is not something to bitchily chortle over, as many reviewers did; it is something to *mourn*. All that hard work, fine acting by Pacino, great period detail—what a picture *Revolution* could have been!

It would be four years before Al Pacino would make another movie.

Sea of Love

UNIVERSAL, 1989

Producers, Martin Bregman and Louis A. Stroller; director, Harold Becker; director of photography, Ronnie Taylor; editor, David Bretherton; screenplay, Richard Price; music, Trevor Jones; associate producer, Michael Scott Bregman; production designer, John Jay Moore; costume designer, Betsy Cox. Running time: 112 min.

CAST

Al Pacino (*Frank Keller*); Ellen Barkin (*Helen*); John Goodman (*Sherman*); William Hickey (*Frank Sr.*); Michael Rooker (*Terry*); Christine Estabrook (*Gina Gallagher*); Richard Jenkins (*Greber*); Michael Fischetti (*Doorman*); Michael O'Neill (*Raymond Brown*); Patricia Barry (*Older Woman*).

After the debacle of *Revolution* four years earlier, *Sea of Love* was considered by many to be Pacino's "comeback" film.

The movie begins with the murder of a nude, panicked man who is shot in his bed as the record "Sea of Love" plays on the phonograph. Called in to investigate is Detective Frank Keller (Pacino), who is embittered because his ex-wife married another cop, with whom he often crosses paths. Keller teams up with another detective, Sherman (John Goodman), who has had a similar murder in his own jurisdiction. The two cook up a scheme to catch the killer by placing a personal ad in a singles' publication. One clear suspect emerges: Helen (Ellen Barkin). As Keller finds himself sexually and romantically drawn to the woman, things keep happening which make him more and more suspicious of her, especially the fact that she dated all (by now) three murdered men.

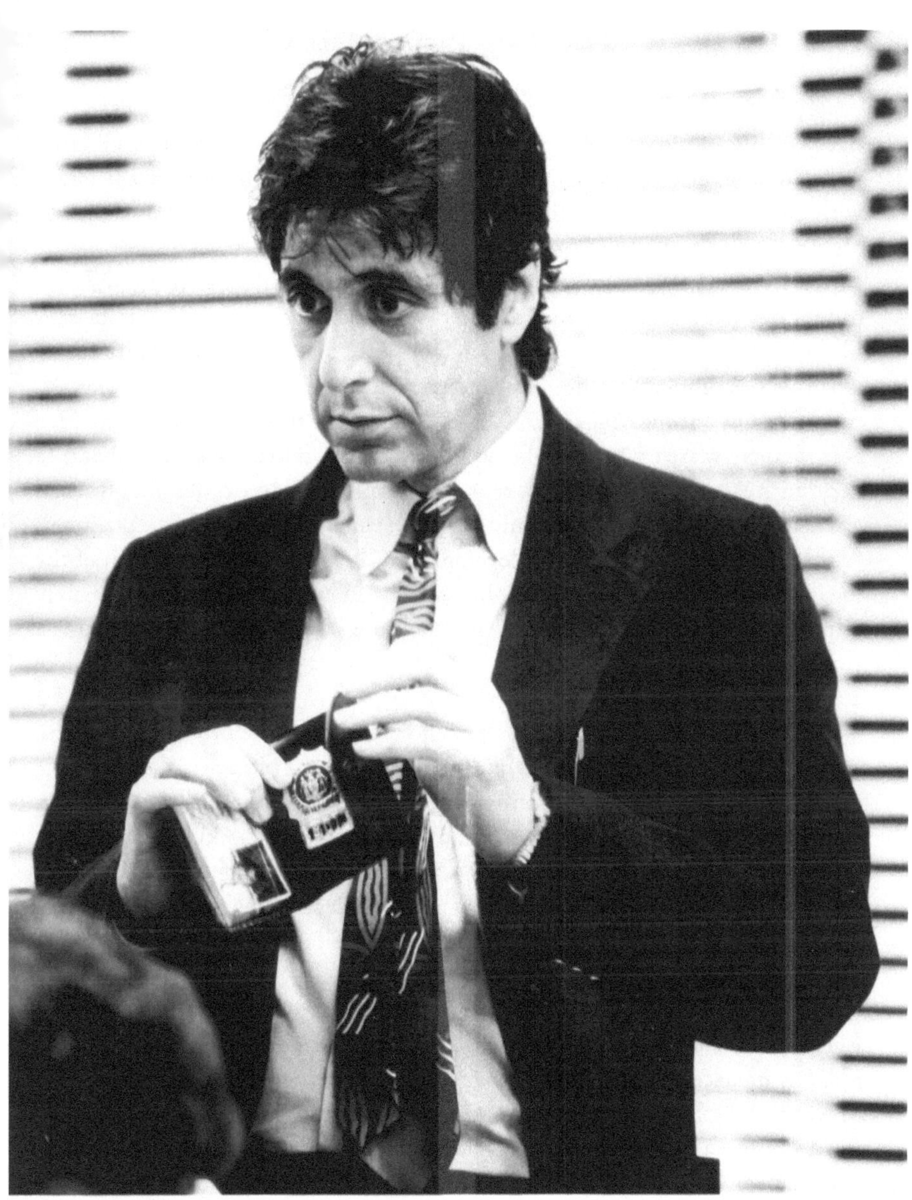

In the erotic thriller *Sea of Love* (1989), Pacino was back on familiar territory as a street-wise cop. This was hailed as his comeback film.

Helen is furious to find out that he's a cop and breaks up with him. The killer is eventually unveiled: Helen's jealous ex-husband. Keller patches things up with Helen.

Pacino is a bit (deliberately) schlumpy in *Sea of Love*, but he looks good and acts well. He gets into some hot, animalistic love scenes with Barkin—

rough, slightly kinky, up against the walls, and so on—which reveal that Pacino has kept himself in good shape. It's quite possible that Pacino did this picture when he was pushing fifty just to show he could keep up his vital, virile image with the best of them. That plus the fact that it seemed like a sure crowd pleaser after the more "acquired taste" of *Revolution*.

Richard Price's screenplay is no world-beater by any objective standards, but it does give Pacino a chance to quietly (for a change) practice his craft. He's like a little lost puppy begging Barkin not to be mad at him and quite funny when he has dinner with her at a fancy restaurant where there are no waiters, no menu, but an annoying violinist. "Can you get the waiter?" he asks him. He's convincingly scared when he's being beaten by the murderous ex-husband (a very enthusiastic Michael Rooker) at the climax. He exudes that special charisma of his when he drunkenly goads Sherman (Goodman) to "take it off" as the latter dances at a police reception. And there's even a milder form of the Pacino blast when he gets in a fight with his ex-wife's husband immediately after the reception. The world-weary, lonely, regretful, semi-alcoholic cop is a tired old stereotype, but Pacino does his best to make Frank Keller seem like a real human being.

Ellen Barkin, with her odd, crooked smile, is like the proverbial martini. In her first appearance she looks like a hooker, and the picture makes her little more than a sex object—albeit an aggressive one—for most of its running time. Since she is supposed to be a woman of mystery—did she kill those men or didn't she?—the movie can't reveal too much of her. Getting into the spirit of things, Barkin felt the film revealed too much, such as Helen's apartment, child, and mother. As it is, Helen is half real, half femme-fatale icon. Barkin plays her as well as anyone could.

John Goodman is, as usual, ingratiating, if only on the surface. William Hickey is as reliable—and as creepy—as ever as Keller's father. Michael Rooker radiates menace as Helen's ex-husband, Terry. Michael O'Neill has a nice bit as Raymond (the family man addicted to singles' ads who becomes the killer's third victim), as does Patricia Barry as the "older woman" who answers Keller's personal ad. Actually, Barry doesn't look much older than Pacino. All the smaller parts are well cast, in fact.

The picture has a few highlights, such as an early scene when Pacino welcomes a group of men into a gymnasium where they think they are going to meet the New York Yankees. "I know who you are!" one fellow says to Pacino. "Look," he tells his pals, "it's Phil Rizzuto!" But the "meet the Yankees" business is just a ploy, and the invitations are phony. The men have actually been rounded up because there are outstanding warrants out on all of them. A closet bleeding heart, Keller lets one guy go who is wanted on two counts of grand theft auto because his little son is with him. (What a role model!) *Sea of Love* works up some mild suspense during Pacino and Barkin's first bedroom scene. When Helen leaves the room, Keller is sure she's going to get her gun and make him victim number four. He panics, but finds only a starter pistol in her purse. The climax, with Pacino battling the real killer, has some well-orchestrated fisticuffs, involves guns and barbells, and is fairly exciting, thanks to some good stunt work.

Although *Sea of Love* has a light touch, it doesn't quite come off as a comedy-thriller, and some supposedly humorous moments—such as Keller discussing why his wife left him for her new husband while leaning over the first corpse—are ill-advised. Worse yet are the many moments of illogic. First, Barkin bluntly tells Keller that he's not her type, rudely walking out on him, but the next time she sees him, at a fruit stand, she picks him up! This creates suspense but makes little sense. Did the daylight turn him into "her type?" Keller makes dates with several of the women who answered his ad, at the same bar, *on the same night*. While this facilitates Sherman's retrieving their fingerprints (he's disguised as a waiter), it seems incredible that all of the women would dutifully walk off at the appropriate time so that Keller would be free to meet the next on his list. (If each date occurs on a different night, the editing certainly doesn't make that clear.)

Price's screenplay is virtually mindless, without having the clever denouement or fascinating elements that might compensate. The ending, the solution to the murders, is flat and no surprise. Keller and Sherman laugh at one of the victims' poems in a personal-ad magazine, but the film never examines their jealousy of these cocksmen or says anything fresh or novel about the situation. What's more, it completely lacks the visceral power *of Fatal Attraction*, its obvious model.

At least Price drops in some good dialogue now and then. When Keller gets a punk would-be customer to leave the shoe store where Helen works and she learns that Keller is a police officer, he says: "You let creeps like that in here, but you're upset because I'm a cop? People find out I'm a cop—suddenly I'm a nonperson." After Keller points out different apartments in which murders have been committed in a building across the street as he and Helen take a walk, she looks at him and says, "This is one big city of the dead for you, isn't it?" There's some saucy dialogue from the women who answer Keller's ad but don't believe his made-up stories. "If you're a printer," one says, "I've got a dick."

"You probably do," Pacino mutters as she storms off.

The fatal ingredient in *Sea of Love* is Harold Becker's direction, which betrays absolutely no style or pacing whatsoever. Alfred Hitchcock probably would have rejected this script, but if he hadn't he would have made a picture that moved and had suspense. Instead of Bernard Herrmann on the score, we get Trevor Jones, whose music is forgettable. "Sea of Love," performed by Phil Phillips and the Twilights, is a catchy tune from the '50s, but it won't make people rush out to buy the soundtrack.

None of this mattered to the critics and fans, who made *Sea of Love* a hit. Pacino got some of the best reviews of his life, and his career and popularity were back on track. But one suspects that years from now *Sea of Love* will not be one of the pictures for which he is best remembered.

Dick Tracy

TOUCHSTONE, IN ASSOCIATION WITH
SILVER SCREEN PARTNERS IV, 1990

Executive producers, Barrie M. Osborne, Art Linson, and Floyd Mutrux; producer, Warren Beatty; director, Beatty; director of photography, Vittorio Storaro; editor, Richard Marks; music, Danny Elfman; original songs, Stephen Sondheim; screenplay, Jim Cash and Jack Epps, Jr., based on characters created by Chester Gould; production designer, Richard Sylbert; art director, Harold Michelson; set decorator, Rick Simpson; costume designer, Milena Canonero. Running time: 105 min.

CAST

Al Pacino (*Big Boy Caprice*); Warren Beatty (*Dick Tracy*); Glenne Headly (*Tess Trueheart*); Charlie Korsmo (*Kid*); Madonna (*Breathless Mahoney*); Paul Sorvino (*Lips Manlis*); Charles Durning (*Chief Brandon*); William Forsythe (*Flattop*); Dustin Hoffman (*Mumbles*); Ed O'Ross (*Itchy*), R. G. Armstrong (*Pruneface*); Dick Van Dyke (*D.A. Fletcher*); Michael J. Pollard (*Bug Bailey*); James Caan (*Spaldonf*); Mandy Patinkin (*88 Keys*); Estelle Parsons (*Mrs. Trueheart*).

Warren Beatty's production of *Dick Tracy* is due for a re-evaluation. *Dick Tracy* got mixed reviews upon its release because too many critics reacted to what it wasn't instead of to what is was. Audiences were expecting a rollicking roller-coaster ride à la *Indiana Jones and the Temple of Doom* or *Batman*; they wanted their comic-book movies to be one cliffhanger after another. Because the first episode of the 1937 serial *Dick Tracy* had more thrills than the entire Beatty movie, many deemed his *Dick Tracy* a failure. Once you accept that *Dick Tracy* is an adventure movie but not a rat-a-tat-tat action flick, its pleasures are more readily apparent.

Al Pacino was chosen for the pivotal role of Tracy's prime antagonist, Big

Boy Caprice. Caprice rubs out his rival Lips Manlis (Paul Sorvino) and takes over both his territory and his girl, the singer "Breathless" Mahoney (Madonna). Dick Tracy (Warren Beatty) declares war on the Mob, to which Caprice reacts by trying to kill him. Tracy's life is saved by a mysterious figure known only as "the Blank." The Blank kidnaps Tracy's girlfriend, Tess (Glenne Headly), and frames Tracy for the murder of the district attorney (Dick Van Dyke). Tracy rescues Tess and unmasks the Blank as voluptuous Breathless, who was playing both sides against each other in an effort to take over the city for herself. Caprice's reign of criminality is brought to a halt.

Playing a miserable warthog of a man, Pacino was certainly outfitted for the occasion. A body suit gives him a massive chest and upper body and a tremendous ass. Along with plastered-down hair complete with Hitlerian bangs, he has thick, ugly lips, a pencil mustache, an oversized honker, and an expanded, witchlike chin with a cleft. He walks hunched over all the time like a miniature Quasimodo. He ain't pretty, but his acting is superb. Pacino obviously had a ball playing Big Boy, and his performance garnered him an Oscar nomination for Best Supporting Actor.

Played by Pacino, Big Boy Caprice is almost lovable in his own rodent-like way. Pacino does a terrific, energetic parody of himself. Whether he is rubbing his hands together like a little kid and practically cackling after planting a fake message on a tape or urging Breathless to give "more, more, *more*" to her song number (appropriately entitled "More"), he proves that he's very adept at *broad*, high-impact comedy. Larger than life in *Dick Tracy*, Pacino is in a Rossini mode as opposed to the Verdi mode of *The Godfather* or *Scarface*.

But Pacino knows when to underplay. After rival Spaldoni's (James Caan) car is blown up after their meeting, Pacino quietly says, "Very upsetting," and gently pats the table. (It's an inspired touch and great fun to have Michael Corleone and Sonny Corleone facing each other down from opposite ends of the table.) Pacino also gets off some blasts as Big Boy: "There is one Napoleon!" he shouts. "One *me*!" and, "I want ... Dick Tracy ... *dead*!" Big Boy is absolutely hilarious as he and Tess Trueheart ride on their stomachs in a getaway underground railway car and *he never stops talking* the whole time!

Pacino's is the showiest performance, no doubt, but he is surrounded by a generally talented supporting cast. The nominal star, Warren Beatty, actually isn't bad as Dick Tracy, even if he doesn't seem as perfect for the role as his predecessor, Ralph Byrd, was. (Byrd starred as Tracy in several serials, feature films, and even a television series.) Glenne Headly is perfect—sweet, but a little saucy, too—as Tess Trueheart, who temporarily goes home to Mother when Tracy fails to propose and get a desk job. Little Charlie Korsmo is excellent as Kid, the young boy who comes into their lives, saves Tracy's life, and chooses

"Dick Tracy, Jr." as his official moniker. Dick Van Dyke scores in an unusual role for him, as the corrupt district attorney. Beatty even gave small parts to his old *Bonnie and Clyde* costars Michael J. Pollard (a 1930s version of a wiretapper) and Estelle Parsons (Tess's mom); both deliver. "It takes a lot of understanding to love a man like that," Parsons counsels her daughter.

After Beatty and Pacino, the actor who got the most press was Madonna. Madonna is able to put over Stephen Sondheim's catchy songs (without having a particularly good voice), but as an actress she radiates more style than substance. She comes *this close* to being effective, but doesn't quite cut it. To be fair, she has a credible scene at the docks with Tracy. "Tell me you want me!" she says to him, hinting at the vulnerability and pathos beneath the surface sexiness. Beatty might have gotten even more of an *on-screen* performance out of Madonna if he hadn't been so busy romancing her at the time.

"No grief for Lips?" he asks Breathless after the murder of her former boyfriend.

"I'm wearing black underwear," she replies. Madonna is in her ersatz Marilyn Monroe mode throughout.

As previously stated, *Dick Tracy* lacks any really magnificent action set pieces à la the James Bond or Indiana Jones series, but it is not without its highlights just the same. One near nail-biter has Tracy tied to a chair in a basement next to a boiler that is about to explode; Kid comes to the rescue just in time. A shootout between the cops and a bunch of crooks firing from their cars with tommy guns is exciting. The business with a kidnapped Tess tied to a drawbridge's turntable and nearly crushed isn't milked for enough suspense, but it is still tense and compelling. The picture has a sense of fun, too: Tracy is called from watching a musical show to investigate the murder of Lips Manlis and others; when he returns to the theater, they're still doing the *same number*.

A stunning visual feast, *Dick Tracy* is a study in charm and whimsy and cinematic artistry. Beatty's direction is assured and confident, and editor Richard Marks gives the picture fluidity and pacing. Harold Michelson's sets and Richard Sylbert's production design are outstanding, as are the special effects and matte paintings employed to bring the wonderfully colorful (in every sense of the word) proceedings to life. Kudos also to Danny Elfman's score, Stephen Sondheim's nifty songs, and Vittorio Storaro's cinematography, which throws a glossy, striking sheen over everything.

Those who dismissed *Dick Tracy* when it was first released may find it genuinely delightful on second viewing. One thing that can't be dismissed: Pacino *is* a delight as Big Boy Caprice. He practically walks away with the picture, no mean feat indeed.

The Godfather Part III

Paramount, 1990

Executive producers, Fred Fuchs and Nicholas Cage; producer, Francis Ford Coppola; director, Coppola; director of photography, Gordon Willis; editors, Barry Malkin, Lisa Fruchtman, and Walter Murch; screenplay, Mario Puzo and Coppola; music, Carmine Coppola; additional music, Nino Rota; associate producer, Marina Gefter; coproducers, Fred Roos, Gray Frederickson, and Charles Mulvehill; production designer, Dean Tavoularis; costume designer, Milena Canonero. Running time: 170 min.

Cast

Al Pacino (*Michael Corleone*); Andy Garcia (*Vincent Mancini*); Eli Wallach (*Don Altobello*); Talia Shire (*Connie*); Sofia Coppola (*Mary*); Franc D'Ambrosio (*Anthony*); Diane Keaton (*Kay*); George Hamilton (*Harrison*); Bridget Fonda (*Grace*); John Savage (*Andrew Hogan*); Donal Donnelly (*Archbishop*); Raf Vallone (*Cardinal Lamberto*); Mario Donatone (*Mosca*); Joe Mantegna (*Joey Zasa*); Al Martino (*Johnny Fontaine*); Helmut Berger (*Frederick Kelmszig*).

Sixteen years had passed since *The Godfather Part II*; it was time for the next—and, thus far, final—chapter in the saga of the Corleone family. The story begins in New York City in 1979. Michael Corleone (Al Pacino) is receiving an award for his charitable work through the Corleone Foundation, which helps the impoverished and is dedicated to the rebirth of Sicily. Kay (Diane Keaton) has divorced Michael and remarried. Daughter Mary (Sofia Coppola) is chairman of the Corleone Foundation, while son Anthony (Franc D'Ambrosio) is about to make his debut as an opera singer. Sonny's illegitimate son, Vincent Mancini (Andy Garcia), Michael's nephew, makes it known that he wants to advance in the family. He and cousin Mary begin an affair.

Michael agrees to cover losses in the Vatican bank in return for control of Immobiliare, the Vatican corporation. His former partners want in on the deal to "purify their money," but Michael is after total legitimacy and must turn them down. He also meets resistance from the other board members of Immobiliare. After suffering a diabetic stroke, Michael tells Vincent that he'll make him head of the family but he must give up Mary. During Anthony's debut in *Cavalleria rusticana* in Palermo, the Corleones strike to take care of their assorted enemies and attempt to save the life of Pope John Paul I, who has ratified the Immobiliare deal but is promptly murdered by opposing Vatican factions. On the steps of the opera house Michael and his daughter are both shot by assassins.

Pacino inexplicably wanted to wear his hair down to his shoulders in *God-*

father III, but director Francis Ford Coppola wisely told him *no*. Instead, he wears a more appropriate gray brush cut. His voice is very raspy, and he seems more "common" than he was in the first two films. But he absolutely *dominates* the picture, even over such competition as the younger, energetic and sexy Andy Garcia, as his nephew. Pacino plays with his usual assurance and charisma and has several especially fine scenes, such as when he gives his confession to Cardinal Lamberto (Raf Vallone), who later becomes Pope John Paul I. Collapsing into tears, he says, "I murdered my mother's son, my father's son." He is also excellent reacting to Mary's death on the steps of the opera house, emitting a potent outcry of remorse and anguish. One of the few Pacino blasts in the picture occurs when Michael learns that his nephew "whacked" someone without his permission: "It was not what I wanted!" he screams.

Of the supporting cast, Andy Garcia, with slicked-back hair and intense expression, makes the strongest impression as the bastard nephew Vincent. While he represents the younger generation, he's an old-fashioned mafioso at heart. Michael orders Vincent to make peace with Joey Zasa (Joe Mantegna), who now owns what used to be the Corleone family business. But as Vincent grudgingly hugs his nemesis Joey, he gives the latter a bloody bite on the ear. This culminates in Vincent disguising himself as a cop on horseback and carrying through on his threat to whack Zasa by shooting him during a violent blowout in Little Italy. Later, as Vincent watches his cousin perform in *Cavalleria rusticana*, there's an amusing cut to his laughing in appreciation after he sees Anthony's Turridu biting the ear of Alfio, the man who married his lover while Turridu was in the army (and with whose wife Turridu is now sleeping).

Diane Keaton's Kay is the voice of common decency in the *Godfather* movies, especially in this installment. Keaton is quite effective in her confrontation with ex-husband Michael at the reception that takes place after he receives his award and is also good later in the picture when she and Michael have a few quiet moments in Sicily before their son's operatic debut. Kay and Michael are fond of each other but no longer in love—but there's still a lingering feeling and a bond. This was exactly the situation in real life. Keaton and Pacino, who had been involved with each other at different times over the years, broke up, got back together, and finally broke up for good during the shooting of *The Godfather Part III*.

Julia Roberts had been first choice for the part of Mary Corleone, but there were scheduling conflicts. Winona Ryder was subsequently signed, but she had to bow out due to illness from an overcrowded schedule. Finally, Coppola chose his daughter Sofia, to the amazement of Hollywood insiders, who thought he was crazy to give such an important part to an amateur. Sofia received scathing reviews, but she is actually more than adequate in the part.

Just like the character she portrays, Sofia is equal parts innocence and sensuality, a full-lipped beauty with strong carnal appeal. While you wouldn't want to cast her as Blanche Du Bois in a revival of *A Streetcar Named Desire,* she's perfect as Mary Corleone.

Robert Duvall wanted too much money, so his Tom Hagen character was written out. Instead, there were small roles for John Savage as Hagen's son Andrew, a priest, and George Hamilton, as a new Corleone family adviser, Harrison. Eli Wallach is charming malevolence personified as the traitorous Don Altobello. Bridget Fonda appears very briefly as a reporter who sleeps with Vincent and is okay in the part. Joe Mantegna certainly makes his mark as the slimy Joey Zasa in an energetic, on-target performance. Resurfacing in a bit part as Swiss banker Frederick Kelmszig is Helmut Berger of *The Damned*. Franc D'Ambrosio hasn't much to do as Anthony Corleone, but he reveals a nice enough voice as Turridu, if not quite on the Pavarotti level. And Talia Shire emerges as a tougher, more active Connie in her ruthless portrayal of Michael's sister.

The aforementioned shootouts in Little Italy and on the opera house steps are highlights of *The Godfather Part III* to be sure, but the most exciting scene, bar none, takes place in Atlantic City, where Michael has gathered bigwigs from all the families. Just as this gangland convention is breaking up, a sort of hurricane wind whips through the meeting hall, and an inexplicable racket fills the air. The next moment, the fleeing hoods are spattered with bullets as helicopters with machine guns fly past and over the balconies, spurting death and mayhem. Michael, of course, survives to pay back the man who has dared to try to wipe out all competition in one fell swoop.

The ending of *The Godfather Part III* is a reprise of the climaxes of *The Godfather* and *The Godfather Part II,* with the Corleone family "taking care" of all their enemies in one evening. Targets include a hit man, Mosca (Mario Donatone), who tried to murder Michael in Sicily, and Don Altobello, who was behind the superhit in New Jersey. (Connie feeds the unsuspecting don some poisoned pastries.) As they watch Anthony in the opera, the Corleones are unaware that assassins are taking out their bodyguards, strangling and shooting them in draperied alcoves and deserted boxes, thereby setting up the hit on Michael on the opera steps afterward. This opera sequence is one of the best scenes in the film, but it is not comparable to its obvious model, the Albert Hall assassination attempt in Hitchcock's remake of his own *The Man Who Knew Too Much* (1956). Coppola's opera scene, like the picture in general, needs tightening and pacing to really make it *sing*.

Speaking of singing, a word is in order on *Cavalleria rusticana,* the opera chosen for the background of this sequence. Composer Pietro Mascagni's 1890 masterpiece takes place in Sicily (birthplace of the Mafia) and deals with betrayal and revenge (and, most especially, unrequited love). But that's where its resemblance to the film ends. *The Godfather Part III*, like its two predecessors, is essentially just a glossy, generally well-made potboiler and nothing more. *Cavalleria rusticana* is an immortal work of genius, depth, passion, and *sensitivity*, a brilliant examination of pathetic lives. Franco Zeffirelli's film version with Placido Domingo makes the admittedly entertaining *Godfather Part III* seem like junk in comparison.

Al Pacino is himself an opera buff, which may be why Coppola built the opera sequence into the picture in the first place. A funny sequence in *The Godfather Part III* has Michael Corleone proudly announcing to friends that his son will make his debut in *Cavalleeria rusticana*. "Uh, that's *Cavallereeeah rusticana*, Dad," corrects Anthony. Presumably, Pacino would never commit such a pronunciational faux pas. Coppola's faux pas is to present the great opera *out of sequence* in *The Godfather Part III*. Although Carmine Copolla and Nino Rota are credited as composers for *The Godfather Part III*, all of the great music heard in the last twenty or so minutes is from Mascagni's opera.

Does *The Godfather Part III* glorify the Mafia? In this picture it's the Corleone family against the rest of the Mob—making them "heroes." They even try to save the life of the pope! Their actions are continually justified, and time and again we're supposed to believe that members of the Mafia are just like everyone else. The picture makes comparisons to politics and crime that are a bit self-serving. One thing the movie doesn't gloss over is the fist-in-glove relationship between the Mafia and the Catholic Church. Cardinal Lamberto doesn't even look stricken as Michael confesses his many disturbing sins (not wanting to "bite the hand that feeds him," one supposes). But the main problem with *The Godfather Part III* is its length and deliberate pacing. The picture would be more effective tightened and trimmed of at least a half hour's running time.

Most critics and audiences were pleased with *The Godfather Part III* nonetheless. It received seven Academy Award nominations (including Best Picture and Best Director), but Al Pacino wasn't included. British film critic Alexander Walker boldly declared *The Godfather Part III* a "masterpiece."

Hardly. It was just good dirty fun.

The Local Stigmatic

20TH CENTURY FOX VIDEO; 1990

Producers, Michael Hadge, Timothy Marx, and Al Pacino; director, David F. Wheeler; screenplay, Heathcote Williams, from his play; cinematography,

Edward Lachman; music, Howard Shore; editing, Norman Hollyn. Running time: 56 minutes.

Cast

Al Pacino (*Graham*); Paul Guilfoyle (*Ray*); Joseph Maher (*David*).

The Local Stigmatic was a short film based on a play by Heathcote Williams, who also wrote the screenplay. The play was originally written and produced in the 1960s, with Pacino in one of the lead roles. It is a question why he or anyone else felt the play needed to be immortalized on film, as despite some good dialogue, it is forgettable, with barely developed characters. The film was made in the '80s, shown at the Museum of Modern Art in 1990, and has had a few other select screenings, but has never been theatrically released, although it is now on DVD. Part of the problem is that it is only a little over fifty minutes long. Another problem is that it isn't very good, although Pacino gives a more than credible performance.

In London, Graham (Pacino) and Ray (Paul Guilfoyle) are roommates. Graham is in a bad mood because a guy gave him a tip for the dog races that didn't pan out. Graham and Ray go out for a drink, when on the street Graham sees an old drunken man (Michael Higgins) who reminds him of the guy who gave him the tip. Graham harasses the man, who hollers at them, but ultimately they let him walk off. Graham is angry with Ray for not joining him in harassing the fellow, but Ray seems to have some compassion for the drunk. "What if he just lost his wife?" he asks. At the pub, Ray reads some gossip items about celebrities to Graham; they then spot a film actor, David (Joseph Mayer), sitting at the bar and go over to him. The conversation is friendly, if a bit edgy, and Graham offers to walk along with David when he leaves; Ray follows. When Graham gives a command, Ray attacks David, knocking him to the ground and stuffing a handkerchief in his mouth to keep him from shouting for help. Graham then slashes David's face with a knife, and the two walk off. Some weeks later Ray tells Graham that he walked by David and he didn't recognize him. Angry at this, Graham tells Ray to call David's private number and taunt him. Graham is pleased that Ray will do whatever he tells him.

There are the bones of an interesting story in *The Local Stigmatic*, but the problem is that Williams can't quite make his characters come alive. They exist only for the time it takes to tell the story, and are too insubstantial to have any life beyond that. Pacino was concerned that they not be seen as homosexual characters. Whether this was because he feared negative reaction from the gay community as with *Cruising*—Graham and Ray are borderline sociopaths—or because he felt that that was simply the wrong interpretation, or both, is unknown. The characters do often seem like a (non-stereotypical) gay couple, except they never touch, and Pacino's almost flirtatious performance only adds to the ambiguity. One could argue that straight men often engage in mock-homosexual flirtation, often to belittle one another, but this behavior just as easily can hide true homosexual feelings. Ray has a girlfriend (which is not proof of anything) and Graham does not; perhaps he has repressed feelings for his friend.

Although homosexuality had been dealt with in the theater long before the '60s, even in that period it could be handled in a coy manner. Perhaps Graham and Ray are presumably straight Williams's dated conception of a (loose) homosexual couple. In the end, it doesn't matter, because they have no resonance beyond the fifty minutes they occupy our time. One does have to wonder why Pacino, in the bar scene, says the line, "They're all fuckin' faggots" when it isn't even in the play. If the intention was to make it clear that Graham isn't gay, it almost has the opposite effect, making him seem full of the self-hatred that often characterizes the homophobe. Perhaps Pacino was subconsciously expressing contempt for the gay community and their alleged part in the failure of *Cruising*, although his public comments indicate otherwise.

Although Pacino was criticized for his cockney accent, it sounds perfectly okay to American ears—although he's hard to understand at times. His performance is imbued with equal measures of charm and menace; despite the broad smile, his eyes are crazy and it seems like there is something unpleasant in him that is barely restrained—you don't know what he's going to do next. It's very strong and compelling work, if only a better script had been built to surround it. Paul Guilfoyle is quite good as Ray, the less dominant personality, who often seems in thrall to his roommate's darker psyche. The casting of Joseph Maher as David is problematic, however. Maher is good, and he played the part with Pacino on the stage many years earlier. But while the fact that in the film Graham and Ray are approaching middle-age—Pacino was nearing fifty—instead of being in their twenties (as in the play) may not be too destructive, Maher being nearly sixty (instead of in his thirties) is a different story. If the play is about envy, as Williams has suggested, why are they so envious of a *slightly* famous actor who is comparatively *old* on top of it? One can imagine Ray, who showed compassion for another older man, more readily going along with Graham's orders if David were young, with many good years ahead, but now his actions seem a bit inexplicable. It could be argued, of course, that this still illustrates Graham's increasing influence over Ray. But in the end, this also doesn't matter because of the essential wispiness of the characters.

It is possible that Pacino was attracted to the play in his post-stardom period because he had felt the envy and indeed hateful jealousy of people who hadn't achieved the major success that he had. Perhaps he should have chosen another vehicle to explore it.

Frankie and Johnny

PARAMOUNT, 1991

Executive producers, Alexandra Rose and Charles Mulvehill; producer, Garry Marshall; director, Marshall; director of photography, Dante Spinotti; screenplay, Terence McNally; based on McNally's stage play *Frankie and Johnny in the Clair de Lune*; editors, Battle Davis and Jacqueline Cambas; coproducer, Nick Abdo; music, Marvin Hamlisch; production designer, Albert Brenner; costume designer, Rosanna Norton. Running time: 118 min.

CAST

Al Pacino (*Johnny*); Michelle Pfeiffer (*Frankie*); Hector Elizondo (*Nick*); Nathan Lane (*Tim*); Kate Nelligan (*Cora*); Jane Morris (*Nedda*); Fernando Lopez (*Jorge*); Glen Plummer (*Peter*); Sean O'Bryan (*Bobby*); Tim Hopper (*Lester*).

"New York City can be a dangerous, hostile place," the warden says to Johnny (Pacino) as the latter leaves jail after serving his sentence.

"It'll be a nice change," Johnny says.

And indeed, the New York City of *Frankie and Johnny*—one of Pacino's nicest pictures—is not the New York of *The Panic in Needle Park*, with its drug addicts; *The Godfather* and sequels, with their elegant hoodlums; *Serpico*, with its corrupt police officers; or *Cruising* and *Sea of Love*, with their brutal serial murderers. Not since *Author! Author!* in 1982 had Pacino done a warm, comic film. Even better, *Frankie and Johnny*—unlike *Author! Author!*—was a *good* picture.

Johnny has spent one and a half years in jail for forging a check. He goes to work as a cook at the Apollo Restaurant at Ninth Avenue and Twenty-third Street and is almost immediately smitten with a pretty blonde waitress, Frankie (Michelle Pfeiffer). But Frankie finds Johnnie too intense and "needy"; she's had too much bad luck with men. Her gay friend and neighbor, Tim (Nathan Lane), reminds her that her phone hasn't exactly been ringing off the hook. Agreeing to a date, Frankie is charmed by Johnny but reluctant to get involved in a full-scale relationship. At her apartment one night, the two admire a lovely piece (Debussy's "Clair de Lune") on the radio, and Johnny calls the station to ask them to play it again. Against all odds, the piece is reprised minutes later. Perhaps, the lovers think, their relationship will also work in spite of the odds against it. *Fade out.*

Playing mid-forties at age fifty-one (and getting away with it), Pacino is simply terrific in one of his most delightful pictures. He and Pfeiffer give very

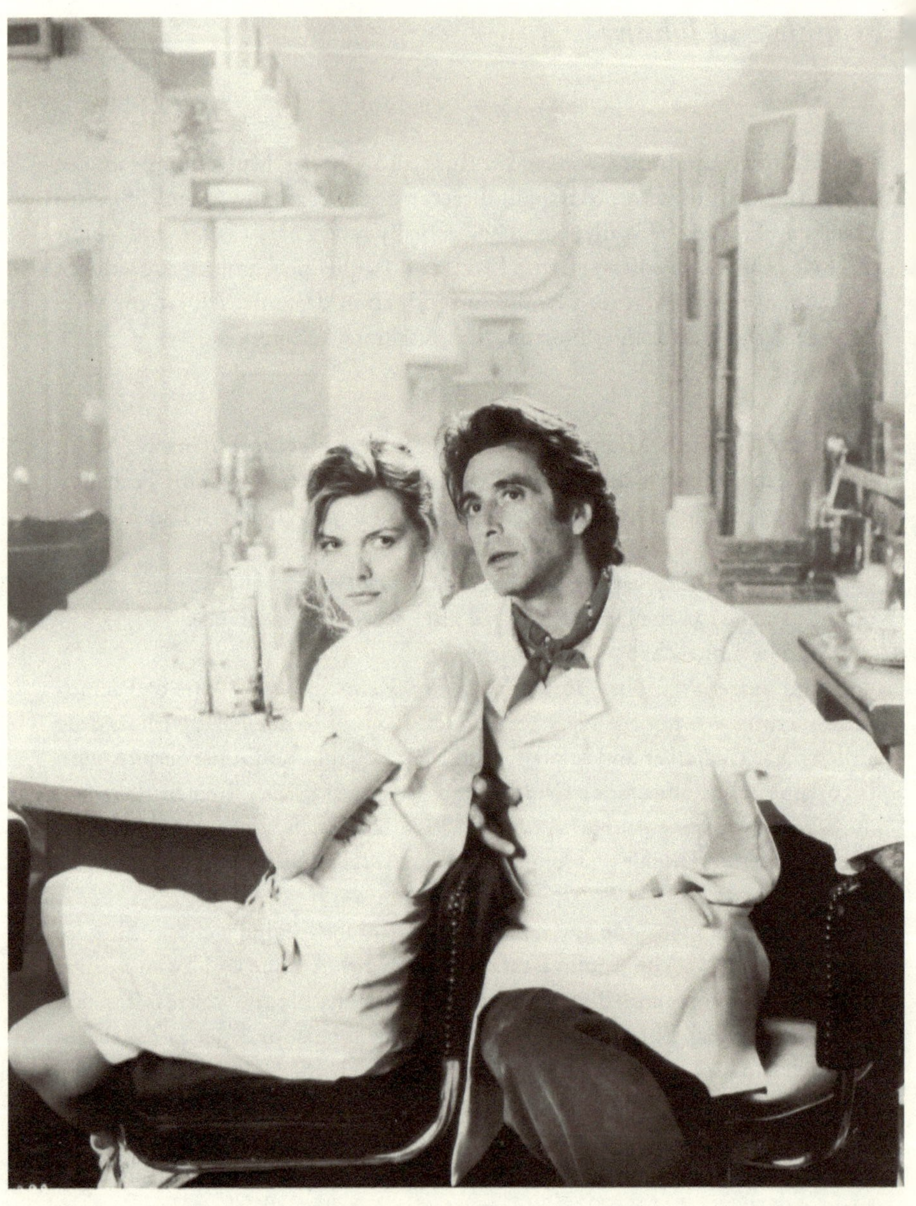

Two lonely New Yorkers, Frankie (Michelle Pfeiffer) and Johnny (Pacino), meet and fall in love while working together in a diner. This romantic comedy (a Hollywood version of the Off Broadway play *Frankie and Johnny in the Clair de Lune*)—a rarity in the Pacino canon—scored with moviegoers. *Frankie and Johnny* (1991).

realistic depictions of "uncertain" lovers—she, not wanting to offend him but with deep reservations; he, hoping he's charming her but afraid that he's not. Pacino is actually very charming in this picture, whether he's telling another waitress, Cora (Kate Nelligan), why he doesn't cry out or moan during an orgasm or assuring Tim that he, Johnny, has a gay cousin. To Cora, whom he beds, he explains that he was in a place where "full-throated orgasm would have been inappropriate." "Like a monastery?" Cora asks.

To Tim, he says of his cousin: "I just found out he was gay a couple of months ago."

"I'll look him up in the directory," Tim says wryly. "Under the new listings."

Later, Pacino pulls out the stops when he expresses his full-fledged orgasm with accompanying verbalizations and his joy at having same. Pacino is also wonderful dancing to Greek music with the "stiff" but fun-loving waitress Nedda (Jane Morris) at a party celebrating a busboy's selling his first script to Hollywood. Morris and Pacino seem to be having so much *spontaneous* fun that they make the scene one of the standouts in the picture.

In Terrence McNally's stage play *Frankie and Johnny in the Clair de Lune* (Light of the Moon), upon which McNally's screenplay was based, the part of Frankie was essayed by Kathy Bates as an "unattractive, middle-aged woman who had given up on love." The *New York Times* said: "The casting of the conspicuously young, exquisitely beautiful, and very bankable Michelle Pfeiffer [in the film] provoked scorn in the theater community." Yet Pfeiffer—while she may be different from the original conception—is quite good in the picture and has several outstanding scenes. A lonely woman (who is to say pretty women can't be lonely?), she watches other people's lives—among them a woman who is beaten by her husband—through the windows of the building across the street and at one point tries to give herself the Heimlich maneuver. Pfeiffer movingly gets through the fear and desperation and loneliness of her character as she tells Johnny about the previous men in her life, including one who fell for her best friend and one who beat her so severely that she miscarried. True, Kathy Bates, plain and overweight, might have been more pathetic in these scenes, but Pfeiffer is no less touching.

Of the rest of the cast, Kate Nelligan is excellent, completely different from her usual self and totally convincing as Cora, the hard-boiled, likable sexpot with whom Johnny dallies for some sexual hijinks. Jane Morris as the slightly weird Nedda is so realistic and irrepressible that one could imagine her being snatched not from central casting but out of some greasy spoon on Broadway. Nathan Lane is delightful as Frankie's confidant Tim, never descending into stereotype, dashing off lines with perfect timing and breezy skill. Sean O'Bryan is also good as Tim's lover, Bobby. Of the coffee-shop staff, Hector Elizondo is fine, as usual, as Nick, the owner, while Fernando Lopez, Glen Plummer, and Tim Hopper, among others, turn in nice jobs as cooks, busboys, and so on.

McNally's screenplay has only a few false notes, such as when Johnny asks Frankie for a date while they're huddled over an epileptic customer's body waiting for an ambulance to arrive. And how does Johnny manage to talk the suspicious, insular Frankie into taking him home to bed on the night of their first date? The two stand talking in front of a truck filled with flowers, but we aren't allowed to hear the dialogue. Which is a shame, because McNally's dialogue is usually excellent, from the witty gags and trenchant observances to Pacino's explaining to Pfeiffer that he feels like "the only person in the world trapped inside this body, only bumping into people but not connecting with the only other people in the world trapped inside their bodies." In many ways *Frankie and Johnny* is only an updating of all those '40s comedies with likable lunatics trying to win over more reserved heroines. Unlike those old films, *Frankie and Johnny* makes good points about smothering, self-centered love.

Some critics felt that the film's ending wrapped things up too neatly. Not only do Frankie and Johnny agree to commit to each other in "the light of the moon," but the battered wife in the next building leaves home the same night. But it is hardly a typical Hollywood happy ending: Frankie and Johnny have only agreed to *try* and make things work, to open themselves to love and all its vulnerabilities and risk heartbreak. Who really knows what will happen in the months ahead? For that matter, who knows what will really happen to the battered wife who has left home?

Garry Marshall's direction is quietly effective and moves things along nicely. Marvin Hamlisch's pleasant music and funky pop tunes on the soundtrack are fine, but, of course, Debussy's "Clair de Lune" is what really makes the ending work.

Why is Pacino so much better in *Frankie and Johnny* than in his earlier romantic comedy (of sorts) *Author! Author!*? (Not that he was *bad* in the former film.) First, there's the fact that McNally's script is far superior to Horovitz's. Second, a naturalistic actor like Pacino is much better playing a real person like Johnny than an unreal *type* like Ivan Travalian. Besides, as Johnny, he didn't have to strain to be funny; Johnny *is* a man of charm and humor, and Pacino just had to play him that way, not emote in a certain "style."

Frankie and Johnny was a nice change of pace from the "blood and guts" pictures, as would be Pacino's next two films.

Glengarry Glen Ross

NEW LINE CINEMA, 1992

Executive producer, Joseph Caracciolo Jr.; producers, Jerry Tokofsky and Stanley R. Zupnik; director, James Foley; director of photography, Juan Ruiz Anchia; screenplay, David Mamet, based on his play; editor, Howard Smith; music, James Newton Howard; coproducers, Morris Ruskin and Nava Levin; production designer, Jane Musky; costume designer, Jane Greenwood. Running time: 100 min.

CAST

Al Pacino (*Ricky Roma*); Jack Lemmon (*Sheldon Levene*); Alec Baldwin (*Blake*); Ed Harris (*Dave Moss*); Alan Arkin (*George Aaronow*); Kevin Spacey (*John Williamson*); Jonathan Pryce (*James Link*); Bruce Altman (*Mr. Spannel*); Jude Ciccolella (*Detective*).

While it undoubtedly worked even better on the stage, the film adaptation of David Mamet's Pulitzer prize–winning play *Glengarry Glen Ross* is noteworthy if for no other reason than that it gives the audience the opportunity to see several fine actors really putting on a *show*. In particular, Al Pacino, Jack Lemmon, and Ed Harris seem to be in a three-man acting contest, with accompanying pyrotechnics—and these gents *deliver*!

The agents in a real estate firm are told by a slick operator, Blake (Alec Baldwin), from "downtown," that they are, in effect, "fired" and have one week to get their jobs "back." In other words, unless their performances improve, they're through. They must close a deal before the week is up, or else. The men complain that they don't have good enough "leads" (names of people to whom they might be able to sell property), and all are hungering for leads to a property in Florida known as the Glengarry Highlands. The manager, John (Kevin Spacey), insists that the Glengarry leads are reserved for those agents who have gotten the best—and most—deals. The likely contender is Ricky Roma (Al Pacino), who has been wining and dining a client, Link (Jonathan Pryce), in a nearby Chinese restaurant.

The most desperate of the group is Shelley Levene (Jack Lemmon), whose daughter's hospital bills have to be paid. John agrees to give the Glengarry leads to Shelley for 25 percent of the commissions and fifty dollars a lead, but Shelley can't come up with the money. Meanwhile, Dave Moss (Ed Harris) and a reluctant George Aaronow (Alan Arkin) plot to steal the leads, which are missing from the office the following morning. When John lies to Ricky's client, Link (who has changed his mind), and tells him that his check was cashed and the contract sent downtown, Shelley makes a blunder, telling John that he should never make anything up unless it will be helpful. For once John went home early instead of going downtown with the contracts and demands to know how Shelley knew he was lying. Shelley confesses that *he* stole the leads and sold them to a rival broker. John tells the detective investigating the break-in who the guilty party is; the broken, defeated Shelley will be fired and arrested.

Pacino is very convincing as a somewhat sleazy, oily real estate operator, someone who has developed a certain style but never really had any class. Ricky Roma is more polished than, say, Scarface or Pacino's later Carlito, but only superficially. He's a "cool guy." Pacino looks good, if a little battered, in the role, smooth and urbane. *Glengarry Glen Ross* presents mostly fine-tuned ensemble acting, but Pacino has several standout moments in the picture, such as when he talks to a nervous Link, trying to placate his fears and convince him not to pull out of the deal. Or when he tells off John for giving him bad leads: "Where did you get this one from—a morgue?" Later, he gets angry at John for ruining his deal with Link by saying the check has been cashed. "You *never* open your mouth until you know what the shot is!" he screams at the manager. Ricky is properly furious, but Pacino seems too restrained, merely simmering when a real Pacino blast might have been called for. Otherwise, his performance is excellent; he was nominated for an Academy Award, in fact.

Pacino's chief competition is from Jack Lemmon as Shelley Levene. A hypnotically fascinating actor, Lemmon is superb as the tired but still frantically energetic salesman at the end of his rope. Trying to sell property to a potential but disinterested client, Mr. Spannel (Bruce Altman), Lemmon registers charm, grace, hope, defeat, and despair in equal measure. In their best scene together, Lemmon pretends to be another satisfied client so that Pacino can clinch the deal with the almost hysterical Link. The two men, such different types of actors, clearly play well together and are having fun. These are two thespian powerhouses at their peak. (Decades later, Pacino played the Shelley Levene role on the stage.)

Ed Harris is also dynamic as Dave Moss, tough, macho, but essentially a complaining loser. Harris manages to make a man who would probably not be very interesting in real life seem fascinating, subtly revealing the weakness beneath the strong, masculine exterior. Alec Baldwin really makes the most of his one scene as Blake from "downtown," who threatens everyone with dismissal. Baldwin took a risk in playing it in a more stylized, slick manner than the others' naturalistic emoting, but it pays off in the long run: his Blake emerges as menacing, powerful, larger-than-life-loathsome, almost a force of nature, all the conscienceless "winners" in the world combined into one obscene, smirking *presence.*

Although their roles are less "showy," the other actors also score, particularly Kevin Spacey as the manager, John, and Jonathan Pryce (with a convincing American accent) as James Link, Ricky's client. Both actors have been powerhouses in other roles, but here they underplay, slowly building up to their bigger scenes: Pryce, weak but determined, walking away from the deal with Ricky; John telling Shelley that he basically set him up because he just doesn't like him. Alan Arkin as quiet George, Bruce Altman as Mr. Spannel, and Jude Ciccolella as the detective are also just right.

Glengarry Glen Ross is not exactly *Death of a Salesman*, but it is absorbing and occasionally powerful. The opening scenes, with all their tedious, confusing real estate chatter, hardly draw one in, but the movie eventually builds in tension and interest. The storyline is basically old-fashioned; as in Rod Serling's *Patterns*, we're handed the creepy boss who wants his employees to improve business or *leave*. The picture is well edited by Howard Smith and briskly directed by James Foley. The jazz rifts James Newton Howard composed for the score are forgettable, however.

Scent of a Woman

Universal; a City Light Films production, 1992

Executive producer, Ronald L. Schwary; producer, Martin Brest; director, Brest; director of photography, Donald E. Thorn; screenplay, Bo Goldman; editors, William Steinkamp, Michael Tronick, and Harvey Rosenstock; music, Thomas Newman; production designer, Angelo Graham; costume designer, Aude Bronson-Howard. Running time: 137 min.

Cast

Al Pacino (*Frank Slade*); Chris O'Donnell (*Charlie Sims*); James Rebhorn (*Trask*); Philip Seymour Hoffman (*George Willis Jr.*); Nicholas Sadler (*Harry Havemeyer*); Richard Venture (*W. R. Slade*); Bradley Whitford (*Randy*); Margaret Eginton (*Gail*); Rochelle Oliver (*Gretchen*); Tom Riis Farrell (*Garry*); Gabrielle Anwar (*Donna*); Leonard Gaines (*Freddie Bisco*); Ron Eldard (*Officer Gore*).

By 1992, Al Pacino had received Academy Award nominations for Best Actor or Best Supporting Actor for, among others, such pictures as *Serpico*, *Dog Day Afternoon*, and *...And Justice for All*. What an irony that he should finally *win* the Best Actor Oscar for *Scent of a Woman*!

Certainly Pacino gives a fine performance in the film as retired colonel Frank Slade, a charming, blind reprobate obsessed with "pussy" and suicide.

But the part could hardly have been tailor-made for the miscast Pacino. As written, Frank Slade is more of a role for Charles Durning or even the older (than Pacino), grizzled Ben Gazzara. Played by Pacino—however winningly—Frank Slade never seems quite like a real person. But then Bo Goldman's script does little to make the colonel seem real to begin with.

Charlie Sims (Chris O'Donnell) is a student at the Baird prep school in New Hampshire. For extra money, he agrees to "baby-sit" for the disagreeable and vulgar Frank Slade, a blind middle-aged man who lives with his niece and husband, while they go on vacation. Charlie expects this to be an easy—if unpleasant—assignment, but Slade surprises him by insisting he accompany him to New York City. After Slade has a good meal at the Oak Room, dances a tango with a sexy restaurant patron, and sleeps with a high-class call girl, he attempts suicide in his hotel room. Charlie prevents him from blowing his brains out.

"Why shouldn't I kill myself?" asks Slade, who is ready to exit after his final fling.

"Because you can dance a tango and drive a Ferrari better than anyone I've ever seen," says Charlie (typical of the picture's often puerile dialogue).

The two return to New Hampshire, where further adventure awaits. It seems that Charlie knows who participated in a practical joke on the headmaster, Trask (James Rebhorn), and is threatened with expulsion unless he reveals their identities. The headmaster practically guarantees his entry into a superior university if he does snitch. At a public hearing over the matter, who should advance up to the stage but Frank Slade, who argues in Charlie's favor and commends his integrity. "He won't sell anybody out to buy his future." The students applaud Slade, and the board votes not to expel Charlie. *Finis*.

Frank Slade is an utterly self-centered person—at times, he seems pathetic; at others, a borderline psycho—but as played by Pacino, he slowly begins to grow on you ... to a point. As has often been the case in his career, Pacino's personal charm makes an unpleasant character more bearable. Conversely, it is also possible that Pacino tries *too* hard not to sentimentalize the colonel. Pacino's jivey, vaguely Southern accent that comes and goes also seems a little odd.

Chris O'Donnell is okay as the shy, shuffling Charlie, with his hangdog look, but he doesn't seem nearly nervous enough at the climactic hearing. It is hard to imagine the very shy Charlie able to lead Pacino over to a strange beauty in a restaurant (without at least having had a beer or two first) and being so at ease. A budding bleeding heart, Charlie tells Slade, "You're not bad; you're just in pain." Slade's words of wisdom for Charlie: "There are only two syllables in this whole wide world worth hearing: pussy." (To his cat, Slade opines: "When in doubt, fuck.")

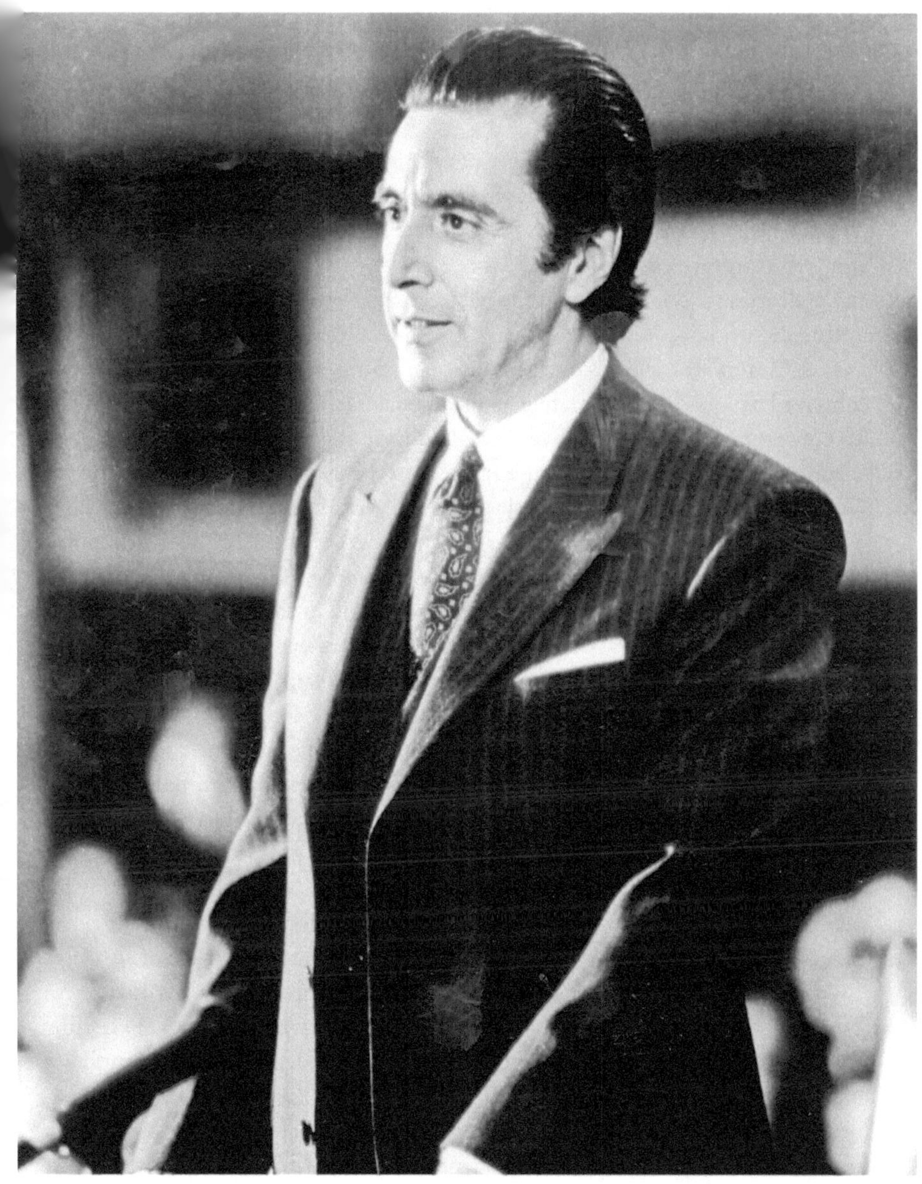

"Hoo-ah!" Pacino won his only Oscar (thus far) for his bravura performance as blind ex-army colonel Frank Slade in *Scent of a Woman* (1992).

A tense Thanksgiving dinner scene—Slade just shows up at his brother's house, uninvited, with Charlie in tow—is one of the best segments in the movie, illustrating the dual nature of Slade's personality. On the one hand, he is admirably frank and earthy, fun-loving. On the other hand, he can be overbearingly obnoxious. His relatives are undeniably "uptight," but Slade goes too far.

His nephew Randy (Bradley Whitford) declares: "He was an asshole before; now he's a blind asshole."

Slade *is* an asshole and, in many ways, unsympathetic. He lost his eyesight during a grenade-juggling contest when he was drunk! While in New York with Charlie, he convinces a dealer to let them take a Ferrari out for a spin and speeds along the streets in it, not caring what happens to himself, young Charlie, or any pedestrians. The scene is supposed to be "cute"; instead (like so many scenes in this picture), it's irritating.

A "drama" for the sitcom generation, *Scent of a Woman* is as phony and contrived as a bad made-for-television movie. Far too many scenes are put in for confrontation value but have no real point to them. The headmaster, Trask, is supposed to be such a villain, but we are told more about him than we are *shown*. Considering the humiliating joke played on him (a big balloon filled with paint poured over his new car and him before the assembled students), his determination to get the pranksters seems more than reasonable. But the picture really implodes at the climactic hearing and as the result of Pacino's big speech, which is embarrassingly overdone. "If it were five years ago," he says, "I'd take a flamethrower to this place!" The students applaud Pacino, but in real life they would probably find him laughable.

And what about the hearing? Certainly Charlie has been placed in an extremely difficult position by the headmaster, who is being unfair. But what about the students who actually perpetrated the practical joke (or, more accurately, the mean-spirited act of vandalism)? What about *their* integrity? They sit smirking in the audience, perfectly willing to let Charlie be expelled for his silence, absolutely unwilling to take responsibility for their actions. It never occurs to anyone connected with *Scent of a Woman* that its message of so-called integrity is patently phony. Why should Charlie throw away his future for "friends" (with friends like these...) who are willing, if not anxious, to let him take the fall, who don't have the guts to come forward, admit their complicity, and let Charlie off the hook? By not getting Charlie out of trouble, regardless of the consequences (they *did* commit the deed, after all), they prove their unworthiness. Charlie *should* have turned them in once he realized they were not going to do the right thing.

At 137 minutes, *Scent of a Woman* is much too long, and Martin Brest's direction (along with three editors) isn't able to prevent tedium from setting in long before the conclusion. Some of the supporting cast certainly do their best to help pep things up: Richard Venture expertly limns the affectionate exasperation he feels for Slade as his brother; Bradley Whitford is fine as the not-so-affectionate nephew; James Rebhorn is solid as headmaster Trask; and Leonard Gaines makes the most of his bit as Freddie Bisco, the Ferrari dealer who is reluctant to let Slade and Charlie take one of his cars out for a spin. Gabrielle Anwar got some press as Donna, the lady with whom Slade dances the tango; she has little to do in the film but does it well. Ditto for Ron Eldard as a handsome cop who fails to notice that Pacino is blind when he pulls up to the Ferrari. The college students and assorted relatives of Slade are also well cast. Donald E. Thorn's photography is excellent and crisp, making the most of great-looking New York City locations, not to mention New England. Thomas Newman's theme music, with its lively bells and guitars, is irresistible.

One reason Pacino may have done the picture is to accept the challenge of playing a blind person, a challenge he is more than up to. You never question that Frank Slade is without sight; Pacino *is* blind, or seems to be. He plays a "visually impaired" person so naturally that it never seems like a stunt. Undoubtedly, it had much to do with his winning the Oscar. *Scent of Woman* was also nominated for Best Director and Best Screenplay, as well as Best Picture; only Pacino won.

Scent of a Woman was based on the 1974 Italian film *Profumo di Donna.*

Carlito's Way

UNIVERSAL/EPIC PRODUCTIONS, 1993

Executive producers, Louis A. Stroller and Ortwin Freyermuth; producers, Martin Bregman, Willi Baer, and Michael S. Bregman; director, Brian De Palma; director of photography, Stephen H. Burum; screenplay, David Koepp; based on the novels *Carlito's Way* and *After Hours* by Edwin Torres; editors, Bill Pankow and Kristina Boden; music, Patrick Doyle; production designer, Richard Sylbert; costume designer, Aude Bronson-Howard. Running time: 145 min.

CAST

Al Pacino (*Carlito Brigante*); Sean Penn (*David Kleinfeld*); Penelope Ann Miller (*Gail*); John Leguizamo (*Benny Blanco*); Ingrid Rogers (*Steffie*); Luis Guzman (*Pachanga*); James Rebhorn (*Norwalk*); Joseph Sirayo (*Vinnie Taglialucca*); Frank Minucci (*Tony Taglialucca*); Viggo Mortensen (*Lalin*); Jorge Porcel (*Saso*); Adrian Pasona (*Frankie*).

It was back to the world of sleaze and drugs and nefarious characters for Pacino and director Brian De Palma, who had previously teamed for *Scarface.*

In New York City's court of appeals in 1975, the judge heartily lambastes the district attorney's "unfortunate investigative techniques" that are allowing criminal Carlito Brigante (Pacino) to go free after serving only five years of his thirty-year sentence. Brigante has had enough of jail and tells everyone that he intends to go straight. Back in his neighborhood, a crony, Pachanga (Luis Guzman) bemoans how things have changed, how the kids in the game refuse to play by the rules and are much more violent. Halfheartedly, Carlito accompanies his young cousin, who is a delivery boy in a drug deal, and gets firsthand knowledge of the ugly new world he is now living in. The dealers murder his cousin and try to kill him, but he fights back successfully, absconding with $30,000 that no one is left to claim. He uses the money to buy an interest in a disco; as soon as he has saved up $75,000, he intends to head for Florida and open a legitimate car dealership.

But the fates seem to conspire against Carlito. His lawyer, David Kleinfeld (Sean Penn), has been told by a tough client to help spring him from Riker's Island *or else* and enlists a grateful but reluctant Carlito in the scheme. Carlito is stunned when Kleinfeld murders both the client and his son because the lawyer kept a million-dollar payoff he was supposed to forward to another party. Soon both the police and the client's other son are hunting Carlito; Kleinfeld betrays him to the D.A. to save his own skin; his business partner in the disco tries to appropriate all his savings; and his buddy Pachanga also turns traitor. Carlito manages to outwit his many pursuers and make it to Grand Central Station, but he's shot to death by a punk and would-be kingpin he once insulted just as he is about to board a train to Florida with his girlfriend. (Some days you just can't win.)

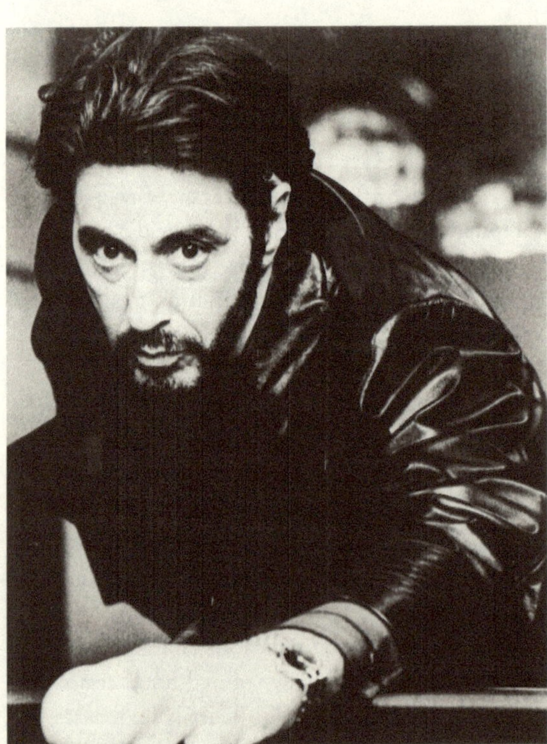

Pacino shooting pool, *Carlito's Way* (1993).

Although it is questionable whether his acting could really be described as "great," Pacino swaggers through *Carlito's Way* with all his star charisma intact. He is sensational as Carlito, registering force and dynamism in every scene. He looks great in a beard and a seventies hairstyle, although the Hispanic accent he employs sort of comes and goes. Pacino gives a ludicrous character much more dignity than he deserves.

Sean Penn proves again that he is one of our greatest young actors with his performance as mob lawyer David Kleinfeld. Penn never lays all his cards on the table; he never telegraphs his character's actions (which some actors do regardless of the script). There's no clue that nerdy Kleinfeld can be as brutal as the gangsters he represents, that he can be sexually aggressive and viciously underhanded. Penn unveils each loathsome layer with great skill and authority and is totally convincing every step of the way. Penelope Ann Miller, as the dancer, Gail, with whom Carlito renews his relationship, is a bit too glossy and superficial in the part, not exhibiting the surface hardness that such a woman would have to have to be in love with a man in Carlito's profession. (To be fair, the character is unconvincing to begin with.) Miller does have a hot love scene with Pacino, with whom she had a brief liaison during filming. (De Palma's revolving camera during this sequence is yet another variation of the Jimmy Stewart–Kim Novak kiss in Hitchcock's *Vertigo*, but at least it is more effective than the one in De Palma's *Body Double*.) Ingrid Rogers certainly scores as the sexy, brazen disco dancer, Steffie, who eventually becomes Kleinfeld's lover.

James Rebhorn (D.A. Norwalk) was a brief adversary of Pacino's as the headmaster in *Scent of a Woman*; here he's really out to get him and plays each scene with his customary verisimilitude. Frank Minucci registers so much menace as the dreaded Tony Taglialucca, the incarcerated client of Kleinfeld's who was cheated out of a million by his own lawyer, that he's one of the best—and most frightening—things in the picture. John Leguizamo hits the mark as Benny Blanco, the punk who kills Carlito, and Luis Guzman is also notable as Carlito's crony Pachonga. Also good are Jorge Porcel as Carlito's disco partner, Saso, and Joseph Sirayo and Adrian Pasona as Tony Taglialucca's sons, Vinnie and Frankie.

An actor who deserves special mention is Viggo Mortensen, as Lalin, a hood who has been condemned to life in a wheelchair and wears a wire to a meeting with Carlito. When Carlito learns of his duplicity, Lalin breaks down into blubbering begging and self-pity. Mortensen manages to make you feel sorry for someone who doesn't deserve much sympathy and plays with such strength and conviction that he positively steals the scene from Pacino.

Although, like *Scarface*, *Carlito's Way* doesn't have much of the famous camera trickery De Palma employs in his shockers, there are several outstanding scenes. Among them is the tense sequence when Carlito accompanies his cousin to the den of the drug dealers behind the barbershop. There's a game of pool going on. The friendly head of the drug gang wants Carlito's cousin to bend down and get a soda out of a large ice chest by the wall. Somebody goes to the bathroom. Everything seems absolutely normal, and yet something's *not quite right*. De Palma milks the scene for so much suspense that it is almost a relief when the dealers show their true colors and the violence finally begins.

Also outstanding is the sequence involving Kleinfeld and Carlito's alleged "rescue" of gangster Taglialucca from the river after he manages to escape from the Riker's prison barge. Pretending to offer Taglialucca a helping hand up into the boat, Kleinfeld instead bashes his brains in and lets him drown. He also murders one of his sons who is on board before Carlito can stop him. The only misstep occurs early in this scene when a nervous Kleinfeld is preparing to set sail with Carlito, who doesn't really want to be a part of it but feels he has a debt to pay. "Untie the fuckin' rope, you spick!" screams Kleinfeld. While Carlito may not be the mad dog Tony Montana of *Scarface*, it's unlikely that he would let such a slur go by without comment, especially when you consider that he'd rather be anywhere else at that moment.

The film's lengthy chase climax, which begins at the disco and culminates at Grand Central, is also memorable. First, there's a suspenseful bit with Carlito attempting to get his savings from a hiding place without Taglialucca's surviving son—who wants both him and Kleinfeld *dead*—seeing him retrieve it *and* to leave the club. Then there's a protracted sequence when Carlito tries to elude his pursuers in the subway. Finally, the shootout in Grand Central, where Carlito disposes of the gang that's after him but falls victim to the inimitable Benny Blanco just when he thinks he's home safe. The whole trip is very exciting, but the bit with Pacino lying down horizontally on the escalator to the Graybar Building to avoid detection is a bit much. A quieter but equally intense scene has Carlito checking up on his lady love, Gail, whom he has not seen for five years, as she dances in a studio to the strains of Delibes's *Lakme*. Carlito, thinking he has lost her forever, watches from outside in the pouring rain with only a garbage-can lid for cover.

David Koepp's screenplay certainly keeps things percolating, and De Palma never fails to bring to vivid life all the twists and turns of the story. Stephen H. Burum's cinematography sharply illuminates the New York City locations, such as the village, uptown, and a very early morning (or expert re-creation of) Grand Central Station. Patrick Doyle's music adds tautness to the subway chase and other scenes. However, it is a little overdone at the end when Carlito dies, trying to summon up a sense of inappropriate pathos; Carlito is hardly some tragic hero, after all.

Like *Scarface*, *Carlito's Way*, with its world of dealers and losers, is enormously entertaining. Also like *Scarface*, it pretty much avoids dealing with the morality of it all. *Carlito's Way* is a good B movie but nothing more.

Two Bits

MIRAMAX, 1995

Executive producers, Willi Bar, David Korda, Joseph Stefano; director, James Foley; writer, Joseph Stefano; cinematography, Juan Ruiz Anchia; music, Carter Burwell; editing, Howard E. Smith. Running time: 85 min.

CAST

Al Pacino (*Grandpa*); Jerry Barone (*Gennaro*); Mary Elizabeth Mastrantonio (*Luisa Spirito*); Joanna Merlin (*Guendolina*); Andy Romano (*Dr. Bruna*); Donna Mitchell (*Mrs. Bruna*); Geoff Pierson (*Dr. Wilson*); Mary Lou Rosato (*Aunt Carmela*); Joe Grifasi (*Uncle Joe*); Alec Baldwin (*narrator*).

Two Bits covers one eventful day in South Philadelphia in 1933 when a new movie theater, La Paloma, is having its grand opening in the flavorful Italian neighborhood. Young Gennaro (Jerry Barone) hopes to raise the money—a quarter, or "two bits"—to buy a ticket to the movie house or get it from his widowed mother, Luisa Spirito (Mary Elizabeth Mastrantonio), or his grandfather, Gaetano (Al Pacino), who is waiting to die and has a very close relationship with his grandson. As Gennaro tries to get his quarter through various means, we see slices of life in the neighborhood: a wedding and a funeral have been scheduled for the same church at the same time, leading to a fist fight; a woman steals some potatoes that she desperately needs for her starving children; a pretty street singer with a very nice voice warbles a torch song at a busy intersection. Going into the basement of his grandfather's strange doctor, Bruna (Andy Romano), to do some work for him, Gennaro encounters his equally strange wife (Donna Mitchell) and later finds her hanging from the rafters, a suicide. Gaetano agrees to give Gennaro a quarter if he will carry out an errand for him. He wants the boy to go speak to Guendolina (Joanna Merlin), the woman he slept with so that he wouldn't be a virgin on his wedding night ("If a man is a virgin on his wedding night, he'll be a virgin the rest of his life"), and ask for her forgiveness. Gennaro does as he is told, gets his quarter, but when he gets to La Paloma he discovers that the price has gone up to fifty cents because it's now evening. He returns home to find that his grandpa has taken a turn for the worse, and is being attended by a new doctor. Gaetano dies as Gennaro watches him, and another quarter that he was keeping for his grandson rolls out of his hand. In the way of the very young, a grieving Gennaro takes the quarter—he now has fifty cents—and goes to the movies.

Told in these simplistic terms, the story of *Two Bits* sounds charming, and there are some fine moments in the picture, such as the scene with the mother stealing potatoes. But other scenes, such as the fist fight at the church, are awkwardly staged and don't work. The whole business with Dr. Bruna and his wife seems dragged in from another movie. Apparently Bruna is a pedophile, and his wife tells Gennaro that her husband "has never touched me, not anywhere, not once." True, the woman—who kills herself not much later—is emotionally disturbed, but her pouring out her heart to a twelve-year-old still seems improbable, merely contrived so that the audience can have a clue as to what's going on (or not going on) in the marriage. In this way the movie is overly theatrical and not always convincing. The whole business with Guedolina is perhaps more gross than anything else. Although this is by no means unrealistic, the movie is steeped in an oppressive Catholicism.

Pacino was third-billed above the title. His presence lends star power to the picture, but he is not well cast. Playing an elderly man much older than his years—Pacino was only fifty-five at the time—he is certainly not bad but most of the acting in the film is arch and obvious. Little Jerry Barone actually makes the best impression as Gennaro, and Alec Baldwin makes a first-rate narrator, the adult Gennaro looking back on these events. Todd McCarthy of *Variety* had an interesting reaction to Pacino: "Grizzled and rumpled, sitting in an overgrown garden and dispensing advice in a rough, muted voice, the elderly Italian gent is a virtual dead ringer for Marlon Brando's aged Don Corleone in the garden at the end of *The Godfather*. Of course, the other person in that scene with him was Pacino, nearly a quarter-century ago." Many critics found Pacino simply too youthful and vigorous to be convincing as a dying elderly man while others even found him hammy.

The screenplay was written by Joseph Stefano—most famous for *Psycho*—and was inspired by his boyhood reminiscences. Most of the film's critics felt that *Two Bits* was simply too slight to work as a major motion picture. However, there were notable contributions from composer Carter Burwell, and the cinematography of Juan Ruiz Anchia is splendid, although some felt it prettified things a bit too much. Stephen Holden opined in the *New York Times*: "Depression-era poverty has rarely been made to look so clean and wholesome and the effects of a heat wave so unsweaty."

Whatever the flaws of *Two Bits*, Pacino gets credit for tackling a role quite different from those he'd played before.

Heat

WARNER BROS., 1995

Producer-director-writer, Michael Mann; cinematography, Dante Spinotti; music, Elliot Goldenthal; editing, Pasquale Buba, William Goldenberg, Dov Hoenig, and Tom Rolf. Running time: 170 min.

Cast

Al Pacino (*Lt. Vincent Hanna*); Robert De Niro (*Neil McCauley*); Val Kilmer (*Chris*); Diane Venora (*Justine*); Kevin Gage (*Waingro*); Tom Sizemore (*Michael*); Amy Brenneman (*Eady*); Ashley Judd (*Charlene*); William Fichtner (*Roger Van Zant*); Dennis Haysbert (*Donald*).

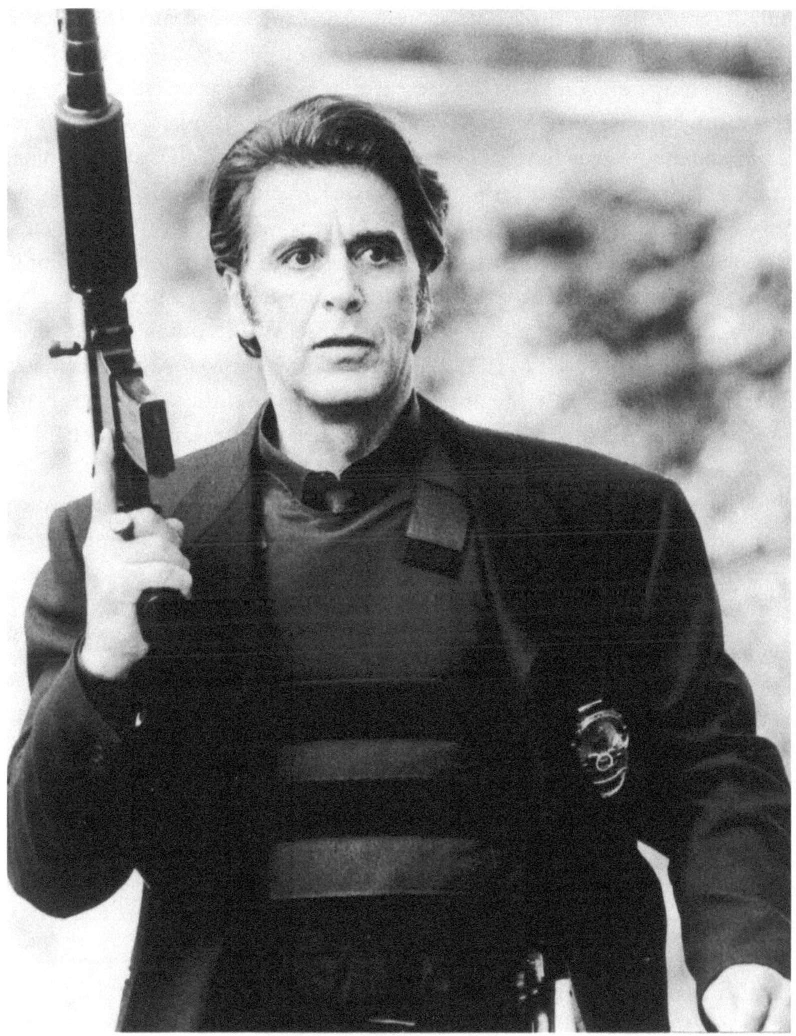

Pacino is Lt. Vincent Hanna in *Heat* (1995), the film that re-teamed him with his *Godfather Part II* co-star Robert De Niro. Unlike the earlier film, the two actually appeared onscreen together (albeit briefly) in this riveting cops-and-robbers saga.

Lt. Vincent Hanna (Pacino), a cop with the LAPD, is called to the scene of an armored car robbery in which three security guards were slaughtered. The mastermind of the heist is Neil McCauley (Robert De Niro), who is so angry at Waingro (Kevin Gage), the man who shot the guards, that he tries to kill him in a parking lot. Waingro escapes and occupies himself with beating prostitutes to death until he gets the idea of joining forces with money launderer Roger Van Zant (William Fichtner), to whom McCauley tried to sell back the bonds he stole during the heist; at first Van Zant agreed and then double-crossed him. Hanna, whose marriage is in difficulty due to his devotion to his job and its long hours, follows the gang around with his associates, and tries to figure out what they're planning next. McCauley, who thinks it's best for men like him to have no attachments as they might have to flee police at any moment, falls for a clerk named Eady (Amy Brenneman). Hanna pulls McCauley, against whom he has no real evidence, over on the highway and the two have a cup of coffee, where they admit to each other that they can have no other way of life, and that each will kill the other if the need arises. McCauley's next job is a bank robbery which goes spectacularly awry because Waingro has tipped off the police after torturing Neil's associate Trejo (Danny Trejo) for the information. Neil tries to flee with Eady, but abandons her when he realizes Hanna is closing in—the two have a final encounter near an airport runway in which Neil is shot to death.

Heat, written and directed by Michael Mann, is one of the best movies Pacino has ever appeared in; an exciting, suspenseful cops-and-robbers epic with richer characterizations than usual and which is never boring for its nearly three-hour running time. Pacino's performance is excellent, handling a wide variety of emotions with aplomb, getting across Hanna's almost manic need to catch McCauley combined with his disheartened fatigue caused by the strain of his difficult marriage. One of Pacino's best scenes is when Hanna goes to a crime scene where a young prostitute, butchered by Waingro, is dumped like so much garbage in an alley and the hardened detective takes the time to comfort her disconsolate mother (a very effective Hazelle Goodman). Some of Pacino's typical jive talk sneaks into his speech on occasion, and Hanna is no charm boy. One of the highlights of the film is when Hanna and McCauley share a cup of coffee in a diner, a scene that is contrived if irresistible.

Robert De Niro is also fine in the picture, as are Val Kilmer and Tom Sizemore as other gang members. As the psychotic Waingro, Kevin Gage offers a portrayal that is vivid and vital. There is also solid work from Jon Voight as an associate of McCauley's; William Fichtner as the slimy Van Zant; Dennis Haysbert as an ex-con whose life turns even more tragic; Ricky Harris as a snitch named Albert and Tone Loc as his brother; and Danny Trejo as Trejo (*sic*), who is tortured by Waingro for information. The female characters have less to do in the film but do it well: Diane Venora as Justine, Hanna's wife, who's taken a lover; Ashley Judd as Kilmer's wife; and Amy Brenneman as McCauley's confused lady friend, Eady (Brenneman later appeared with Pacino in *88 Minutes*).

Heat holds the viewer's attention throughout the lengthy film, but there are certain especially outstanding sequences, such as a bank holdup which leads into a protracted chase and gun battle on city streets. The climactic battle between McCauley and Hanna takes place in a field near a runway where the two antagonists play a deadly game of hide and seek behind bunker-like structures. *Heat* received generally excellent reviews, with the two lead actors getting especially high marks. According to John Hartl in the *Seattle Times*: "The quintessential scene in *Heat* is a coffee chat between a professional thief, Neil McCauley (De Niro), and a veteran Los Angeles detective, Vincent Hanna (Al Pacino) ... Unlikely their truce may be, but it dramatically underlines what they share. The law and the lawless have so much in common here...."

On the other hand, Stephen Rea of the *Philadelphia Inquirer* opined: "So why doesn't *Heat*, with its elaborately staged, tautly edited robberies, its killer cast, edgy score and elegant cinematography, offer more satisfaction? It's the script, stupid.... *Heat*, for all its sparks and stars, never catches fire."

City Hall

Columbia Pictures, 1996

Producer/director, Harold Becker; writers, Ken Lipper, Paul Schrader, Nicolas Pileggi and Bo Goldman; cinematography, Michael Seresin; music, Jerry Goldsmith; editors, David Bretherton and Robert C. Jones. Running time:111 min.

Cast

Al Pacino (*Mayor Pappas*); John Cusack (*Kevin Calhoun*); Bridget Fonda (*Marybeth Cogan*); Danny Aiello (*Frank Anselmo*); Martin Landau (*Judge Stern*); David Paymer (*Abe Goodman*); Anthony Franciosa (*Paul Zapatti*); Roberta Peters (*Nettie Anselmo*); Larry Romano (*Tino Zapatti*); Angel David (*Vinnie Zapatti*).

On a New York City street a young black boy, James Bone (Jaliyl Lynn), is accidentally shot to death during a shoot-out between cop Eddie Santos (Nestor Sarrano) and hood Tino Zapatti (Larry Romano), both of whom are also killed. Mayor John Pappas (Pacino) uses the boy's funeral to make a speech, promising that tragedies like this will not happen again. His deputy mayor Kevin Calhoun (John Cusack) wonders why Zapatti—whose uncle Paul (Anthony Franciosa) is a crime boss—was out on the street in the first place and begins an investigation. Marybeth Cogan (Bridget Fonda), who works for legal aid, is representing Santos and his family and tries to get a pension pay-out for the grieving widow, but things are complicated when $40,000 is found in Santos's cabin with no explanation of where it came from. Unbeknown to the others, Paul Zapatti has had Brooklyn politico Frank Anselmo (Danny Aiello) frame the dead cop. Calhoun learns that when probation officer James Wakely (Rob LaBelle) recommended ten to twenty years for Tino, he suddenly found himself transferred way upstate. Tino's new parole officer, a discomfited Larry Schwartz (Richard Schiff), may have the answers, but then he's murdered. It becomes clear that the major's friend and former law partner, Judge Stern (Martin Landau), who gave Zapatti probation instead of jail time, is on the take, and must resign. Paul Zapatti tells Anselmo that his family will suffer if he tells what he knows, so Anselmo commits suicide to protect them. Then Kevin confronts Mayor Pappas, now knowing that he arranged the pay-out to Stern, and is responsible for Zapatti being free, and ultimately for James Bone's and Eddie Santos's deaths. Kevin makes it clear that the ambitious man, whom he once idolized, will have to take himself out of the running or face the consequences.

City Hall has the bare bones of a decent plot, but despite the murders, betrayals, and bar room scheming, it just never comes alive. You can't fault the actors: Pacino and Cusack are excellent, and Danny Aiello is riveting as Anselmo. There are memorable scenes featuring these players, such as when Pappas and Anselmo meet during a performance of *Carousel*—both men are Rodgers and Hammerstein fans (although it's hard to believe they would walk out during the middle of "If I Loved You.") "You got what you wanted," John tells Frank, and gives him a kiss. Pacino nearly works himself up to a blast during the scene when Pappas is furious with Kevin for meeting with another member of the Zapatti family—"You're the *deputy mayor*. What the fuck are you doing?" Their confrontation at the end is also well-handled, but it and everything else in the film is too low-key; there's no real climax to the movie. Pacino gives a solid performance, but the script just doesn't give him enough to sink his teeth into; the main character is played by Cusack. Anselmo commits suicide in his car to the strains of "You'll Never Walk Alone," a nice touch.

Director Harold Becker fails to make *City Hall* hum—which it could have—just as his work on *Sea of Love* was equally unsatisfying. Another problem with the movie is that the dead black boy and his family are sort of shunted to the side, a situation that, sadly, could have occurred in real life. Most critics opined that the acting is what put the movie over and deemed it a disappointment. Jack Kroll of *Newsweek* wrote of Pacino: "At 55, he has a haggard, life-wrestling beauty and a street eloquence that has more innocence than De Niro and more sincerity than Nicholson."

Roger Ebert wrote on his website: "There are a few scenes of great power ... a strong, although curiously tentative, late scene between the mayor and his deputy. Pacino and Cusack are effective together throughout the movie—the older man wise and tough, the younger one eager to learn, but with principles that don't bend."

Michael Dequina of *The Movie Report* opined: "With a solid cast and strong behind-the-scenes talent, Harold Becker's *City Hall* has all the ingredients for a solid drama but instead comes out a half-baked disappointment.... Pacino [is] excellent as the charismatic mayor; his rousing oratory at the funeral of the dead boy is by far the film's highlight."

Looking for Richard

Fox Searchlight, 1996

Executive producer, William Teitler; producer, Al Pacino; cinematography, Robert Leacock; music, Howard Shore; editing, William A. Anderson, Ned Bastille, Pasquale Buba, and Andre Ross Betz. Running time: 112 min.

Cast

Al Pacino (*Himself/Richard III*); Penelope Allen (*Herself/Queen Elizabeth*); Alec Baldwin (*Himself/Duke of Clarence*); Kevin Conway (*Himself/Hastings*); Larry Bryggman (*Himself/Lord Stanley*); Kevin Spacey (*Himself/Earl of Buckingham*); Estelle Parsons (*Herself/Queen Margaret*); Winona Ryder (*Herself/Lady Anne*); Richard Cox (*Himself/Catesby*); Paul Guilfoyle (*Himself/Second murderer*).

Pacino made his directorial debut with this documentary about Shakespeare and his play *Richard III*, scenes from which are interspersed with comments from the actors Pacino works with, other famous Shakespearean actors, and even the Man on the Street. "It has always been a dream of mine to communicate to other people how I feel about Shakespeare," said Pacino to explain why he made the film. If there's any problem with this quite excellent documentary, it's that it leaves you longing to see the whole play as interpreted and filmed by Pacino and his actors. Pacino only wanted to film scenes, however; a mistake he would not make when he later directed both Oscar Wilde's *Salome* as well as a documentary about the play. As for *Richard III*, Shakespeare based

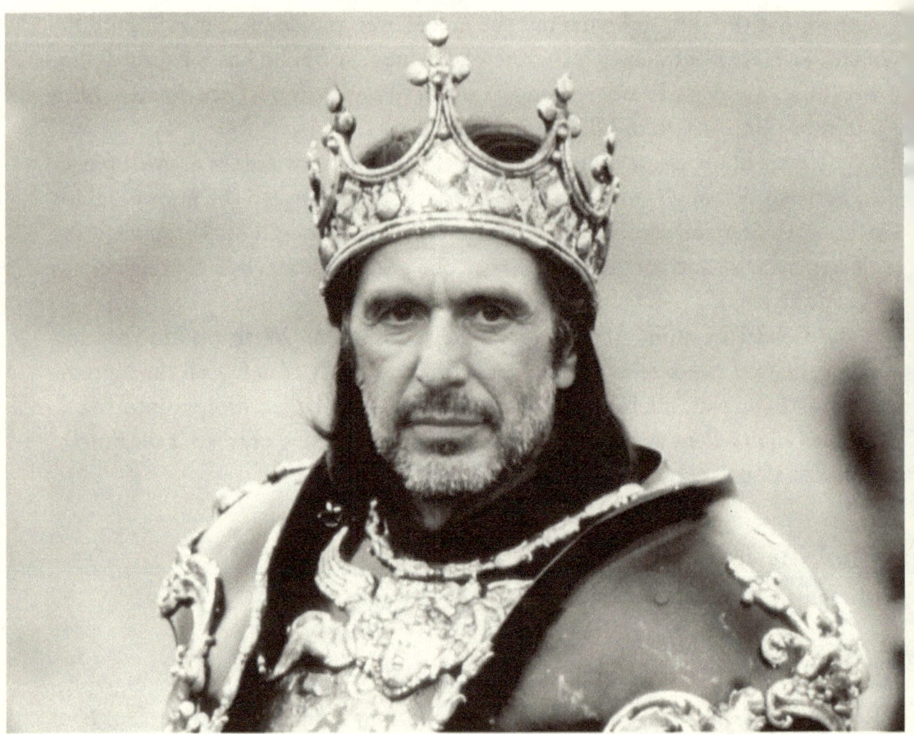

In *Looking for Richard* (1996), director and star Pacino takes on one of the Bard's most memorable characters, Richard III. This fascinating documentary-style film also serves as an exploration of Shakespeare's relevance to people in every walk of life.

his masterpiece on historical facts and figures. His main character was determined to be the king of England, and everything he does, every betrayal, every false word, every murder or death he engineers leads him to the throne until his death in battle where he loses his horse and cries, "My horse! My Horse! My kingdom for a horse!" It has always been believed that Richard was responsible for the deaths of his young nephews, the princes whose very lives threatened his ascendancy, and who disappeared from the Tower of London, never to be seen again.

Pacino famously appeared on the stage as *Richard III*; for those who did not see that production, this may provide the only chance to get some idea of how Pacino portrayed the infamous murderer, Richard. Pacino himself never watched the 1955 film version of the play which both starred and was directed by Laurence Olivier. While comparisons may be odious, it is interesting to compare the two interpretations; surprisingly, Pacino comes off the better of the two. Olivier is fascinating, playing Richard like a malevolent imp, almost humorously, ferociously charming as he plots and plans behind the scenes; he's so in love with the language that he often rushes through the lines. Pacino's delivery is slower, he is not only more adept at getting across Richard's rage but the meaning of the lines as well. His interpretation is more virile and romantic. Shakespearean scholars can argue over which interpretation comes closer to Shakespeare's vision, or which is the more effective, but these two very different actors are both very interesting to see in the play. At times—at least in this film—Pacino reminds one of Olivier when he raises his voice to a higher pitch, especially in the scene when Buckingham asks Richard to give him what he promised.

The scenes from the play only whet the appetite. Of special note is a superb sequence when Richard accuses and condemns Lord Hastings, who is beautifully played by a dynamic Kevin Conway. Pacino chose his cast wisely, using not only very famous actors but those he worked with in the past. In the former category are Kevin Spacey as Lord Buckingham; Alec Baldwin as Richard's doomed brother, George; Winona Ryder as Lady Anne; and Estelle Parsons as Queen Margaret. In the latter category are the remarkably gifted Penelope Allen, who is simply superb as Queen Elizabeth; Paul Guilfoyle from *Chinese Coffee* as the second murderer; Larry Bryggman from *...And Justice for All* as Lord Stanley; and Richard Cox from *Cruising* as Catesby. Playwrights Ira Lewis (*Chinese Coffee*) and Heathcote Williams (*The Local Stigmatic*) also had small parts.

The above actors are also seen as themselves, commenting on the play and its meaning, along with Vanessa Redgrave, Derek Jacobi (who says that Americans are intimidated and think they can't do Shakespeare when they can), Sir John Geilgud and Viveca Lindfors. Producers Michael Hadge and the talkative James Bulleit are also seen, the former as himself and the latter playing himself and also Lord Ellis. Pacino is shown scouting locations, such as the Cloisters, and arguing in friendly fashion with Bulleit. Pacino also includes people on the street, most of whom have little if any knowledge of Shakespeare and have nothing of importance to say.

Jonathan Rosenbaum was especially negative about the film in the *Chicago Reader*: "A 1996 documentary by a movie star (Al Pacino) about his own entitlement as a movie star.... Just to show you what a regular guy he is, he plays Richard with and without a Bronx accent and speaks to people on the street.... This runs 118 minutes, but it felt like six or seven hours."

However, Geoff Andrew of *Time Out* wrote: "Pacino's first film as writer/director is a marvelously intelligent, witty and imaginative exploration of the problems faced by anyone wishing to act in Shakespeare or translate the plays to film.... Pacino seduces us with his enthusiasm, energy and passion."

As for Pacino's famous New York accent? He is able to successfully bury it as Richard III—most of the time.

Donnie Brasco

TRISTAR, 1997

Executive producers, Alan Greenspan and Patrick McCormack; director, Mike Newell; writer, Paul Attanasio; cinematography, Peter Sova; music, Patrick Doyle; editing, Jon Gregory. Running time: 127 min.

CAST

Al Pacino (*Lefty Ruggiero*); Johnny Depp (*Donnie Brasco/Joe Pistone*); Michael Madsen (*Sonny Black*); Anne Heche (*Maggie Pistone*); Robert Miano (*Sonny Red*); Gretchen Mol (*Sonny's girlfriend*); Val Avery (*Trrificante*); Bruno Kirby (*Nicky*); James Russo (*Paulie*); Brian Tarantina (*Bruno*).

Benjamin "Lefty" Ruggiero (Pacino) is a low-level Mafioso in New York who takes a ring he wants to sell to "Don the Jeweler," a thief and fence named Donnie Brasco (Johnny Depp). When Brasco reveals that the diamond is phony and helps him get restitution, Lefty is impressed and takes the younger man under his wing. What Lefty doesn't know is that "Donnie Brasco" is an alias for Joseph Piscone, an FBI agent who is working undercover to infiltrate the mob. Pistone carries a tape recorder everywhere he goes and passes on the information he picks up to his fellow agents. Because he is away from home for weeks at a time, and even gets involved in operating a mob-owned club-casino in Florida, his wife, Maggie (Anne Heche), who is raising three daughters on her own, is tormented and considers getting a divorce. During the past few months, Lefty and Donnie have become very close, but Sonny Black (Michael Madsen), who has gotten a promotion since the big boss was whacked, tells Donnie that schlumpy Sonny may be the wrong person to sponsor him; he has been passed over time and again and is not respected. When the Florida operation goes south, Black and his team, including Lefty, are marked for extermination, but they turn the tables on their assassins and murder them instead. Joe narrowly manages to get out of performing a hit on the son of the one of the victims. The FBI wants Joseph to drop out of the operation as it is becoming too dangerous, but he goes AWOL instead, as he knows that as soon as the Mafioso learn the truth about him Lefty will be whacked for bringing him into the fold. The FBI agents, hoping some of the hoods will want to make a deal, tell them the truth about Brasco, but at first they don't believe them. It is implied that Lefty is killed while Joe gets a commendation, as dozens of arrests and convictions result from his work.

Donnie Brasco was based on the memoirs of Joseph Pistone, who was a real-life FBI agent who spent six years working undercover. The movie compresses the time period and eliminates some of the minor players to tell a tighter story. Pistone first infiltrated the Columbo family and then entered the ranks of the equally infamous Bonnano family. In real life Sonny Black, whose real name was Dominick Napolitano, was murdered because of Pistone—he was shot and his hands cut off—but Lefty Ruggiero did not die. The movie makes it seem as if the FBI couldn't care less about Pistone's concerns over Lefty's fate, but in order to save his life he was picked up and taken to jail. He refused to testify against his peers so a contract that had been put out on him over the Brasco business was canceled. After serving many years in prison, he died of lung cancer three years before the film came out.

Donnie Brasco is an absorbing, well-made and well-acted drama that features excellent performances from Pacino and Johnny Depp. As played by

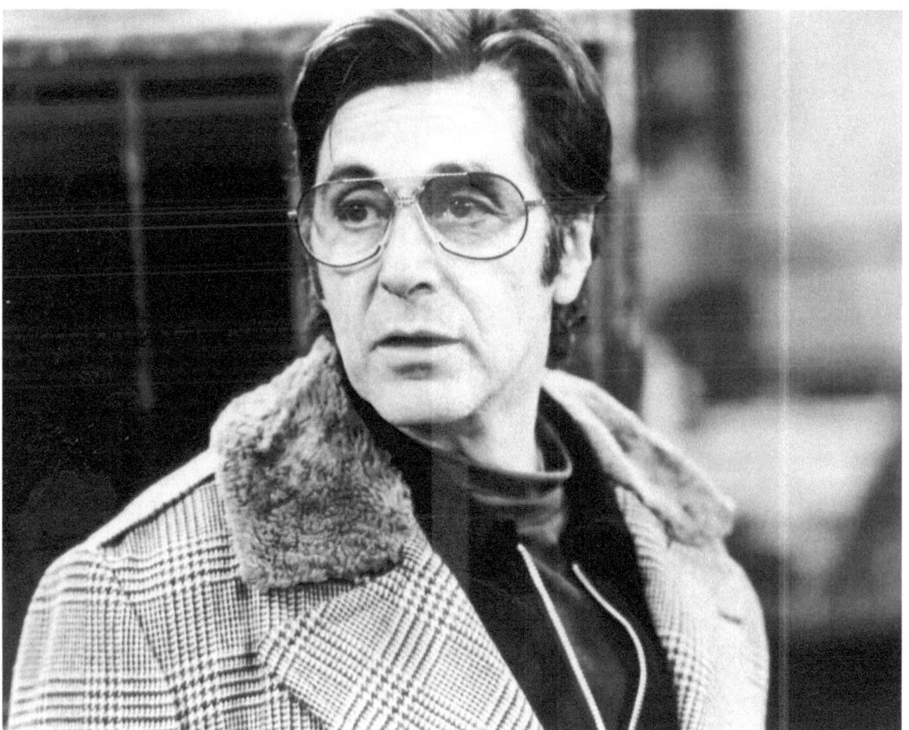

Unlike his character's stature in *The Godfather* films, Pacino's role as "Lefty" Ruggiero in *Donnie Brasco* (1997) is that of a low-level member of an Italian crime family. His protégé (the title character, played by Johnny Depp) is actually an undercover agent for the FBI.

Pacino with his customary insouciance, Lefty is quite a character. When the *coq au vin* he's preparing catches fire, he backs up and has his wife put out the flames. Talking about Sonny, Lefty says "He's got a family, he's got a mistress, he's got a mistress for the mistress." Efforts to make him a sympathetic figure don't quite work, however. "Thirty years I've been busting my hump," he moans. "Even a dog gets a piece of the sidewalk. I ought to have something to show for it." And the mood music turns all phony-touching but fails to negate the fact that Lefty is a murdering creep and loser. It seems incredible that his wife (Ronnie Farer) is as attractive as she is, although his son, Tommy (Larry Romano), is a screwed-up junkie. This is yet another Pacino role that illuminates and sympathizes with lowlifes.

In what is really the lead role Johnny Depp is quite impressive, with his hair all slicked back and his attitude on overdrive. The movie explores—although not enough—how undercover agents can begin to bond with and even act like their intended victims, and even start to resemble them in their speech and behavior. Attending a session with a marriage counselor, wife Maggie notices that her husband is a "college man, but says "nuttin'" instead of nothing. At one point Joe whacks Maggie in the face the way a "wise guy" would do. The film's most disturbing scene occurs when Donnie accompanies Sonny, Lefty and others to a Japanese restaurant. Donnie is afraid to take off his shoes as the eatery requires because he has a tape recorder hidden there, so he makes a scene, hollering about how his father died at Okinawa, which leads to the men—five of them versus one guy half their size—beating up the Japanese waiter in the men's room. Donnie hangs back for awhile while the others take their licks, but then viciously kicks the poor man as he lies helpless on the ground. We never learn his subsequent fate, and are never shown Joe contemplating the immorality of his actions, which don't seem justified even to maintain his cover.

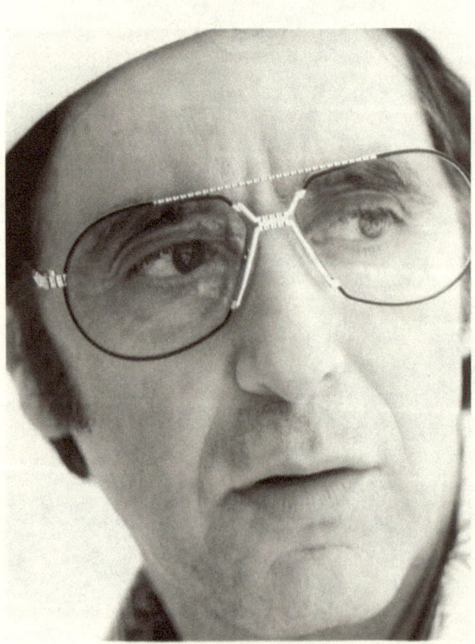

Another pensive character study of Pacino, here as "Lefty" Ruggiero in *Donnie Brasco* (1997).

Michael Madsen is quite effective as the lizard-like Sonny Black, an ambitious and handsome dude who wants to take over Donnie's sponsorship. But perhaps the strongest performance in the film—which is a surprise as this is basically a buddy movie—belongs to Anne Heche as Pistone's wife. Maggie is not given short shrift in the movie, but has several good scenes in which she tries to cope with constantly being alone and to convey her anger and frustration to Joseph, who can only see that he has a job to do. One might think that Maggie isn't accepting of the fact that her husband hardly has a normal nine-to-five job, but his extreme absences—and his keeping her in the dark most of the time—are enough to drive her nearly crazy. There are also flavorful supporting performances from Bruno Kirby, Terry Serpico (no relation to the Frank Serpico that Pacino played), Rocco Sisto, James Russo, Gerry Becker, and others. Val Avery is hard to miss as the flamboyant Florida mobster Trafficante, cavorting in a hot tub on a boat with several "babes."

Two other scenes stand out in the movie. The first is the reverse hit in the basement when Sonny, Lefty and so on are called to a meeting with "Sonny Red" (actually Alphonse Indelicato), played by Robert Miano, who plans on murdering them because they know he deliberately screwed up the Florida club deal. Instead, Black and the others arrive first, hide in the basement, and in a graphic and hard-hitting sequence slaughter Indelicato and his associates when they come down the stairs. Donnie has been told to wait in the car, but afterward he has to come inside and help dismember the bodies. In the second scene Lefty takes Donnie to a boat where Indelicato's son Bruno, who dodged the massacre, is hiding out, and there is considerable suspense over whether or not Donnie will whack Bruno or find some way to get out of it.

The film garnered mostly positive notices, but there were some naysayers. Bridget Byrne of *Boxoffice* opined, "It's hard to develop any sympathy for the film's nasty manipulative humans, despite the best efforts of all involved in this newest slant on the mean-streets crowd." Rita Kempley of the *Washington Post* felt that "unfortunately, the story isn't inventive and Newell's methodical approach to it verges on monotony." Todd McCarthy of *Variety* had praise for Pacino: "Although perhaps familiar in its outer trappings, Pacino's fine work is the key to the film succeeding to the extent that it does."

Pistone changed his name after the operation was over and a contract for $500,000 was put on his head. He served as a consultant to the movie, and has written several other books, fiction and non-fiction, inspired by his experiences.

The Devil's Advocate

WARNER BROS., 1997

Executive producers, Taylor Hackford and Barry Bernardi; director, Taylor Hackford; screenplay, Jonathan Lemkin and Tony Gilroy; cinematography, Andrzej; music, James Newton Howard; editor, Mark Warner; production design, Bruno Rubeo; art direction, Dennis Bradford. Running time: 144 min.

CAST

Al Pacino (*John Milton*); Keanu Reeves (*Kevin Lomax*); Charlize Theron (*Mary Ann Lomax*); Jeffrey Jones (*Eddie Barzoon*); Judith Ivey (*Alice Lomax*); Craig T. Nelson (*Alexander Cullen*); Heather Matarazzo (*Barbara*); George Wyner (*Meisel*); Tamara Tunie (*Jackie Heath*); Christabella Andreoli (*Connie*).

Kevin Lomax (Keanu Reeves) is a Gainsville, Florida, lawyer representing a client, Gettys (Chris Bauer), whom he first believed to be innocent but comes to realize is guilty of molesting one of his young female students. When his client is acquitted, Lomax is disgusted. Afterward, Kevin is approached by a huge law firm in Manhattan that is interested in instituting a criminal division. Kevin and his wife, Mary Ann (Charlize Theron), are brought to New York, wined and dined, and meet the head of the firm, the charismatic John Milton (Al Pacino). Impressed with the salary and the beautiful apartment they will occupy in Milton's building, Kevin decides to take the job. One of his first assignments is representing Alexander Cullen (Craig T. Nelson), who has been accused of murdering his wife and two others. Kevin is so busy with the case that he neglects his wife, who dreams—or is it a dream?—that she has been ravaged by John Milton; Mary Ann is so distraught that Kevin has no choice but to put her in a psycho ward, where she slashes her wrists. After winning an acquittal for Cullen, Kevin not only discovers that his firm is involved in a great many illegal activities, but his religious fanatic of a mother, Alice (Judith Ivey), confides in him that she had an one-nighter with Milton years before and that Milton is his father. Worse, in a confrontation with Daddy Dearest, he learns that Milton is no ordinary man, but the incarnation of Satan himself, who wants his son to father the anti–Christ.

The Devil's Advocate began life as an entertaining paperback penny dreadful by Andrew Neiderman. In the novel the pedophile client was a woman, a lesbian, and it was strongly implied that she was guilty, although many of the characters seemed to think it was bad enough that she was a lesbian. The film wisely made the character a male pedophile and thereby removed the distasteful homophobic taint. (In sharp contrast to this old-fashioned attitude toward

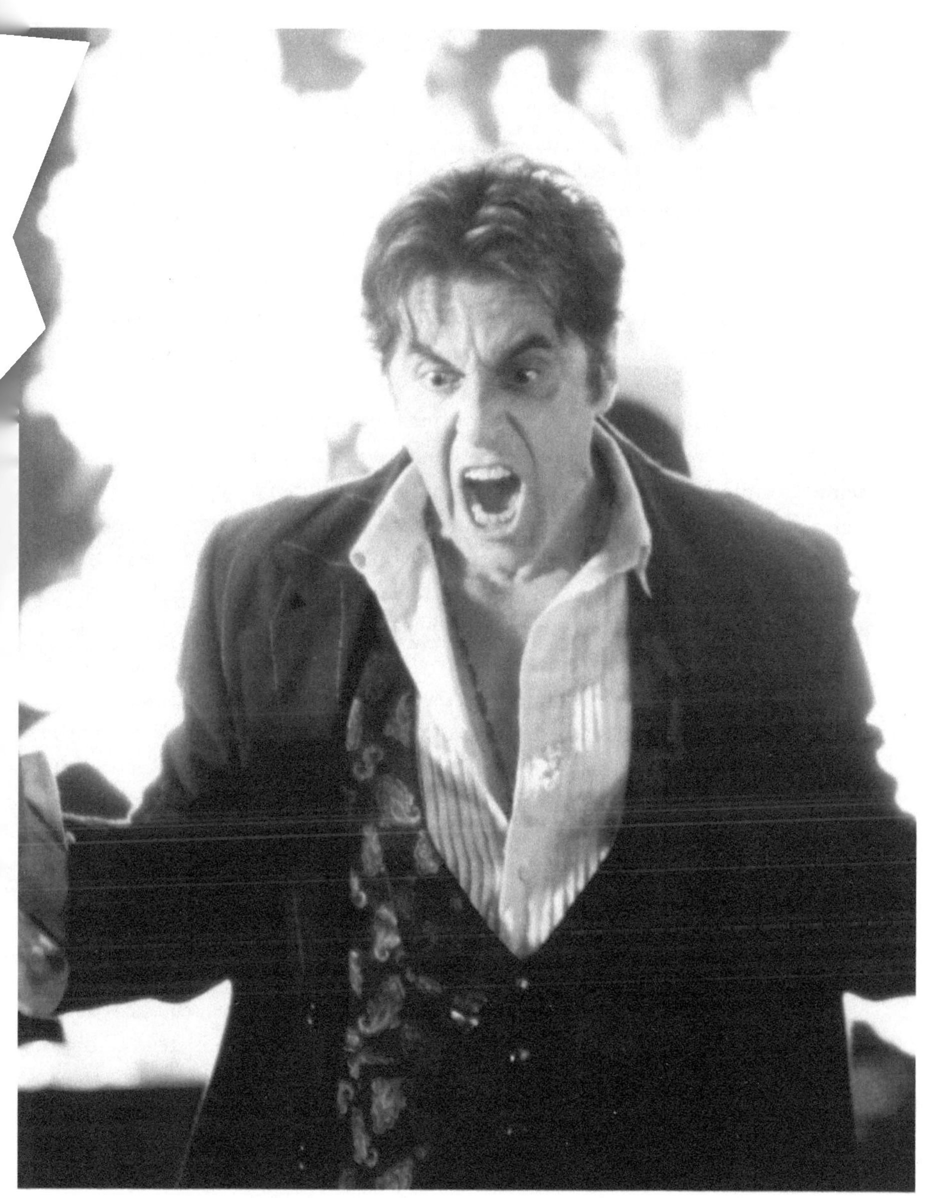

Pacino, as Satan (a.k.a. John Milton), turns up the heat in *The Devil's Advocate* (1997), an over-the-top horror-satire of corporate America.

homosexuality betrayed in the novel, one scene in the movie has Milton in an elevator with two women who are engaged in some hot homoerotic action.) In the novel Milton was not Kevin's father, and the business with the anti–Christ was similarly an invention of the screenwriters, who no doubt had seen *Rosemary's Baby* and *The Omen* once too often.

Like many of these devil movies, the supernatural aspects are slowly introduced into a film that is already compelling as a legal drama. Kevin and Mary Ann both notice unusual things about Milton and his associates. Mary Ann has been befriended by an associate's wife, Jackie (Tamara Tunie)—"You got three choices, the holy trinity: you can work, you can play or you can breed," she tells her—but when she looks at her from a different angle the pretty woman appears to be hideous and demonic. Kevin begins to wonder exactly what kind of man Milton is when the two are riding the subway; Milton successfully stands down two threatening subway riders, and seems to know more about one of them than he does himself, as if he's looking into the angry man's soul.

Satan's perverse plan is for Kevin to mate with his own half-sister, Christabella (Connie Neilsen)—to whom he had been undeniably attracted—and bring the anti–Christ into being. Satan wants his firm to bring acquittal after acquittal to the most evil clients, until "the stink reaches up to Heaven." Satan rationalizes that Kevin cannot blame *him* for his actions vis-à-vis defending his pedophile client and Cullen, actions which were motivated by his own ambition and greed. "I told you to take care of your wife," Milton tells his son. "You could have saved her anytime you wanted; you were too *busy*." Kevin commits suicide rather than submit to his father's plan, and winds up back in Florida where the film began; this time he risks disbarment by refusing to represent Gettys any further. When a reporter comes up to Kevin and asks for an interview and says she wants to give him a major play-up, Kevin agrees. Later the reporter turns into Milton/Satan and remarks to the audience how vanity is his favorite sin.

Pacino gives a wonderful modern-style performance as Satan sans horns and pitchfork and melodramatic pronouncements. He is like an imp, a funny prankster, who sees morality and life itself as a great comedy. Despite the character he plays, and a couple of moments of rage, there are no real classic "Pacino blasts" in the movie as the actor plays with subtlety and charm instead of bombast, and even has great fun dancing and lip-syncing to Sinatra. In the aforementioned subway scene Milton/Pacino deals with the menacing riders with quiet but no less deadly intensity. This is Satan as the great jester, marvelous when he says that God's attitude of self-abnegation is: "Look but don't touch; touch but don't taste; taste but don't swallow."

Keanu Reeves is perfect as Kevin, expertly limning this role of an essentially good man who is seduced by evil. Charlize Theron is highly effective as a woman driven mad by literal demons, and the other supporting performances in the film are all well-delineated. The film makes good use of New York City locations, and acrophobes in the audience undoubtedly squirmed a bit at the scene when Milton and Kevin confer on the very high rooftop of Milton's building, where there's a pool and waterfall, but no railing.

The Devil's Advocate is not a great movie as such, but it is colorful and fun, and well worth a viewing or two, although one could argue that ultimately it's rather silly and perhaps not entirely worthy of Pacino's talents. If nothing else, Pacino can say that, yes, he has made an honest to goodness horror movie (as opposed to the occasional *horrible* movie). "The movie's greatest strength is that it becomes more complex and rewarding as it goes along," wrote Mick LaSalle in the *San Francisco Chronicle*, while Mike Clark of *USA Today* felt, "As the movie approaches 2 1/4 hours, it begins feeling like eternal damnation." Nigel Floyd in *Time Out* opined: "As the epitome of charismatic evil, Pacino is perversely attractive, his seductive performance making Reeves' temptation all the more believable.... Regrettably, an overblown finale and redundant trick ending undercut the mild subversiveness of what's gone before."

The Insider

TOUCHSTONE, 1999

Producers, Pieter Jan Brugge and Michael Mann; director, Michael Mann; screenplay, Michael Mann and Eric Roth; cinematography, Dante Spinotti; music, Pieter Bourke and Lisa Gerard; editing, William Goldenberg, David Rosenbloom and Paul Rubell. Running time: 157 min.

CAST

Al Pacino (*Lowell Bergman*); Russell Crowe (*Jeffrey Wigand*); Christopher Plummer (*Mike Wallace*); Diane Venora (*Liane Wigand*); Philip Baker Hall (*Don Hewitt*); Lindsay Crouse (*Sharon Tiller*); Debi Mazar (*Debbie De Luca*); Gina Gershon (*Helen Caperelli*); Michael Gambon (*Thomas Sandefur*); Rip Torn (*John Scanlon*).

The Insider began life as a *Vanity Fair* article by Marie Brenner entitled "The Man Who Knew Too Much." Both article and movie are the true story of Jeffrey Wigand (Russell Crowe), head of Research and Development for a tobacco company who blows the whistle on his former employers for the show *60 Minutes*. The Brown and Williamson tobacco company consciously ignored the health issues that Wigand presented to them, and intentionally made their cigarettes more addictive. According to Wigand, nicotine is "more rapidly absorbed into the lungs and affects the brain and nervous system." Wigand knows that the CEOs of all the major tobacco companies lied to Congress about the addictive qualities of their product. After Wigand is fired, he is contacted by *60 Minutes* producer Lowell Bergman (Al Pacino), who wants to run a story on the tobacco industry and needs an insider's cooperation and input, but

Wigand is hesitant. He is threatened not only with legal action if he talks, but if he betrays a confidentiality agreement he signed, his family could lose their health insurance and he could lose his severance pay. Meanwhile Wigand's family find death threats on their computer. Another attack comes in the form of a dossier prepared on Wigand, which is full of malicious fabrications and exaggerations in an attempt to discredit him. Then CBS is threatened with a potentially devastating lawsuit. Wigand is furious when an abridged *60 Minutes* segment is aired, and feels manipulated and betrayed by Bergman. Bergman leaks the story of CBS's cowardice to the *New York Times*, which accuses the show of "betraying the legacy of Edward R. Murrow," while the *Wall Street Journal* discredits the dossier and prints Wigand's deposition in its entirety. The full interview is eventually aired on *60 Minutes*, but Lowell Bergman decides it's time for him to move on.

The Insider is the story of a true American hero, a man who did the right thing at great cost to himself. Fed up with all the harassment that he and his family are undergoing due to Brown and Williamson, Wigand agrees to testify even though he would be violating a court order filed in Kentucky, and could be arrested when he returns there from Mississippi. He is pleased to finally be speaking out against his tormentors, but his elation doesn't last when he discovers his wife has left him due to the pressure and taken the kids with her. "Deglamorized" Russell Crowe—he gained weight, pushed back his hair line, and wore aging make-up to look like a man in his fifties—gives an excellent performance and is the true star of the film, but Pacino matches him in passion. Christopher Plummer also turns in a fine performance as Mike Wallace.

Rob Gonsalves of ecritic.com opined that "... though the movie is constructed as Bergman's story—his struggle, his fight to get Wigand on the air—Pacino plays his hand close to the vest, exploding only at key moments.... He essentially (and subtly) plays Bergman as if he were the supporting actor ... he understands that it's really Russell Crowe's movie." Which is exactly why when one thinks of great and exciting Pacino performances, *The Insider*, as good as it is, doesn't come to the top of the list.

The long and leisurely film itself is not a masterpiece but it presents an absorbing portrait of evil in its true-life depictions of tobacco men who really don't care how many people get cancer as long as their coffers are enriched. The sequence with the hostile FBI agents investigating the harassment of his family is overstated, however, their obvious hostility overplayed as if they are practically admitting to Wigand that they're sided with the bad guys. (Wigand fears that the agents are in collusion with former comrades who now work for B & W.) One of the best scenes occurs when CBS is threatened with a lawsuit from Brown and Williamson—"They could own CBS," says lawyer Caparelli (Gina

Gershon)—and *60 Minutes* producer Don Hewitt (Philip Baker Hall) decides to eliminate the interview with Wigand from the tobacco segment. Bergman is furious because he knows that Caparelli and the CBS president stand to gain financially from an upcoming sale of CBS which a lawsuit could threaten, and asks Mike Wallace (Christopher Plummer) to join him in his protest. Unfortunately, Wallace, nearing eighty and fearing the fallout, sides with Hewett.

Of the very large supporting cast, Michael Gambon turns in a highly flavorful performance as Thomas Sandefur, the CEO of B & W who fires Wigand. Colm Feore and Gary Sandy are notable as, respectively, a private attorney who represents the State of Mississippi against the tobacco industry, and Sandefur's lawyer. There are appearances by Rip Torn, Michael Moore and Pete Hamill. But women don't have much to do in the movie. Gina Gershon as the CBS lawyer and Debi Mazar as a *60 Minutes* assistant have limited dialogue, and Bergman's significant other is barely seen. As Wigand's wife, Liane, Diane Venora has a little more to do and is effective. Disney studios was hoping for another box-office blockbuster like *All the President's Men*, but the movie did not earn back its costs, possibly due to its length, or its rather grim subject matter. Pacino and Crowe generated considerable star power, but even that didn't seem to help.

The critics were virtually unanimous in praising the film, however, but the rave reviews didn't pull enough people into the theater. The film received several Academy Award nominations, including nods for Crowe and director Mann, but didn't win any. Wrote Andrew Sarris in the *New York Observer*: "What I didn't expect was an intelligently absorbing entertainment that ran for two hours and 40 minutes, during which I didn't once look at my watch—just about the highest praise I can bestow upon a film these days." Garth Franklin wrote in *Dark Horizons*: "Crowe and Pacino give solid and engaging performances, but neither is particularly memorable. While it gets to show off each of their talents, they're playing roles very similar to ones they've done before—and so these turns don't stand out. The chemistry between the pair is good, far superior than the Pacino–De Niro mix in Mann's previous film, *Heat*."

Some found the film a little pompous or remarked that its story had already been too well covered by the press for the movie to be riveting. Pacino had played real-life characters before (Frank Serpico and Sonny Wortzik, for instance) and would do so afterwards (Jack Kevorkian, Phil Spector), but all were much more bizarre and attention-getting than Lowell Bergman, which doesn't detract from his performance but ultimately—and arguably—makes it a less interesting Al Pacino Movie.

Any Given Sunday

WARNER BROS., 1999

Executive producers, Richard Donner and Oliver Stone; director, Oliver Stone; screenplay, John Logan and Oliver Stone; cinematography, Salvatore Totino; music, Richard Horowitz and Paul Kelly; editing by Stuart Levy, Tom Nordberg, Keith Salmon and Stuart Waks. Running time: 162 min.

CAST

Al Pacino (*Tony D'Amato*); Dennis Quaid (*Jack Rooney*); Jamie Foxx (*Willie Beamen*); Cameron Diaz (*Christina Pagniacci*); James Woods (*Dr. Mandrake*); LL Cool J (*Julian Washington*); Matthew Modine (*Dr. Powers*); Jim Brown (*Montezuma Monroe*); Lawrence Taylor (*Luther "Shark" Lavay*); Bill Bellamy (*Jimmy Sanderson*); Ann-Margret (*Margaret Pagniacci*); Charlton Heston (*Football commissioner*); Aaron Eckhart (*Nick Crozier*).

Tony D'Amato (Pacino) is the coach for the Miami Sharks, a football team whose glory days seem to be in the past. Their star quarterback, Jack "Cap" Rooney (Dennis Quaid), is thirty-eight, and his assorted injuries over the years, including a new back problem, are catching up with him. But Rooney has the team spirit, which is lacking in the team's best new hope, a cocky African American named Willie Beamen (Jamie Foxx). Willie angers his teammates and Tony with his attitude, and sees the latter as a washed-up old man, "Coach Stone Age." Tony and the team's manager and co-owner, Christina Pagniacci (Cameron Diaz) nearly come to blows deciding which quarterback—Rooney or Beamen—will lead the team in their big game against the Dallas Knights. A reluctant Rooney, who only wants to retire, summons up the resources to play magnificently, impressing Willie, who takes over in the second half—the Sharks win and are on top again, but Tony moves on to coach a new team, taking a more respectful Willie with him.

With flashy editing, over a two-and-a-half-hour running time, vignettes of the game and all of its trappings, and some fine performances from a large and adept cast, *Any Given Sunday* almost manages to disguise the fact that the basic plot is as old as the Dead Sea Scrolls. There have been countless movies made about the brash newcomer who lets success go to his head, sees himself as an independent star, then learns the error of his ways, while the aging former star has to deal with his own demons. The milieu for this basic story can be anything from a sports arena to a movie set to the Broadway stage or even Wall Street. That being said, *Any Given Sunday* still manages to be a fairly entertaining picture, even if it takes quite a while to get started.

Pacino gives an excellent performance as the coach. Standing amid the husky football players he seems like a withering Lilliputian, but he towers over them when he opens his mouth. D'Amato is a lonely man who has given up any semblance of life out of love of the game, and has nothing else going for him—another stereotype, of course, but Pacino brings him to life. His greatest moment occurs when he gives an impassioned pep talk to his team just before the big game, telling them that in football as in life one inch either way can make a difference. Pacino employs two major blasts in the film, when Tony learns that Dr. Mandrake (James Woods) covered up information about a player's health, and when he thinks Christina, with whom he's always battling, has made an indiscreet remark in front of the players.

Although fifth-billed, Jamie Foxx plays the next major character and is wonderful as Willie, making his perhaps unrealistic conversion from cocky asshole to caring and vulnerable human being more believable. Willie has a degree of black pride which is nearly overwhelmed by his own ego. "Either you're number one, or you ain't shit!" he feels. He points out that while 70 percent of football players are African American, few coaches (and none of the owners) are black. Foxx has a particularly good scene with Pacino as Tony tries to bond with him, but it is clear that Willie just sees him as an old fart who has nothing to offer. Dennis Quaid is also memorable as Rooney, his best moment coming when he tries to tell Tony that he wants out, that he's falling apart, but Tony convinces him to give it one more shot. Cameron Diaz scores as Christina, who seems perfectly capable of handling not only Tony but all of the macho men on the team. There are other good performances from James Woods and Matthew Modine as doctors; Lawrence Taylor and Bill Bellamy as players; Lauren Holly as Rooney's wife, who slaps him when he talks of retiring; and Elizabeth Berkley, as a hooker, Mandy. Mandy comes on to Tony, saying she "digs" older men, then hits him with the news that it will cost him a grand. Later in the picture, Tony does buy Mandy's services, and wonders if she'll consider seeing him for free. ("Don't go there," she tells him.) Ann-Margret has the small role of Christina's mother, while Charlton Heston shows up for a couple of minutes as a football commissioner; both are fine.

A note about the editing of *Any Given Sunday* is in order. The film consists chiefly of quick cuts, one thing interspersed with another, which makes it move fast and keeps the football sequences humming, but in certain scenes the frenetic cutting is unnecessary. For instance, there is a fine, well-acted sequence when Willie comes to Tony's house for dinner, and the two have a confrontation. It's a good scene as it is, but it's intercut with shots from *Ben-Hur*, the 1959 Charlton Heston movie that happens to be playing on Tony's TV. It's a heavy-handed way of comparing football players to ancient gladiators, but the scene doesn't need it. (Besides, *Ben-Hur* is a better movie, and you never want to remind an audience that the movie they're watching isn't nearly as good as the one they're seeing in clips.)

Even some of the movie's biggest fans felt director Stone went over the top with a sequence when one of the opposing players has his entire eyeball and its optic nerve popped or ripped out on the field during the climactic game. It was probably meant to illustrate how rough the tackles can get, with eye-gouging and finger-breaking not unknown, but not only is such a thing completely unlikely, it has never happened in the history of football. Eye injuries, yes, but nothing that extreme. The scene was cut from the theatrical release but can be seen on the DVD.

Whatever the flaws of *Any Given Sunday*, Pacino's work in it is solid and he got the lion's share of the praise, even from reviewers who didn't particularly care for the movie. "Only Al Pacino could give a quiet, thoughtful performance while screaming so often and so loudly," opined Joe Lozito of *Big Picture, Big Sound*. "In fact, Mr. Pacino is wonderful as an aging star who, in trying to get his ailing Miami Sharks into the playoffs, is forced to re-evaluate nearly every choice he's made in his life." Audiences liked the movie better than the critics, who were divided, some suggesting that the ever-controversial Oliver Stone had come up with nothing less than a major critique of American sports. But *Any Given Sunday* doesn't really seem to have anything so weighty on its mind, being more a paean to the Great God Football, and telling a simple and oft-told tale.

Chinese Coffee

FOX SEARCHLIGHT, 2000

Executive producer, Anne D'Amato; director, Al Pacino; screenplay, Ira Lewis, from his stage play; cinematography, Frank Prinzi; music, Elmer Bernstein; editing by Michael Berenbaum, Pasquale Buba, and Noah Herzog. Running time: 99 min.

CAST

Al Pacino (*Harry Levine*); Jerry Orbach (*Jake Manheim*); Susan Floyd (*Joanna*); Ellen McElduff (*Mavis*); Libby Langdon (*Julie*); Paul Butler (*Barney*); Michel Moinot (*Maurice*); Maria Gentile (*Sarah*); Judette Jones (*supermarket cashier*); Joel Eidelsberg (*Harry's brother*).

Al Pacino not only starred (with Jerry Orbach) in this adaptation of Ira Lewis's play, in which he had appeared in 1992, but also directed. Harry Levine

(Pacino) a middle-aged writer in Greenwich Village in the early '80s who had two books published but hit a career slump, is fired from his job as a doorman. Down to his last $1.50 he goes to his friend, Jake Manheim's (Orbach), apartment to see if he can get back a few hundred dollars that Jack owes him. Jake, who takes pictures of actors but isn't making much of a living at it, tells him that he's broke and three months behind on his rent. The two men review their lives and friendship, as well as the women they were involved with, as Harry tries to find out what Jake thinks of his new unpublished novel, which he dropped off several weeks before. Harry had a lovely girlfriend named Joanne (Susan Floyd), but she left him due to his unpleasant moods. Jake is divorced from his wealthy ex-wife, Mavis (Ellen McElduff), and no longer has her monetary protection. At first Jake tells Harry that he hasn't read his manuscript, but then admits that he has and trashes it, telling Harry that it will never sell and indeed he must find a new way to make a living. Later it develops that Jake, who also fancies himself a writer, is actually furious because he feels Harry "stole his life" by using both of them as the book's main characters; the book is trash but it will make money. Their friendship over, Harry gets a job as a dishwasher, then goes home to his basement apartment to continue work on his manuscript.

Ira Lewis based the play on events in his own life. *Chinese Coffee* presents strongly etched and acted portraits of two unsuccessful middle-aged men who are getting older and are scared of what the future holds in store for them. They are well-drawn Greenwich Village characters, true Bohemians who shun the nine-to-five workaday world while struggling on a constant basis to make ends meet. They are unfulfilled and unsatisfied, all the more difficult for Harry because he seems to have some talent. Jake considers himself a writer as well, but only had two short stories published in his youth, and hasn't written anything since. Harry feels that his friend's true forte is photography, which Jake has practiced to varying degrees of success over the decades. For many years he was a photographer for a nightclub, taking pictures of drunken patrons. His attempt to start his own photography business is not generating much income, but unlike Harry, he probably can no longer abide the thought of a boss.

People like Harry and Jake, ever on the fringes of an artistic life, exist in other places besides Greenwich Village, but the village was once famous for its "starving artists," most of whom could no longer afford to live there; even in the early 1980s things were changing. *Chinese Coffee* (the title refers to the coffee Harry gets in Chinese restaurants, which he thinks is superior) benefits greatly from being filmed in Greenwich Village locations, including Arthur's Tavern on Grove Street—although many places are gone, a surprising number of night spots still exist as they did years ago. It was Pacino's idea to open up the stage play by shooting scenes which illustrate what the actors are talking about and it works, as many of these quickly intercut flashbacks add much not only to the film's impact, but to its humor.

Although the two leads at first seem a bit over-rehearsed and theatrical, the performances in the film are excellent. As *Chinese Coffee*, despite its rather grim subject matter, is essentially a comedy, Pacino and Orbach act "cutesy" in spots but when it comes time for the more serious sections they really deliver. Harry is depressed because he looks so awful that he was confused with a "sub-human murderer" from Queens that the police were looking for. When he goes to the Strand to ask for copies of his books, the clerk asks him if "Harry Levine" is a living author. His brother (Joel Eidelsberg), who despairs of how he lives in a small basement room, is utterly condescending. Harry is determined to keep plugging away, hoping against hope for success, no matter the odds against him. He is not a loser as much as he is an aging struggler at a time in his life when he should be already collecting the rewards of his profession.

It could be argued that Orbach gives the better performance of the two, that he is a bit more successful at immersing himself into his character (even though both actors brought much of themselves to their performances). Orbach and Pacino both come from the theater, and Pacino in particular had some dark and hungry early years. But Pacino became extremely successful at a relatively young age, while Orbach found his greatest success—after some winning performances in Broadway musicals—on TV's *Law and Order* in later life. The lean years might have been fresher in Orbach's mind. In any case, while Pacino is wonderful, at times you sense he's playing Al Pacino, at least the Pacino who might have been had he not had his talent and drive and gotten a few lucky breaks.

Chinese Coffee is a comedy but it is not—as so many modern plays are—a sitcom; its characters are richer than those in situation comedies, where the lines they speak are dictated more by the demands of the laugh track than anything deeper. It is full of wonderful and amusing dialogue, such as this interchange between Harry and Jake:

> **HARRY**: What does it mean when you can't fall asleep?
> **JAKE**: Severe depression.
> **HARRY**: And when you keep waking up?
> **JAKE**: Severe anxiety.
> **HARRY**: Any remedy?
> **JAKE**: Death.

A crazy scene develops when Harry stops off at a supermarket to buy detergent, lugging his laundry bag behind him. "We don't redeem cans until 10 a.m.," says the female clerk, repeating this each time Harry protests that it's *his* laundry in the bag and not empty cans for redemption. Undoubtedly this scene, albeit exaggerated, was taken from real life.

The ladies in the men's lives are very well played by Susan Floyd and Ellen McElduff. (Harry is briefly given another post–Joanne girlfriend who is much too young, the film trading reality for the Hollywood nonsense of casting very young women with much, much older men.) Paul Butler makes an impression as the poet-bartender Harry talks to in the film's post-credit epilogue.

An odd scene has Jake talking about "twelve-year-old virgins in South America who satisfy your exotic desires," and seems absolutely delighted at the thought of it. This seems to come out of nowhere, and makes Jake seem like a pedophile, but if he is the movie doesn't deal with it.

Insomnia

WARNER BROS., 2002

Executive producers, George Clooney and Steven Soderbergh; director, Christopher Nolan; screenplay, Hillary Seitz; cinematography, Wally Pfister; music, David Julyan; editing, Dody Dorn; production design, Nathan Crowley; art direction, Michael Diner. Running time: 118 min.

CAST

Al Pacino (*Will Dormer*); Robin Williams (*Walter Finch*); Martin Donovan (*Hap Eckhart*); Hilary Swank (*Ellie Burr*); Paul Dooley (*Chief Nyback*); Maura Tierny (*Rachel Clement*); Crystal Lowe (*Kay Connell*); Lorne Cardinal (*Rich*); Nicky Katt (*Fred Duggar*); Larry Holden (*Farrell*).

Will Dormer (Al Pacino) and Hap Eckhart (Martin Donovan) are Los Angeles homicide detectives who are under investigation, especially the former, for manufacturing evidence to convict a child molester. Eckhart wants to make a deal, and Dormer tells him he should do whatever he feels he has to. They have both been sent off to Alaska to investigate the murder of a teenage girl named Kay Connell (Crystal Lowe). Chasing after a suspect, Dormer accidentally shoots and kills Eckhart, but covers it up even as Ellie Burr (Hilary Swank) begins her own investigation into what happened. Dormer then enters into a cat-and-mouse game with writer Walter Finch (Robin Williams), who murdered Kay but is aware of Dormer's duplicity regarding his dead partner. Uneasy allies of sorts, the two make a deal and concoct a scheme to frame Kay's boyfriend Randy (Jonathan Jackson) for her murder. But Dormer is ultimately appalled at everything he's doing, and he and Finch have a climactic and decisive confrontation.

Insomnia is based on a creditable 1997 Norwegian film of the same name which starred Stellan Skarsgard as a Swedish detective named Engstrom. Engstrom is a somewhat edgier character than Will Dormer. Whereas Dormer shoots a bullet into a dead dog as part of his cover-up, Engstrom simply shoots and kills a dog. Dormer has an interesting scene with Kay's friend Tanya (Katharine Isabelle) that has some erotic undertones, but Engstrom outright molests "Tanja" when she's riding in his car with him. But the American *Insomnia*, courtesy of a screenplay by Hillary Seitz, has a richer screenplay with more interesting elements and details, and is a better picture.

Pacino's performance is good, if not one of his greatest, although this can be hard to judge due to certain aspects of the storyline. Living and working in an area where there are "white nights" and no nighttime, Dormer has trouble sleeping and is becoming more and more exhausted (hence the title). This may explain why Pacino often at least *seems* to be too casual, unengaged with the material, considering everything that's going on—yet his character *is* befuddled due to lack of sleep. His phone call to his partner's widow to give her the awful news about Hap's death is disappointing, but Pacino still has some good moments—in fact, the more tired Dormer gets the better Pacino is—such as when he finally has it out with Finch at the climax. Hilary Swank isn't given enough to do but does it well, Donovan is solid, and Robin Williams—cast against type—is excellent as the sociopathic Finch and makes a worthy opponent for Pacino.

The film is well directed by Christopher Nolan, and remains one of his better films. The pace never drags and the suspense is sustained; there are some exciting scenes such as when Dormer is trapped underwater beneath a bunch of logs. Critical opinion was largely favorable, but some critics were unimpressed. According to Stuart Klawans of *The Nation*, "Pacino behaves ridiculously, as he typically does when the script's a laugh.... Who allowed these performances, or maybe even encouraged them? [Christopher Nolan] was so intent on dolloping pizazz onto this story that he didn't notice the visual syrup was drowning a six-inch stack of toaster waffles."

Continues Klawans, "I'm sure *Insomnia* will have its champions, even so. They'll claim the picture is About Something, namely the importance of never, ever breaking the rules. That's the one, big idea of *Insomnia*. As we may learn from life and better movies, it's wrong."

Richard Schickel in *Time* had a better opinion of the film: "What we have here is your basic good-cop-bad-cop story, except that those two characters are wrapped into one, with Pacino giving one of his terrific tormented performances in the role—impatient, arrogant and, in the long watches of the night, almost pathetically vulnerable."

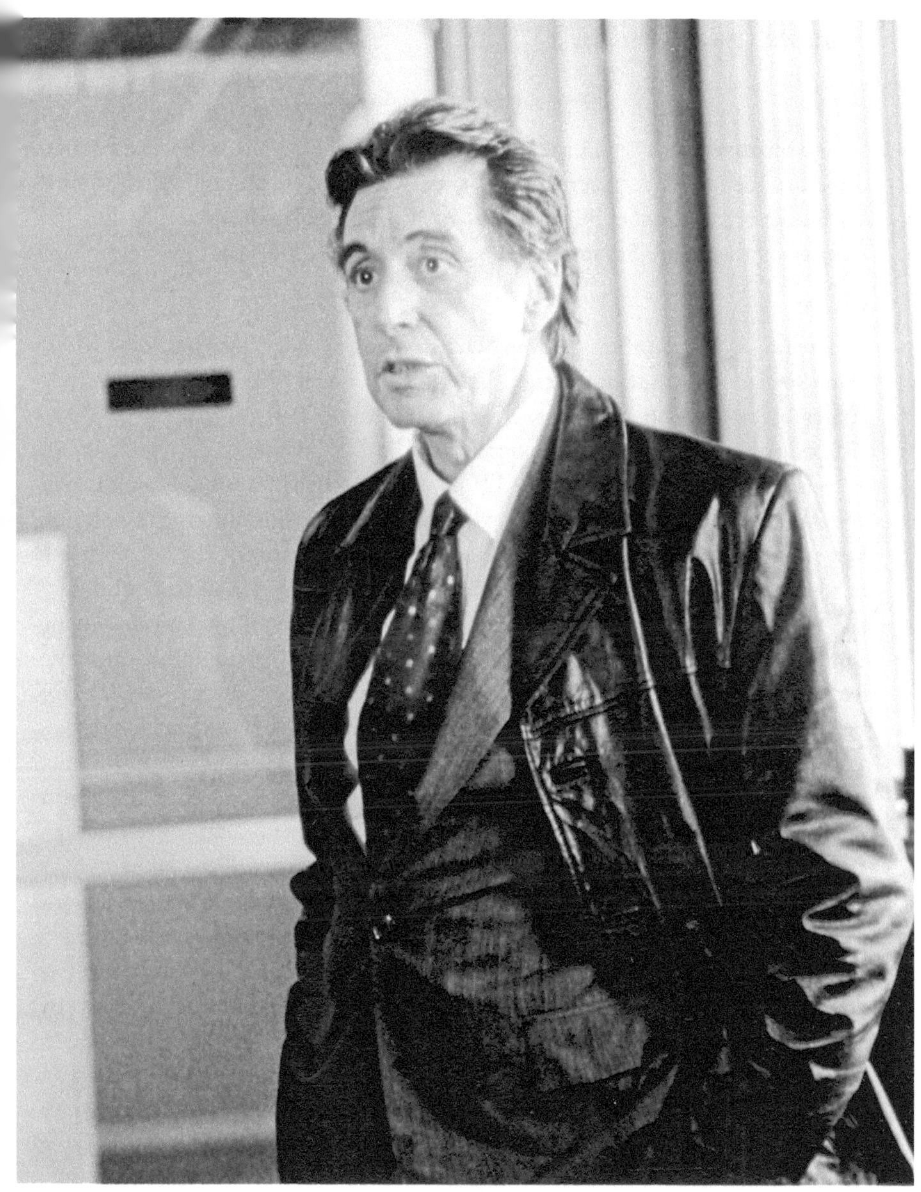

LAPD Det. Will Dormer (Pacino), sent to investigate a grisly murder in a small town in Alaska, finds it increasingly difficult to adapt to the region's endless daylight. *Insomnia* (2002) is generally thought to be better than the 1997 Norwegian film of the same title. This is due in no small measure to the onscreen chemistry between Pacino and his co-star, Robin Williams (cast against type as a sociopathic writer).

Simone (aka *S1m0ne*)

NEW LINE CINEMA, 2002

Executive producers, Bradley Cramp, Michael De Luca, and Lynn Harris; director, Andrew Niccol; screenplay, Andrew Niccol; cinematography, Edward Lachman; music, Carter Burwell; editing, Paul Rubell; production design, Jan Roelfs; art direction, Sarah Knowles. Running time: 117 min.

CAST

Al Pacino (*Viktor Taransky*); Evan Rachel Wood (*Lainey Taransky*); Jay Mohr (*Hal Sinclair*); Catherine Keener (*Elaine Christian*); Winona Ryder (*Nicola Anders*); Rachel Roberts (*Simone*); Jeffrey Pierce (*Kent*); Pruitt Taylor Vince (*Max Sayer*); Lotus (*Susan Chuang*); Barry Papick (*Walter*).

Producer Viktor Taransky (Al Pacino) knows he's in trouble when his lead actress, Nicola Anders (Wynona Ryder), walks out on him, sinking the picture he's trying to make. His ex-wife, Elaine (Catherine Keener), the studio head, has so little faith in him that she fires him. "It's not every day you're fired by the mother of your own child," he tells her. However, Viktor knows a dying computer genius named Hank (Elias Koteas), whose technological tinkering has given him a crazy idea. Using Hank's equipment he creates a new star for his film, a computer simulation or virtual actress he calls Simone (for Simulation One), who is beautiful and sexy. This digital creation is manipulated to interact with the real actors in the film, who never actually meet her. When the film is released, the movie is a big hit and Simone becomes a major star—even though she doesn't actually exist. As her legions of fans increase, and the money pours in, Viktor finds it more and more difficult to give excuses to keep people, including the cast and crews of her subsequent movies, away from her. Everything catches up to Viktor when the authorities learn that all of Simone's money has gone into his bank accounts, and she herself hasn't been seen in the flesh by anyone but him. Viktor is arrested for murdering Simone, but his daughter, Lainie (Evan Rachel Wood), and her mother come to his rescue by using an anti-virus program to bring Simone back for good. "I was trying to convince the world that you existed," Viktor says of Simone, "but what I was really trying to do was convince them that *I* existed."

Andrew Niccol, who both wrote and directed the film, cooks up interesting ways for Viktor to maintain the deception about his creation. First, he spreads the rumor that Simone is too pathologically shy to sing or emote with anyone but Viktor present. He is able to use his technology to get Simone interviewed—via satellite or closed circuit—on talk shows and news programs, but nobody ever meets her. For one appearance at a party he uses a stand-in who quickly vanishes, although dozens of people later say that they not only met Simone but talked to her at length! Simon embarks upon a vocal career, and is extremely successful at that as well, with Viktor using holographic technology to make her appear to sing in front of thousands of people at a stadium. Doing everything he can to preserve the illusion that Simone is a flesh-and-blood female, Viktor even goes so far as to put on lipstick and kiss her photographs as a real actress might do for her adoring fans.

As comically delineated by a charming Pacino, the stress and weariness of keeping up the mammoth deception along with his fear of discovery eventually affects Viktor and he sets out to destroy his creation. The film has perhaps the most fun showing how Viktor fails in his goal because Simone can seemingly do no wrong. Under Viktor's guidance, she makes outrageous, politically incorrect statements, but still becomes *Time*'s Woman of the Year. She directs her own terrible movie that Viktor hopes will shock and appall the public but they see her as edgy and forthright, a true *artiste*, and cheer her. Finally Viktor erases Simone with a computer virus.

Perhaps the funniest and truest thing about the movie is that—as is often the case—Simone has sex appeal going for her and nothing else. She's a lousy actress, and her singing voice sounds like a hundred others. The movie cannily dissects the cult of celebrity and the skewered reality of L.A. and contains dead-on satiric barbs aimed at Hollywood, such as when the threat of an all-out world war is overshadowed by the comparative trivia of the Oscar nominations. Pacino is marvelous throughout—he has an especially good scene when he tries to tell Elaine the truth about Simone—and is great fun as a man who is both exhilarated and overwhelmed by what is happening to him. The supporting cast, those already named as well as Jay Mohr as actor Hal Sinclair and Claudia Jordan as a Simone lookalike, are all on the money. As for Simone herself, she was played by Rachel Roberts (whose name was left out of the theatrical credits), who plays her well. Some feel it's only a matter of time before real live actors are replaced in films by virtual performers who will come cheaper and hopefully be free of all that thespian ego and angst.

Although *Simone* is a delightful movie, it doesn't quite reach classic status, and it received mixed reactions from the critics. Rick Kisonak in *Film Threat* opined: "Not only has the filmmaker elected to address some extremely well worn themes, he evidently has little new to say about them." Michael Dequina in *The Movie Report* wrote: "Pacino, not one known to be terribly light on his feet, delivers a nimble and uncharacteristically reined-in performance that generates both laughs and genuine sympathy for his character's unusual plight ... [director] Niccol ... reveals said idea to be not at all far removed from reality—as any good satire should."

David Nusair in *Reel Film Reviews* felt that *Simone* was "engaging and enjoyable ... due in no small part to Pacino's terrific performance.... Viktor is a bubbling mess of nerves and worry and Pacino effortlessly steps into his shoes ... one of Pacino's most accessible performances in years, and it definitively proves that he's got the timing to act in more comedies."

People I Know

MIRAMAX, 2002

Executive producers, Robert Redford, Kirk D'Amico, and Philip von Alvensleben; director, Daniel Algrant; screenplay, Jon Robin Baitz; cinematography, Peter Deming; music, Terence Blanchard; editing, Suzy Elmiger. Running time: 100 minutes.

CAST

Al Pacino (*Eli Wurman*); Ryan O'Neal (*Cary Launer*); Tea Leoni (*Jilli Hopper*); Kim Basinger (*Victoria Gray*); Mark Webber (*Ross*); Richard Schiff (*Elliot Sharansky*); Bill Nunn (*Blunt*); Robert Klein (*Dr. Napier*); David Marshall Grant (*Tom Silverton*); Joe Duer (*Michael*).

Eli Wurman (Pacino) is a New York publicist who is originally from Virginia. Wurman's career has been in better shape, and he is down to having only one famous client, Oscar-winner Cary Launer (Ryan O'Neal). Launer asks Eli to do him a favor and bail model-celebrity Jilly Hopper (Tea Leoni), one of his paramours, out of jail, and get her to her hotel room safely. Eli balks, but does as he is told. Jilly insists on taking Eli to a sex-and-drugs party patronized by powerful people, and while there she uses a digital camera, which looks like a toy, to take pictures. She is thrown out of the party, but brags that she has photos of everyone as the elevator door closes. Later she drops the camera, and Eli absently puts it in his pocket. High on booze and opium, Eli has collapsed in the hotel room bathtub when an intruder breaks in and murders Jilly, searching unsuccessfully for the camera. The next day it all seems like a dream to Eli, until he sees news of Jilly's death on TV.

Still in a bit of a fog, Eli is preoccupied by an event for racial unity that he is sponsoring at the Palm, an eastside restaurant, and has to not only deal with the egos of spokespeople but with trying to get Cary and other "names" to show up for the event. His widowed sister-in-law, Vicky (Kim Basinger), wants to start a relationship with him, but he at first finds the idea too strange. His assistant Ross (Mark Webber) tells Eli he's leaving, then Cary fires him and tells him he wants to run for political office, an idea that does not sit well with billionaire financier Elliot Sharansky (Richard Schiff) and his cronies, who were at the party Eli and Jilly attended. Eli is told that he had better turn over the camera but is too befogged to really know what they're talking about, although he suspects he's in deep shit. The event at the Palm is a success, and Eli decides to pack it in, get out of New York, and go with Vicky to her farm in Virginia. But while perusing a paper at a newsstand, Eli is stabbed by a passerby. Not really aware of what has happened to him, Eli makes it back to his apartment, where he succumbs to blood loss.

Despite its flaws, *People I Know* is one of Pacino's best pictures and most notable performances. Pacino himself suggested that it be less of a thriller—and indeed the whole conspiracy business over the camera and the powerful forces who want it, etc., is rather obtuse and confusing—and more of a character study, which worked better for him if not for the movie as a whole. Still, his portrait of the schlumpy, disheveled Eli, who has become lap dog to celebrities and ignored his own health and life, is riveting. In the hotel room sequence he is convincingly wasted, and he gets across Eli's habit of charging ahead on sheer nervous energy while on the verge of collapsing. One minute he is charming the New York City movers and shakers that he wants to attend his event, smoothing ruffled feathers, and the next telling Cary, who's jumping ship, that he "knows where the bodies are buried." One could suggest that Pacino underplays certain scenes, such as the one with Cary, but he is not an evil man who enjoys threatening people, just one who's perhaps a bit weak and somewhat defeated.

In his idealistic youth Eli was involved in civil rights causes, and he continues to work for equality and sponsor events such as the one at the Palm, so that his life is not just taken over by frivolous, self-absorbed people. (Ironically, the activists he encounters can be, in their own way, just as egotistical. It could be said *People I Know* uses the civil rights issue in the same way that Pacino does. The movie touches on these issues but doesn't hit them head-on, being primarily concerned with Eli.) Pacino's Southern accent may seem to come and go, but that often happens with people are who not native New Yorkers. They affect a certain New York-ese, but lapse back into their natural speech patterns during moments of stress or whenever they simply want to.

The supporting cast is generally excellent as well. Tea Leoni is dead-on as the cokehead, obnoxious, difficult Jilly who seems too high and too angry to enjoy her success and meets a dark fate (it is implied that Jilly's corpse is raped after her murder). While there may be some amusement in casting Ryan O'Neal as an Oscar winner, in truth he is quite effective as Cary. Mark Webber is perfection as Ross, Eli's put-upon assistant who just deals in his quiet way with his boss and seems to be always holding back an explosion, a very recognizable type in the business. Richard Schiff makes Elliot Sharansky as subtly menacing as he is attractive and charming. Robert Klein is also notable as Eli's feel-good doctor, Sandy, who in one bizarre touch seems to be in league with Sharansky and his associates. Bill Nunn plays the Reverend Lyle Blunt, a black activist, with a wonderful combination of righteous indignation, pride, and barely suppressed if blatant egomania. As the aspiring actor Michael, who thinks the world of Eli and hopes for his help, Joe Duer makes an impression in his two brief scenes with Pacino. While Kim Basinger's performance contains some good moments, she is simply miscast as Vicky. Why portray Eli as a battered borderline loser and have a sexy woman like Basinger pursuing him? Vicky should have been much older and much less attractive for this whole aspect of the film to be believable.

Jon Robin Baitz's screenplay is full of amusing and trenchant dialogue. "I had a whole list of clients back in the days," Eli tells Jilly. "Monty Clift. Mama Cass." To which Jilly snaps, "Fat lot of good you did them!" She tells him that he "looks like someone who doesn't like to touch other people." The self-absorbed Elsa (a vital Lisa Emery), who used to work for Eli and now wants the large room at the Palm for *her* event that same night, tells him that she's sick of his "tragic causes," summing up the attitude of a lot of egocentric careerists. The movie captures the contempt that the young often have for the old, especially if they are on their way down. One strange bit of dialogue has Eli telling Sandy that "the mayor wants to pick up all the colored without green cards and deport them." Eli's use of the word "colored," considering he has fought, even if obliquely, for civil rights his entire life, is weird, so one can only imagine it is meant ironically, his way of suggesting that it is the powers-that-be who see these people as "coloreds," not him. The more conservative Sandy responds with "all I know is that I can walk in Central Park and not get mugged."

Because *People I Know* was not a conventional thriller, it got mixed reviews, being compared to Stanley Kubrick's *Eyes Wide Shut*, which also had conspiracies, powerful people, and sex parties in it, but otherwise was absolutely nothing like the Pacino film. Pacino's accent was criticized. One of the most ludicrous assertions was that Pacino was too old and tired-looking to be a publicist, even though there are many experienced, middle-aged and even senior people in the public relations business. "The movie is weighted down with an excess of plot points that fail to coalesce," wrote Ruthie Stein of the San Francisco *Chronicle*, echoing many of her peers. Some felt that Pacino was the only reason to see the picture, but even he came in for brickbats. The film and Pacino have some admirers, however, such as Marshall Fine of the Westchester *Journal News*, who wrote that the film is "worth watching for Pacino's hollow-eyed, full-bodied performance and for the strong supporting cast surrounding him."

People I Know may be one of those films that is looked upon more favorably years after its release. It's nothing for which Pacino need ever apologize.

The Recruit

TOUCHSTONE, 2003

Executive producers, Jonathan Glickman and Ric Kidney; director, Roger Donaldson; screenplay, Roger Towne, Kurt Wimmer and Mitch Glazer; cinematography, Stuart Dryburgh; music, Klaus Badelt; editing, David Rosenbloom. Running time: 115 min.

CAST

Al Pacino (*Walter Burke*); Colin Farrell (*James Douglas Clayton*); Bridget Moynahan (*Layla Moore*); Gabriel Macht (*Zach*); Kenneth Mitchell (*Alan*); Mike Realba (*Ronnie Gibson*); Ron Lea (*Bill Rudolph*); Karl Pruner (*Dennis Slayne*).

Al Pacino is teamed with young actor Colin Farrell in a spy movie centering on the CIA and deadly double-crosses. Walter Burke (Pacino), a senior instructor for the CIA at Langley or "The Farm," approaches James Clayton (Colin Farrell) at the bar where the latter works. Clayton is a computer genius who has created a program called Spartacus that can hack into any other program and take control of it. He is also searching for information on his father, who died in a plane crash in 1990 in Peru, and whom he thinks was working for the CIA; he thinks of them as "a bunch of fat old white guys who fell asleep when we needed them the most." In spite of this, Burke recruits Clayton, who joins several other hopefuls for training at the farm. Due to a misadventure, Clayton is shortly after booted out of the program, however. But then Burke approaches him on the outside and tells him that he has not really been discharged, but is actually a NOC (non-official cover) operative. Clayton's first assignment is Layla Moore (Bridget Moynahan), another trainee, who may somehow be sneaking out a new computer program, ICE 9, from her office in Langley—ICE 9 can simply be plugged into any electrical outlet—although Burke assures Clayton it's a phony. It develops that Burke actually duped Layla into stealing a real virus so he could sell it for $3 million. When he realizes the truth has been exposed, Burke pulls his weapon and is gunned down by cops as a way of committing suicide. James later learns that his father was an NOC when *he* was killed.

Top-billed Pacino undoubtedly took the part in *The Recruit* because of some good sequences for him towards the end and a hefty paycheck, because Burke is really just a supporting part, with Farrell playing the lead. While not in the league of his greatest performances, Pacino does have some splendid moments, such as when he explains his reasons for selling out to James at the climax—"I couldn't fake it anymore"—and just before his suicide when he looks down at his chest and sees all the red dots from the weapons of the operatives trained on him and wears a look of infinite resignation and defeat. Otherwise, he tends to fall back on old tricks and mannerisms, because the script just doesn't give him much to work with. Colin Farrell gives a good performance, although at times he seems a little self-conscious. Bridget Moynahan is not only lovely to look at, but is excellent as Layla, and never gives away whether this gal is on the side of the angels or not. The other cast members are all good although none of them really get much of a chance to stand out. Gabriel Macht, who plays trainee Zach, later played *The Spirit* in a dreadful version of Will Eisner's famous comic strip character, but survived that debacle to wind up in the popular series *Suits*.

One might wonder why Burke bothers with James Clayton in the first place. It makes sense that he would inveigle Layla into stealing the virus so he can claim a huge payoff, it even makes sense that he would want computer expert James to check and see if she's accomplishing her mission (although this is never quite spelled out), but it makes little sense that he would expect this genius not to see plainly that the virus was real, and not to realize that the fellow might unravel his entire scheme, which is exactly what happens. Why not wait for Layla to hopefully deliver the program, or better still, get James to steal it on some other pretext? Another problem is that the affair between James and Layla doesn't last all that long, so it's hard to imagine that he's fallen *so* in love with her that he's willing to let this "traitor" just run off and escape during a key sequence.

In spite of the script contrivances, *The Recruit* is an entertaining and fast-paced movie, but critics were divided, with some enjoying the twists and turns and layers of deceit and betrayal (that you get in most spy movies) and others feeling that these didn't make up for the film's essentially second-rate and over-familiar nature. *Reel Film Reviews* wrote that it was reminiscent of "one of those underwhelming straight-to-video flicks that either stars Eric Roberts or Dean Cain," while the *Village Voice* opined that it "weighs in like a porous brick of recycled polypropylene." On his website, Roger Ebert opined, "The senior instructor is Walter Burke, played by Al Pacino in a performance that is just plain fun to watch, gruff, blunt, with a weathered charm.... Pacino works his character for all its grizzled charm."

The Recruit isn't an awful picture, it's just good and forgettable.

Gigli

COLUMBIA, 2003

Executive producer, John Hardy; producer/director/writer, Martin Brest; cinematography, Robert Elswit; music, John Powell; editing, Julie Monroe and Billy Weber. Running time: 121 min.

CAST

Al Pacino (*Starkman*); Ben Affleck (*Larry Gigli*); Jennifer Lopez (*Ricki*); Justin Bartha (*Brian*); Lenny Venito (*Louie*); Christopher Walken (*Detective Jacobellis*); Lainie Kazan (*Mother*); Missy Crider (*Robin*).

Probably because the writer/director of *Gigli*, Martin Brest, had directed Pacino in *Scent of a Woman*, which netted him an Oscar, Pacino agreed to do what amounts to a cameo in this terrible movie, widely considered one of the worst ever made. The plot has to do with a criminal "contractor" or hit man named Larry Gigli (Ben Affleck), who is ordered by a nasty character named Louie (Lenny Venito) to kidnap a mentally challenged youth named Brian (Justin Bartha). Brian is the younger brother of the man who is prosecuting Louie's boss, Starkman (Pacino). Larry is surprised to learn that Louie doesn't quite trust him to do the job, as he has female operative Ricki (Jennifer Lopez) show up at Gigli's apartment to assist. Larry is attracted to Ricki and tries to seduce her, but she tells him that he is not her type and she is a lesbian. Louie wants them to cut off the boy's thumb and send it to the prosecutor, but they balk at this and substitute the thumb of a corpse in a hospital morgue. Larry tells Ricki that he is crazy about her, and the two have sex. Meeting with Starkman, the latter berates them for using the wrong thumb (it had the wrong fingerprints) and kills Louie. Ricki tells Starkman that they will kill Brian so he can't identify who kidnapped him, but she is lying. The two drop Brian off at a beach and decide to leave town. Ricki cannot promise Larry that she will "jump the fence" for him but she can at least give him a lift to wherever he's going.

Gigli is a truly awful movie. First we are asked to accept these two perfectly nice people as mob assassins. Then we're asked to accept that a woman who seems like a committed lesbian—not a bisexual—would hop into the sack with Larry only a short while after she breaks up with her female lover. Characters drop in out of nowhere: a detective (Christopher Walken) shows up at Larry's apartment asking about the kidnapped boy, but never searches the place; Ricki's girlfriend Robin (Missy Crider) also shows up at Larry's apartment out of the blue and slashes her wrists after Ricki breaks up with her. There is absolutely no suspense or tautness; we never see the prosecutor or even learn why Starkman is in trouble. When Ricki and Larry take it on the lam at the end, there's no sense of any danger that Starkman might send someone after them. The movie fails as a thriller and as a romantic comedy, if it can even be called a comedy.

One could argue that critics were disposed to hate the movie because of all the tabloid attention given to its two stars—known popularly as "Bennifer"—who began a relationship while working on the film, and this may account for their bad personal reviews in part, but *Gigli* deserved its excoriation. Utterly contrived, with impossible characters and a wretched screenplay, the greatest actors in the world would have been unable to make the movie believable. Lopez and Affleck have enough charm and sex appeal to make their performances somewhat palatable, but aside from the unreal characters they play they fail to imbue the film with any tension.

Two elements of the film especially earned the scornful wrath of critics and other show biz chroniclers, and that was the offensive and exploitive depiction of a mentally challenged teenager and the whole inane business with Lopez being an on-again/off-again lesbian. Any halfway talented screenwriter who wanted to create sexual tension could come up with half a dozen reasons Ricki might not have wanted to sleep with Larry at first—she didn't want to be a notch on his belt, for instance, or felt it might compromise the operation, etc.—but her being gay seems completely pointless. Brest is trying to be edgy and "hip" but only seems antediluvian. If there *had* to be a sex scene between the two stars—as the studio may have dictated, although Nicki was a lesbian in the original screenplay—a more clever writer may have made it a head game on Nicki's part or some duplicitous part of the plot. Instead it's almost as if the movie is saying, "You're only a lesbian until you meet the right man." Brest inserts some dialogue that is meant to either set up the sex between the couple or confirm that despite what happened Ricki *is* a lesbian and that's that, but it's not enough to counter-act the homophobic effect. More than one critic suggested that if Ricki had to be a lesbian, Brest could at least have inserted some girl-on-girl action for some members of the audience to enjoy.

As for Pacino, he only shows up ninety minutes into the running time. During the measly five minutes that he's onscreen, the movie comes alive and you forget that Lopez and Affleck, who are in the same scene, are even in the same movie. His graying hair cut stylishly with a little pony tail in back, Pacino plays Starkman like a complete sociopath. "I can't go to jail," he tells the couple. "I'm used to the finer things." He goes on a lengthy discourse as to whether a thumb is an actual finger or just a digit. Without any warning he takes out a gun and shoots Louis dead. "I have no compunctions," he explains. He begins quietly and builds himself up to a major Pacino blast as he expresses his outraged feelings towards the whole botched operation. It's not necessarily great acting, but it's riveting and much more than this movie deserves. Had Pacino been given a lot more screen time he might not have been able to save the movie, but surely *Gigli* would not have been quite so tedious.

Although Pacino is the best thing in the movie, even *he* was scalded by the understandable hatred felt for the picture. Cynthia Fuchs of PopMatters opined that Pacino's "embarrassing ostentation stops just short of the hoo-ha that has haunted him since he first ran it in Brest's lamentable *Scent of a Woman*." *Total Film* opined: "As for the cameos from Christopher Walken and Al Pacino—fuhgeddaboudit. These Oscar-winners trot out their usual bag of tricks (Al's coiled fury, Walken's uncoiled nuttiness) and then bail out. It's small change rattling at the bottom of a battered wallet."

The reviews for the film itself were merciless. As Christopher Borrelli of the *Toledo Blade* amusingly and aptly put it: "[In *Gigli*] Ben Affleck has ... the power to attract and convert lesbians into heterosexuality, ... while simultaneously managing one of the worst Tony Soprano impressions ever. Here is a film that exists on another plane. It is so insane, so misguided, so Dadaesque, so Kafkaesque, you'll think I'm exaggerating. I'm not."

In other words, it stunk. Pacino's career was unaffected, but to date Martin Brest hasn't written or directed another picture. Protests from the gay community or advocates for the mentally challenged didn't matter so much to the studio as did the fact that the film was a major loser at the box office, never earning back its costs. Bennifer's inflated salaries hardly helped matters. Reportedly there was much studio tampering with the film before its release because of the media frenzy over the celebrity couple, but one has the feeling that it would never have been a good picture no matter how it was edited.

Angels in America

HBO, 2003 (MINI-SERIES)

Executive producers, Mike Nichols and Cary Brokaw; director, Mike Nichols; teleplay, Tony Kushner, from his stage play; cinematography, Stephen Goldblatt; music, Thomas Newman; editing, John Bloom and Antonia Van Drimmelen; production designer, Stuart Wertzel; art direction, John Kasarda. Running time: 352 min.

Cast

Al Pacino (*Roy Cohn*); Justin Kirk (*Prior Walter*); Ben Shenkman (*Louis Ironson*); Patrick Wilson (*Joe Pitt*); Jeffrey Wright (*Belize*); Meryl Streep (*Ethel

Rosenberg, etc.); Emma Thompson (*Nurse Emily*, etc.); Mary-Louise Parker (*Harper Pitt*); James Cromwell (*Cohn's doctor*); Brian Markinson (*Martin Heller*).

In 1985 New York City several characters begin to converge. Prior Walter (Justin Kirk), a gay man in his thirties, is abandoned by his lover, Louis Ironson (Ben Shenkman), when the former develops AIDS. Joe Pitt (Patrick Wilson) is a young conservative and closeted Mormon wooed for a Washington job by the equally closeted lawyer, Roy Cohn (Pacino). Belize (Jeffrey Wright), a sassy if steel-backed black gay nurse, winds up caring for a dying Cohn in the hospital even as an affair begins between Louis and Joe, who recognizes that he has no attraction for his wife, Harper (Mary Louise Parker). Joe goes back and forth between Louis and his wife, and is thrown out by both; Louis, who hates Joe's politics and homophobic legal decisions, has a violent, physical quarrel with him. Prior has a vision in which he climbs a ladder to Heaven, but opts for going back down to earth and whatever future he may have left. Louis tells Prior that he wants to come back to him, but Prior tells Louis that while he will always love him, he doesn't want him back.

The six-hour *Angels in America* has many other characters, with some of the actors doing double and triple duty in multiple roles. The play and the film that resulted also have many fantasy scenes and hallucinations, as well as discussions of differences in political ideologies, Jewish identity, gay identity, the scourge of AIDS, and the complexity of human relationships. Unfortunately, even in such a lengthy play, much of this is not explored very deeply, with the drama generally taking a backseat to ideology and politics. Because its themes were still fairly raw at the time of the play's premiere, *Angels* was seen by many as a political statement whose proponents would brook no dissension. The only naysayers, it was reasoned, were conservatives and homophobes, even though there were gay Jewish liberals who weren't necessarily carried away by a play that many found pretentious and tedious.

Part of the problem with *Angels*—a problem carried over to the film—was its loose, undefined structure, its too-weird mixture of fantasy with reality, and its blurring or merging of mismatched styles: from the sharply realistic to the fantastical to even a sitcom-like approach. Of course those were just the very things that the play and movie's proponents enjoyed, sitcoms and diatribes being less threatening and more comforting to a contemporary theater audience—as long as there are cute little quips once in a while the many deaths resulting from a terrible epidemic could be endured. (While comparisons can be odious, one must imagine that a critic who boldly states that *Angels* is "the greatest play ever written" has never seen, or possibly even heard of, *Long Day's Journey into Night*.)

The playwright, Tony Kushner, also wrote the screenplay for the HBO two-part mini-series. When he first worked on the screenplay, Kushner made the mistake of inserting camera angles and the like, until Mike Nichols told him that that was the job of the director and the camera man. "And there are things that you couldn't do in a play that you can do on film, obviously," said Kushner. "A lot of language from the play was preserved, but I learned that not all of it could be because of the intimacy of the screen experience ... you don't have the kind of cooling distance of a theatre space."

Not only does the human drama get lost in *Angels*, but there are moments of foolish contrivance, such as when Prior goes to the Mormon HQ to see Joe's mother simply because Joe has become involved with Louis. The whole business with Prior and Mrs. Pitt (an unreal character played badly by Meryl Streep) bonding makes little sense, and seems cobbled together just to give Streep as much running time as possible. The sequence when Mrs. Pitt, lost in Brooklyn, runs into a female street person (Emma Thompson) is pure sitcom and nothing more. At one point an angel (also played by Thompson) not only flies off with Prior, but winds up lifting up and making out with Mrs. Pitt, scenes that may be meant to be striking or theatrical but which only seem ludicrous. On the stage some of these moments may have worked, but in the more literal approach of film they backfire.

One thing that is certain about the film of *Angels* is that Al Pacino gives a superb performance as Roy Cohn, even if at times he appears to be Cohn as filtered through Pacino. That doesn't really make a difference as Pacino offers a mesmerizing portrait of the contradictory, infuriating, right-wing yet homosexual, pitiable, dying yet ever-defiant lawyer who stonily insists to his doctor (James Cromwell) that his illness is not AIDS but another kind of cancer. Cohn is a "heterosexual man who fools around with guys" because thinking of himself any other way means his clout will be, in his eyes, diminished. Cohn is the old-fashioned closet case whose self-hatred informs most, if not all, of his actions. Another top moment for Pacino is when he urges Joe to help him with his possible disbarment because he borrowed $500,000 from a client and never returned it. "I'll be a lawyer until my last day on earth," he says.

An even better scene has Cohn confronting Joe when the latter admits that he is gay and that he has left his wife and has a (temporary) boyfriend, Louis, which outrages and repulses the older man. According to Cohn, he convinced a judge to sentence alleged traitress Ethel Rosenberg to death, and she shows up in his fantasies during his final days when she expresses bemused contempt for him. (The sons of Julius and Ethel Rosenberg have claimed that their father was guilty, but their mother was framed.) Of course, the scenes between Cohn and Joe are just as fictional as the scenes between Cohn and

Ethel's ghost. Pacino has many excellent moments during the hospital sequences, when he lashes out in an almost demented fashion against Belize and other members of the hospital staff; Belize is not quite able to summon up some compassion for the pathetic figure.

The two main characters of the drama are Louis and Prior, with Joe and Harper Pitt being the secondary couple. Louis rails against the conservative Joe, but in some ways is much the better person despite his politics. Louis is a "shit" who walks out on Prior when he gets sick because he can't deal "with the smell and the sores." Ben Shenkman and Patrick Wilson are so good as, respectively, Louis and Joe, that it makes the reprehensible Louis a bit more palatable, and Joe more sympathetic than the playwright probably intended; Wilson especially adds a layer of sensitivity to his performance that informs Joe's confusion and his religious and sexual conflict, although he, too, can be quite selfish. As Prior, Justin Kirk is also good, although he tends to underplay perhaps a bit too much, and while the audience should feel sorry for the cruelly rejected Harper, it is hard to tell if it is her character or Mary-Louise Parker's sitcom-style acting that is the more irritating—but she is *very* irritating.

As Belize, Jeffrey Wright gives a strong performance, although he edges close to parody at times. Belize has a core of strength underneath the borderline "nelly" exterior. (Wright was the only original cast member of the play to appear in the film adaptation.) Emma Thompson is good as Prior's upbeat and compassionate nurse, although one senses Thompson hasn't any idea what she or anyone else is doing as the winged angel. Meryl Streep offers several stunt performances in the film (a male rabbi, the Mormon mother, and the dead Ethel Rosenberg, and is perhaps most successful in the last incarnation), but none of it could be called great acting by any stretch of the imagination.

For Al Pacino fans, one wishes that Pacino had opted out of the often pseudo-intellectual *Angels in America* and simply starred in a biopic of Roy Cohn, where his outstanding portrayal of this often wildly contradictory man could have taken center stage. Todd McCarthy in *Variety* wrote: "Just as there was no real precedent for the achievement *Angels in America* represented in the legitimate theater, so are there few film adaptations of stage works comparable to what Mike Nichols has done.... As Cohn, Pacino gets to percolate, steam and explode, and yet never gets mannered or goes over the top as he can easily do. He's sensational."

Simon Gallagher of *What Culture* had a more negative impression of the telefilm: "I find the series far too pretentious and posturing; it forces itself on the viewer, and doesn't cease until the final credits roll. Admittedly, it features some remarkable acting performances ... but I cannot shake off the unbearable feeling that it is overbearing and insists upon itself terribly."

Angels in America might have been a great play/telefilm if it had focused on the main story of Louis, Prior and Joe—there was certainly more than enough drama in that triangle situation and everything else going on in the three men's lives—but Kushner futzes around with way too much pretentious and unsubtle fiddle faddle that was indeed theatrical but ill-advised in spite of it. Many critics vastly over-rated the series because it was "serious" and "important" and was always on the side of political correctness, and people were afraid they'd seem bigoted toward gay men, insensitive toward AIDS sufferers, anti–Semitic, and—worse—unappreciative of Great Art if they didn't rave about it.

But many of these same admirers probably slept through most of it.

The Merchant of Venice

Sony, 2004

Executive producer, Michael Hammer; director, Michael Radford; screenplay, Michael Radford, from the play by William Shakespeare; cinematography, Benoit Delhomme; music, Jocelyn Pook; editing, Lucia Zucchetti; production design, Bruno Rubeo; art direction, Jon Bunker and Tamara Marini. Running time: 138 min.

Cast

Al Pacino (*Shylock*); Jeremy Irons (*Antonio*); Joseph Fiennes (*Bassanio*); Portia (*Lynn Collins*); Charlie Cox (*Lorenzo*); Heather Goldenhersh (*Nerissa*); Kris Marshall (*Gratiano*); John Sessions (*Salerio*); Gregor Fisher (*Solanio*); Zuleikha Robinson (*Jessica*).

Bassanio (Joseph Fiennes) asks his friend Antonio (Jeremy Irons) to borrow money on his behalf from the Jewish money lender, Shylock (Pacino). Shylock dislikes Antonio but agrees to the loan, insisting that if he doesn't get his money back he will take a literal pound of flesh from Antonio. Shylock's fury is heightened when he learns that his daughter, Jessica (Zuleikha Robinson), has run off with the Christian Lorenzo, and has taken much of his money with her. Despite other suitors, Bassanio wins the hand of the princess, Portia (Lynn Collins). Antonio forfeits on the loan, and Shylock demands his day in court, where Portia and her servant Nerissa (Heather Goldenhersh), disguised as men, argue Antonio's cause. Portia agrees that Shylock must get his pound of flesh, but also that Shylock's life is forfeit if he sheds one drop of Antonio's blood in the cutting. Stymied, Shylock is to lose everything until Antonio steps in. Portia gets her ring back.

Although his performance is by no means terrible, Pacino is badly miscast in *Merchant of Venice* and seems fairly odd throughout the movie, sometimes even perfunctory in his approach. He does have some memorable scenes, however, such as during his "if you prick us, do we not bleed?" speech as he makes a case for Jews being little different from Christians in the Things That Matter. He is also effective enough during the climax in court when he seems to shrivel up as he realizes that he has not only lost the case but may indeed lose everything he has. Shakespeare's play is undeniably anti–Semitic in certain aspects, but one can make a case for a sympathetic Shylock as well. At the start of the film version it is explained how in the Venice of 1596 Jews are locked up in a ghetto by the Christian majority and must always wear red hats when they venture out in public. Shylock's insistence on the pound of flesh may make him seem demented and evil but he is also reacting not only to years of oppression but also to his daughter's betrayal with yet another Christian.

The most impressive performances in the film actually come from Joseph Fiennes and especially Jeremy Irons, who handles every scene with deft perfection. Shakespeare scholars have questioned if Bassanio and Antonio have "special feelings" for one another with Irons disagreeing and Fiennes not only agreeing but planting a kiss on Irons's lips during an early sequence in the film. Antonio and Bassanio pledge that their love is greater than any friend or wife, but this could just as easily imply that wives, no matter how lovely, were second-class citizens in the day as to any homoeroticism. Charlie Cox and Kris Marshall are very good as, respectively, Lorenzo, Jessica's lover, and Gratiano, Nerissa's wife. Lynn Collins and Heather Goldenhersh do what they can as the princess and her friend, but their dressing up as men never quite works. *The Merchant of Venice* is handsomely produced and features beautiful Venetian settings.

The Merchant of Venice was held up for release for five years. Critical reaction was generally favorable, with mixed reactions for Pacino. David Stratton of *At the Movies* found that Pacino's "barnstorming Shylock might be an acquired taste," while Ian Nation of *Empire* found Pacino, "the Shakespeare addict, a joy to watch." Wally Hammond in *Time Out* opined: "This is Al Pacino's show and thankfully his Shylock is absorbing enough to carry the day. Adopting a guttural staccato, he assumes an intriguing figure driven as much by contempt and pride as he is by revenge; an orthodox authoritarian drawing on wells of controlled rage, he's also vulnerable enough to be deeply slighted (and isolated) by the desertion of his beloved daughter." Julian Wood of *FilmInk* wrote: "Pacino manages to lose his New York twang and gangsterish truculence, inhabiting the role in his own riveting way. We see what an actor's actor Pacino can be: he's careful and watchful; respectful of other actors' timing; and says his lines perfectly, resisting all temptation to grandstand." Most critics agreed that the film was tasteful and literate, if not always that exciting and certainly not politically correct.

Two for the Money

Universal, 2005

Executive producers, Dan Gilroy, Guy McElwaine, David Robinson, and Rene Russo; director, D. J. Caruso; screenplay, Dan Gilroy; cinematography, Conrad W. Hall; music, Christophe Beck; editing, Glen Scantlebury. Running time: 122 min.

Cast

Al Pacino (*Walter*); Matthew McConaughey (*Brandon*); Rene Russo (*Toni*); Armand Assante (*Novian*); Jeremy Piven (*Jerry*); Jaime King (*Alexandra*); Kevin Chapman (*Southie*); Ralph Garman (*Reggie*); Gedde Watanabe (*Milton*); Carly Pope (*Tammy*).

Brandon Lang (Matthew McConaughey) was a college football star until an injury on the field gave him a bum knee and derailed his career. "Football wasn't a sport," he explains. "It was my life." Now he has a radio show in which he predicts the winners of games. This brings him to the attention of Walter Abrams (Al Pacino), who runs the biggest sports gambling consultancy business in the country. Walter himself has not gambled in eighteen years due to an addiction, and has a heart condition which occasionally flattens him (but he's not above faking an attack). "Sports betting is a 200-billion-dollar-a-year business," Walter tells Brandon, which is illegal in forty-nine states; however, Walter's clients don't place bets with him but rather are *advised* on which teams and games to put their money on, for a fee. Walter decides the laid-back likable Lang needs a more dynamic approach, so he rechristens him "John Anthony" and has him join him on his TV show where he immediately begins displacing the former fair-haired boy, Jerry Sykes (Jeremy Piven). Brandon becomes more and more popular, keeps picking winners, and brings in more business, but he makes mistakes when he starts simply making hunches instead of doing research and applying what he knows. Walter treats Brandon like a son but also tries to control his life, then gets the paranoid notion that Brandon is sleeping with his wife, Toni (Rene Russo), who helped with "John Anthony's" make-over. Unbeknown to Toni, Walter has started gambling again, betting on Brandon's choices, and losing. After one last high-stakes game in which Brandon's picks, made with the toss of a coin, come true, he leaves the racket and becomes a coach for a junior league football team.

Two for the Money is one of several films in which Pacino's character acts as mentor to, and sort of "seduces," a younger man with dreams of money and power. Both McConaughey and Pacino are excellent—they play very well together—with the latter's charisma in full evidence. For instance, in one scene Walter walks into a meeting of recovering gambling addicts and tells the group that it's not winning they love, but losing, that it's only their "fucked up need to convince yourselves you exist" that drives them—then while they're digesting this he promptly hands out cards for his business! In another scene Walter bets Brandon that he can pick up a beautiful woman sitting with some men in a restaurant, but when Brandon wins the bet she later turns out to be a hooker for whose services Walter already paid. Pacino is fine in *Two for the Money* but his character is essentially glib and superficial, his part colorful yet oddly uninteresting at one and the same time. Because of this it's hard to point out those especially memorable moments that highlight one of his performances.

Rene Russo is given the nearly thankless job of playing Walter's wife in a type of "buddy" movie, but she acquits herself nicely in her several scenes (her husband, Dan Gilroy, wrote the screenplay). The always reliable Armand Assante and Craig Veroni also make their mark. Novian (Assante), urinates on Brandon and has his henchmen beat him up when he loses $30 million after taking Brandon's advice. Craig Veroni plays another client named Amir who is importuned by Brandon to bet much more than is good for him. Winning a lot of money at first, Amir is eventually wiped out—"I had a life!" he furiously tells Brandon.

But while *Two for the Money* is fast-paced, well acted and entertaining, with fine cinematography from Conrad Hall, it has a hollow core that keeps it from registering. The characters, although loosely based on real people, are not individuals the audience embraces or cares about, and the writing and editing do little to help. In one sequence Walter's wife angrily tells him that "we're done!' but the next time we see her she's happily at his side accompanying him—what happened?

The critics were not kind to *Two for the Money*, with Matthew Turner of *ViewLondon* opining that it was "a horribly confused mess, with sub-plots and entire characters simply disappearing into thin air" and Internet critic Cole Smithey stating, "Al Pacino can charm the birds from the trees, but in *Two For The Money* pigeons are the only species visiting." According to Scott Weinberg of *DVD Talk*, "Pacino's performance is only a few degrees shy of full-bore scenery-chewing, but the veteran actor stomps through this movie like a small Italian Godzilla."

Jeff Otto of *IGN Movies* was especially negative on Pacino, and other critics took the opportunity to take the star to task for what they considered an unsubtle approach to his latter-day filmic performances, despite the effectiveness of this approach in so many movies. "Pacino ranting and raving is nothing new," wrote Otto," but he takes the cake here. Not only does he at least tie his own freak-out time on screen in a single film, but he does so without the flair or passion of his past. This is Pacino as a caricature of Pacino. He's calm for the first part of the film, but you can see the ranting just waiting beneath. Once it unleashes, he's no longer intimidating, he's boring. As it goes on and on, it's funny, then sad. We've seen many of the greats go down the tubes in recent years. De Niro's name on a film means nothing these days. With a string [of bombs] like *Gigli*, *Simone* and *The Recruit*, have we lost all hope for the great Pacino, a brand name which has become the gold standard over the past 30 years? *Angels in America* and *Merchant of Venice* give us some hope, but *Two for the Money* is particularly disheartening."

Ethan Alter of *Film Journal International* offered Pacino a kind of backhanded compliment: "As Walter Abrams, New York's top sports-betting advisor, the actor doesn't just chew the scenery—he swallows it whole. While this performance doesn't equal Pacino's legendarily loopy turn in *The Devil's Advocate*, it's the only thing in the movie that holds your attention."

James Bardinelli of *ReelViews* appreciated what Pacino was trying to do: "The role of gambling honcho Walter Abrams is tailor-made for Al Pacino. It's great fun watching Pacino tear into this role, knowingly and calculatingly overacting. By delivering all the expected rants and mini-explosions, Pacino creates in Walter a character who is not only larger-than-life, but intense and charismatic."

As was often the case, audiences seemed to like the movie somewhat more than the critics did.

88 Minutes

Columbia, 2007

Producer, director, Jon Avnet; screenplay, Gary Scott Thompson; cinematography, Denis Lenoir; music, Ed Shearmur; editing, Peter E. Berger. Running time: 108 min.

Cast

Al Pacino (*Jack Gramm*); Alicia Witt (*Kim*); Leelee Sobieski (*Lauren Douglas*); Amy Brenneman (*Shelly Barnes*); William Forsythe (*Frank Parks*); Ben McKenzie (Mike Stempt); Neal McDonough (*Jon Forster*); Stephen Moyer (*Guy LaForge*); Christopher Redman (*Jeremy Guber*); Brendan Fletcher (*Johnny D'Franco*).

Jack Gramm (Al Pacino) is a forensic psychiatrist with the FBI and a professor at a college in Seattle. Nine years ago Gramm's testimony was instrumental in getting serial killer Jon Forster (Neal McDonough)—the Seattle Slayer—convicted and sentenced to death. Now Forster is about to be executed, and Gramm gets a phone call in which a disguised voice tells him that he has exactly 88 minutes left to live. In jailhouse interviews Forster has always maintained that Gramm told lies about him on the witness stand, but a paranoid Gramm wonders which person might be assisting the killer on the outside. Virtually everyone Gramm encounters comes under suspicion: his teaching assistant, Kim (Alicia Witt); brash student Mike Stempt (Benjamin McKenzie); a campus security guard named Johnny D'Franco (Brendan Fletcher); Kim's husband, Guy LaForge (Stephen Moyer). Complicating matters is that an unknown person is committing possibly copycat-style murders à la the Seattle Slayer, leading everyone to wonder if Forster might be innocent after all. Worse, the victims are women Gramm knows: Dale Morris (Kristina Copeland), who was one of his students; Sara Pollard (Leah Cairns), with whom Gramm had a one-night stand. Lauren (Leelee Sobieski), another of Gramm's students, is attacked but survives. Throughout the day, as Gramm tries to uncover who's gunning for him, he finds more menacing messages, and receives a tape recording of his murdered sister's final moments as she was tortured for 88 minutes some years before. When the true killer (actually Forster's appeals attorney using a pseudonym) is exposed, Gramm tells Forster, anxiously waiting to hear from his pawn, that *he* has "twelve hours to live."

88 Minutes was the first twisty psychological shocker that Pacino made since *Cruising*. (The only gay character in the latest movie, Shelley, is a pretty positively drawn lesbian, even if she lets herself get distracted by the murderer, who actually seems to be in love with Forster.) The movie with its plot turns, red herrings, anti-climaxes, and the sub-theme of terrible past incidents affecting the present—plus that fact that no one is who he seems to be—remind one of nothing so much as an American variation of a *giallo* film by Italian thriller director Dario Argento. Slick and fast-paced, it moves too quickly for one to have time to wonder what's actually going on.

Sporting a becoming goatee, Pacino offers a convincing portrayal of a very self-controlled and somewhat egotistical individual. His two most memorable scenes come when he confronts Forster on television, and the affecting sequence when he tells Kim what happened to his kid sister and the crushing guilt he feels because of it. (Gramm left his kid sister alone in his apartment when he went to a meeting.) Although he only has a couple of scenes, Neal McDonough also makes a vivid impression as Forster, and Alicia Witt is competent and appealing as Kim. The other supporting performances are all at least satisfactory.

Although *88 Minutes* is considerably entertaining and even suspenseful, it was skewered by the critics. More than one called it the worst movie of the year. Surprisingly, some critics objected to the gore, of which there wasn't much, aside from an early scene depicting the murder of one twin Asian-American girl and the attempted murder of her sister (but while disturbing, this is not distressingly graphic). Anthony Lane of the *New Yorker* claimed, "Nothing would give me keener pleasure than to reveal the identity of the killer, but a day after seeing the film I have genuinely forgotten," while Michael Phillips of the Chicago *Tribune* opined, "The preposterous *88 Minutes* is a serial killer movie starring Al Pacino's festival of hair." Wrote Matthew Turner in *ViewLondon*: "Ridiculous and ultimately disappointing thriller that stays just about watchable thanks to an amusing pair of performances by Shouty Al and his hairpiece," while David Edwards of the *Daily* Mirror opined, "Pacino looks half asleep throughout, no doubt concentrating solely on his cheque, while the script is a catalogue of clichés and contrivances."

The audiences didn't hate the movie quite as much, though it was probably best enjoyed by horror fans, who had certainly sat through more than their share of far-fetched movies about psycho-killers, and didn't particular object to the less logical turns of the plot. It was probably not apparent to most viewers that once Gramm gets the first phone call, the movie supposedly proceeds in real time—88 minutes—until the conclusion, minus the lengthy credits (which probably didn't add twenty minutes to the actual running time).

Al Pacino was nominated for a Razzie award as "worst actor." His performance is by no means awful, and it's hard to believe that those who tender the Razzies couldn't find a truly wretched performance to nominate in Pacino's place. Leelee Sobieski also got nominated, even though she did her best with an implausible role. *88 Minutes* is not really a totally terrible movie, but because critics felt the material was below Pacino's standards, and a waste of his abilities, they rushed to come out with witty ways of panning the picture. Pacino would make much worse movies—and far better ones as well.

Ocean's Thirteen

Warner Brothers, 2007

Producer, Jerry Weintraub; director, Steven Soderbergh; screenplay, David Koppelman and David Levien; cinematography, Steven Soderbergh (as Peter Andrews); music, David Holmes; editing, Stephen Mirrione; production design, Philip Messina; art direction, Doug Meerdink and Tony Fanning. Running time: 122 min.

CAST

Al Pacino (*Willy Bank*); George Clooney (*Danny Ocean*); Brad Pitt (*Rusty Ryan*); Elliott Gould (*Reuben*); Carl Reiner (*Saul Bloom*); Ellen Barkin (*Abigail*); David Paymer (*V.U.P.*); Matt Damon (*Linus*); Andy Garcia (*Terry Benedict*); Don Cheadle (*Basher*).

Ocean's Thirteen was a sequel to *Ocean's Twelve*, itself a sequel to *Ocean's Eleven*, itself a remake of the 1960 Rat Pack film *Ocean's 11*. In this, Danny Ocean (George Clooney) and his pals team up again to get even with hotel magnate Willy Bank (Pacino) after he screws their friend Reuben (Elliott Gould) in a new casino deal, putting him in the hospital. Manipulating things behind the scenes and secretly paying off some of the staff, they make sure that everything that could possibly go wrong, goes wrong. Knowing how Bank covets all of his hotels winning the Royal Review Board 5 Diamonds Award, the gang ensures that the Royal Review representative (David Paymer) is treated monstrously by the hotel. Clooney goes to his old adversary, rival hotel owner Terry Benedict (Andy Garcia), who also hates Bank, to solicit a loan to buy a machine that, on opening night, can create the illusion of an earthquake. Benedict gives

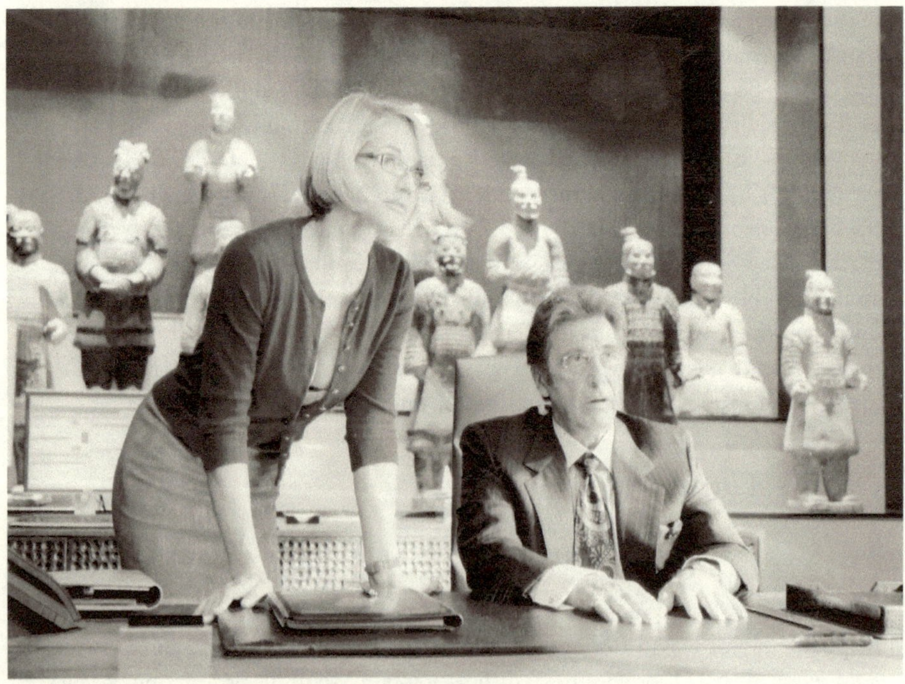

Loathsome casino owner Willy Bank (Pacino) and his right-hand woman, Abigail Sponder (Ellen Barkin), in the comedy-thriller *Ocean's Thirteen* (2007).

them the money, but insists that they rob Bank of the diamonds that he buys each time he wins the award. Trouble is, the Bank hotel and casino has a spanking new security system, so an elaborate scheme unfolds to undermine it at the proper time, when Linus (Matt Damon) is seducing Bank's cougar assistant, Abigail (Ellen Barkin). The crew gets the diamonds, ruin Bank's opening night and his chances of getting the 5 Diamonds award, while the poor put-upon Royal Review representative, who had an absolutely miserable time at the hotel, wins $11 million at a slot machine.

Ocean's Thirteen is amiable nonsense, although its leisurely pacing ensures that it has less suspense than an average episode of *Mission: Impossible*. As the villain of the piece, Pacino basically gives a good performance, out-acting most of the other principals, although on occasion you do get the sensation that he's merely wandering onto the set to say his lines and then wandering off to do something of infinitely higher importance. The best scenes have Pacino interacting with two other old pros, Elliott Gould and Carl Reiner, the elder members of Clooney's team, and the ones who are most impressive in the picture. Compared to them, Clooney and Brad Pitt simply saunter through the movie in imitation of Sinatra and company but altogether in a different league. Matt Damon, Andy Garcia, Don Cheadle, and David Paymer are more on the mark, but, ironically, this buddy movie is almost stolen by Ellen Barkin, Pacino's co-star from *Sea of Love*, in a funny, fascinating turn as Bank's sexy, efficient, if possibly neurotic, assistant, Abigail Sponder.

It's fun to watch Pacino as Bank telling a vaguely interested maid how his hotels *always* win the 5 Diamonds award, and there's a Pacino blast when he's told that the security system is being adversely affected by some device. "Everyone in this room! Empty your pockets *now*!" he screams. Audiences emptied their pockets of some cash to see the movie, which also generally pleased critics who admitted it was no world-beater, but to date there has been no *Ocean's Fourteen*. Michael Atkinson of the *Boston Phoenix* described *Ocean's Thirteen* as "a pastry of a movie, airy, insubstantial, and meant to fill in the gaps between heartier meals." Rene Rodriguez in the *Miami Herald* felt: "When a movie keeps you this entertained without insulting your intelligence, it's hard to complain."

Righteous Kill

OVERTURE, 2008

Producer/director, Jon Avnet; screenplay, Russell Gewirtz; cinematography, Denis Lenoir; music, Ed Shearmur; editing, Paul Hirsch. Running time: 101 min.

CAST

Al Pacino (*Rooster*); Robert De Niro (*Turk*); Carla Gugino (*Karen*); Curtis Jackson/50 Cent (*Spider*); Brian Dennehy (*Hingis*); John Leguizamo (*Detective Perez*); Donnie Wahlberg (*Detective Riley*); Malachy McCourt (*Father Connell*); Barry Primus (*Prosky*); Trilby Glover (*Jessica*).

Turk (Robert De Niro) and Rooster (Al Pacino) have been police officers and partners for many years. They watch with dismay as a child murderer, Charles Randall, walks due to a technicality. Later, Turk confesses to Rooster that he framed Randall for another murder that he didn't commit; at least the monster is in jail. As the movie proceeds, Turk—via a taped video—seems to be confessing to a series of murders of lowlifes, rapists, pedophiles, and drug dealers who have managed to escape the law. As these vigilante killings continue, Lt. Hingis (Brian Dennehy) assigns Turk and Rooster, among others, to investigate. Younger cops Perez (John Leguizamo) and Riley (Donnie Wahlberg) become convinced that it must be a cop that is doing the murders, at which a furious Turk can only scoff. One victim survives his shooting and is placed under watch in the hospital until he wakes up and can identify his assailant. The vigilante breaks in and assaults Turk's girlfriend, Detective Karen Corelli (Carla Gugino). Perez and Riley decide to set a trap for Turk, whom they are convinced is the perp, with the cooperation of drug dealer Spider (Curtis Jackson, a.k.a. 50 Cent). It backfires, however, when Turk shows that he is on to their scheme. Not much later Spider is shot and killed by the vigilante—who turns out not to be Turk, but Rooster. (The tapes actually showed Turk reading Rooster's confession.) Rooster lost faith in his partner and the justice system when Turk stepped outside the law and framed Randall. In a final standoff, Turk shoots Rooster.

The idea of a cop or some other law-enforcement official becoming disgusted with the justice system and turning vigilante is not a new one. In the '90s DC Comics' *Vigilante* presented a prosecutor (then judge) who becomes a costumed force for justice and works outside the law, but that series actually had more on its mind, and delved into the morality of the situation, much more than *Righteous Kill*, which is not really about vigilantism at all. Instead, the film is basically a movie deal: let's get Pacino and De Niro together again—like *The Godfather Part II* and *Heat*—pile on a lot of cop stereotypes and clichés (those nicknames!) and not worry too much if the script even makes sense. After all this is *Pacino and De Niro*—the audience won't give a damn. Such cynical posturing among filmmakers didn't fool the critics and it didn't much fool the fans, either.

First, the film asks us to accept that a veteran like Turk, who's probably seen *many* criminals walk during his career, would risk his job, pension, jail time, etc., to frame a man, knowing this would mean that a) the case would be closed on this particular crime and the real perpetrator would go free, and b) if it ever got out, *every single case* he and his partner had ever handled would have to be reviewed, with the specter of tainted evidence meaning many more criminals they'd arrested would go free. One might almost accept that Rooster would figure if his partner could do something a little haywire, framing somebody, the next logical step would be to simply *kill* the perps, only the film gives no real psychological basis for this conversion from honest cop to multiple murderer. (The film keeps referring to the vigilante as a "serial killer," even though serial killers stalk a certain kind of prey generally for sexual reasons, which is not the case with Rooster.)

Since the audience is led to believe that Turk is the killer, the movie has minimal suspense until the final quarter, when things seem to make even less sense than they do in the beginning. It's never quite explained why Rooster finds it necessary to assault fellow cop and Turk's girlfriend, Karen, unless he's hoping she or Turk will kill him in a rage (he figures the man in the hospital will finger him sooner or later). Even so, she is hardly a drug dealer or rapist. But then the treatment of Detective Karen Corelli is like something out of the '70s, or earlier. She squeals in terror when the (unseen) Rooster attacks her in her home, but doesn't fight back or even seem capable of doing so—an NYPD detective? When Perez rudely slaps her behind she only smiles. The character's whole purpose in the film seems to be to give De Niro someone to have sex with, even though she looks young enough to be his granddaughter. *Righteous Kill* is one of these old-fashioned buddy movies, albeit twisted, in which women are only good for one thing, and the aging actors have to bed young babes on screen to feed their egos. (Couldn't they have cast a perfectly attractive middle-aged lady?) De Niro's half-naked body is not a pretty sight, but at least Pacino spares us that. Then there's some politically incorrect, mostly racist dialogue which some would excuse since "all cops talk that way," only *not* all cops talk that way these days. "Normally $200,000 a year corporate lawyers are smarter than an African American junkie hooker," Rooster tells a pretty coke-snorting witness, and accuses Perez and Riley of watching Turk like "gay hawks," whatever that means.

Still, if nothing else, *Righteous Kill* is slick and fast-paced and holds the attention even as it becomes increasingly silly. One cathartic scene has the vigilante blowing away a pedophile priest in the confessional. The performances certainly don't redeem the film. De Niro has the edge on Pacino, however, who "acts" all through the movie with his usual, often perfunctory, shtick. While it might be unfair to say he phones in his performance—although more than one critic did, as they also did with De Niro—he is severely hampered by the fact that the screenwriter has provided no real—or realistic—character for him to play. The other actors all have too little screen time to make much of an impression.

The critics savaged *Righteous Kill*, calling it a "murky, muddled, miserable mess" (Ali Gray of the movie review site *The Shiznit*) and saying "as far as bad movies go, *Righteous Kill* is something of a zenith" (Rob Humanick of *Projection Booth*). Rene Rodriguez in the Miami *Herald* opined: "The movie, which has more than 10 credited producers, feels like one of those slick, for-the-money projects Hollywood studios cook up via graph charts and marketing surveys." Sonny Bunch in the *Washington Times* declared that "the worst [thing] about *Righteous Kill* is that there's probably a perfectly acceptable procedural thriller somewhere in the mountain of clichés and stupidity that riddle the film."

Too true, unfortunately.

You Don't Know Jack

HBO, 2010

Executive producer/director, Barry Levinson; teleplay, Adam Mazer; cinematography, Eigil Bryld; music, Marcelo Zarvos; editing, Aaron Yanes. Running time: 134 min.

CAST

Al Pacino (*Jack Kevorkian*); Brenda Vaccaro (*Margo Janus*); John Goodman (*Neal Nicol*); Susan Sarandon (*Janet Good*); Deirdre O'Connell (*Linda*); Cotter Smith (*Dick Thompson*); Adam Driver (*Glen Stetson*); Jacqueline Knapp (*Mrs. Gale*): Jonathan Teague Cook (*Hugh Gale*); Todd Susman (*Stan Levy*).

Detroit doctor Jack Kevorkian (Pacino) believes that suffering people have a right to die with dignity, and offers his free services to dying or severely ill people who want help in committing suicide. (Jack sets up the equipment, then lets the patient use it, when they're ready, to kill themselves—in this way he himself is not actually killing anyone, at least at first.) Kevorkian comments that the current method of letting terminal people die—simply allowing them to starve themselves until they expire—is the "Nazi method of execution." His opponents claim that he doesn't give people enough time to change their minds, and that some of his patients—or victims—are not really terminal and are simply suffering from depression. Jack, who can be difficult and dyspeptic, has three important people in his life: his supportive sister, Margo (Brenda Vaccaro); his friend, Neal (John Goodman), a divorced man who is living in a storage unit and who is also supportive; and Janet Good (Susan Sarandon), who founded a chapter of the Hemlock Society in Michigan and who has an almost love-hate thing going with the doctor. Kevorkian becomes known as "Dr. Death," is besieged by crazy religionists, and is arrested more than once, but since there's nothing on the books about assisting a suicide, the charges never stick or he is acquitted. "Who cares what people think?" he argues. "It's what my patient *feels*" that matters. When Janet develops pancreatic cancer, Jack assists her in her own suicide. Kevorkian, who has assisted with 130 suicides, has a sharp attorney named Geoffrey Fieger (Danny Huston), but when he is arrested for murder after he injects a man with lethal chemicals, he foolishly acts as his own lawyer, is convicted, and sent to prison.

Kevorkian is a fascinating and meaty role to play, as he is seen as a hero by some and a demon by others. He helps take people out of their misery, but he is creepily unemotional throughout, almost as if he's a ghoul. Besides being strange, Kevorkian is at times mean and obnoxious to his sister—causing a temporary rift—and to others and is often unpleasant and egotistical, this evidenced by his acting as his own lawyer after his arrest. One senses that something in Kevorkian's character makes him enjoy playing God. Pacino, in an excellent performance, brings all of these contradictory facets of the man to life. Aside from a few cutesy Al Pacino–type moments, he completely loses himself within the character. One of his best scenes is when Kevorkian explains to Janet how he watched his mother suffer—it was as if she had an agonizing "toothache in every bone"—while the doctors did their best to keep her alive, which was not what she wanted. Another excellent and difficult scene is the heartbreaking moment when Kevorkian must take on more of a role in helping the elderly Hugh (Jonathan Teague Cook) expire as his wife, Mrs. Gale (Jacqueline Knapp), tearfully looks on; this leads to his arrest. When the prosecutor compares Kevorkian's actions and euthanasia in general to the genocide of the Holocaust, both Kevorkian and Mrs. Gale are outraged.

Brenda Vaccaro is so good as Margo that she almost walks off with the movie; because of her brother's actions Margo is fired from her job and eventually suffers a fatal heart attack. Susan Sarandon offers a highly memorable portrait of Janet Good. Danny Huston is very effective as the brash lawyer Fieger, as is Logan Crawford as radio host Bob Bender. John Goodman and Cotter Smith are fine as Kevorkian's best friend and chief opponent, respectively. Jonathan Teague Cook and Jacqueline Knapp offer superb and sensitive portrayals of Mr. and Mrs. Gale, and there are other fine vignettes of Kervorkian's patients, would-be patients, and loved ones, including Sandra Seacat as Janet Adkins, a woman with Alzheimer's, and Neil Brooks Cunningham as her husband; and Deborah Hedwall as Melody Youk, the wife of a paralyzed man; among others. One of the most affecting portrayals is by Adam Driver as Glen

Stetson, a young man who set himself on fire when he learned that he would never be able to walk again. Kevorkian tells him that he is understandably depressed, but that there are things that can be done for him, and turns him down. Some of these vignettes are so raw and well acted that they seem like documentary footage, but aren't.

If there is any problem with *You Don't Know Jack* it is that it glosses over the more disturbing criticisms of Kevorkian, not the objections of the religionists, but of opponents who state that many of his patients might have lived quite a while longer, or may have had no serious illness. For instance, Janet Adkins's Alzheimer's does not seem that advanced (of course, she has to be able to consent), and other patients seem to be depressed for very good reasons, but depression alone isn't always a good reason for taking one's own life. Kevorkian feels it's a quality of life issue and feels that if you want to die you have a right to do so; it's only after criticism that he refuses to assist certain people, like the aforementioned Glen Stetson. Kevorkian is shown assisting Janet Good to commit suicide, but it is not known if he was actually at her side at the time. Oddly, the *Detroit News* reported that an autopsy showed that Good had absolutely no signs of pancreatic cancer. This is not mentioned in the movie.

You Don't Know Jack won generally favorable reviews, as did Pacino. "*You Don't Know Jack* presents the maestro [Pacino] a golden thespian opportunity in Jack Kevorkian, the brazen, medically determined pathologist who brought assisted suicide to the front page," wrote Brian Orndorf of *DVD Talk*. "Finding the shadows and the soapbox, Pacino is masterful in this uneasy, thought-provoking drama." On the other hand, Verne Gay of *Newsday* offered this harsh and somewhat inexplicable assessment: "As Kevorkian, Pacino comes perilously close to mimicking Peter Falk as Columbo. He shuffles, mumbles, charms and bloviates.... Pacino's performance feels unmoored because there's no one place to moor it. Or perhaps there are too many."

The Son of No One

ANCHOR BAY, 2011

Producer/writer/director, Dito Montiel; cinematography, Benoit Delhomme; music, Jonathan Elias and David Wittman; editing, Jake Pushinsky. Running time: 90 min.

CAST

Al Pacino (*Detective Stanford*); Channing Tatum (*Jonathan White*); Ray Liotta (*Captain Mathers*); Katie Holmes (*Kerry White*); James Ransone (*Officer Pru-*

denti); Tracy Morgan (*Vincent Carter*); Juliette Binoche (*Lauren Bridges*); Lemon Andersen (*Geronimo*); Brian Gilbert (*Young Vinnie*); Sean Cregan (*Martinez*).

Jonathan White (Channing Tatum) is a young cop with a wife, Kerry (Katie Holmes), and a sickly young daughter, and has been reassigned to his father's old precinct in Queens. He is saddled with an asshole of a partner, a sexist, homophobic jerk named Prudenti (James Ransone). Years ago, when White was a boy nicknamed "Milk" (Jake Cherry), he lived in the Queensboro projects with his grandmother. He shot and killed a junkie who threatened him, then days later kills another man who kicks his dog down the stairs, killing him as well. The only person who knows what he did is his black buddy, Vinnie (Brian Gilbert), who is having sex with his mother's boyfriend and is later institutionalized. Detective Charles Stanford (Al Pacino), who knew Milk's father, questions him, and decides to bury the truth—nobody cared about the two dead men anyway. In the present day, an unknown person is sending letters to *Queens Gazette* reporter Loren Bridges (Juliette Binoche), in which the unsolved murders in the projects are mentioned. The latest letter suggests that a cop's reputation is on the line. Johnathan goes to see the grown-up Vinnie (Tracy Morgan), who swears to him that he never told anyone what happened. He also confronts Loren, who tells him "a mucky pup is the son of a cop. You look like the son of no one"; she is shot to death a short time later. White's boss, Captain Marion Mathers (Ray Liotta), takes Jonathan to see the older Detective Stanford, with Prudenti in attendance, and he is told to go about his business and forget the whole thing—Stanford's pension, and Mather's reputation and future, are both endangered. Realizing that they killed Loren and are sure to kill Vinnie, he goes back to the projects but can't stop Vinnie and Mathers from murdering each other. Vinnie's sister, Vicki (Decorte Snipes), sends White a letter confessing that it was she who sent the notes to the newspaper. Jonathan, who, in essence, did kill two people while still a boy, goes back to his life without benefit of therapy.

The Son of No One combines police corruption, cover-ups, unsolved crimes, several murders, and dangerous old secrets and still manages to be a tedious mess. The first half of the movie meanders back and forth from 1986 to the present day (actually not long after 9/11) in a confusing fashion that nevertheless gives away all of its secrets. There is some passing suspense as to who might be sending the notes to the reporter, but this aspect doesn't amount to much, as there are few suspects. There are no likable characters; even Young Milk and Vinnie are both a little creepy. White's little girl (Ursula Parker) is adorable but hasn't much to do with the story. The film was written, produced and directed by Dito Montiel, who fails except as producer, and there he had help from a whole slew of executive producers/assistants. Channing Tatum walks through the movie looking vaguely troubled and little else. Liotta and Ransone are competent, but the actors who play both the young and older Vinnies make more of a mark. Poor Katie Holmes has as little to do in this as she does in *Jack and Jill,* in which Pacino also appeared. Scenes with actors playing assorted weirdoes and crazy types dealing with nasty cop stereotypes in the precinct house somehow don't ring true. It took two composers, Jonathan Elias and David Wittman, to come up with the sleep-inducing musical score.

As for Pacino, one can't imagine why he bothered with this film unless he was paid awfully well for what might have amounted to two days' work. He is in his bemused mode, which is good enough for the picture, but it has to be said that he does nothing for the movie and the movie certainly does nothing for him. In his "present day" sequence he still shows his wonderful forcefulness at one point, but you get the odd impression that this is simply some strange man doing an Al Pacino impersonation, albeit a damned good one. Critics were deservedly rough on the picture, and a few were even rough on Al. "The end result is yet another ineffective endeavor from a curiously incompetent filmmaker, with Montiel's ongoing ability to receive funding for his efforts nothing short of head-scratching," wrote David Nusair in *Reel Film Reviews.* Stephen Holden, in the *New York Times,* blasted: "Mr. Tatum's performance [is] one of the year's most wooden, expressionless star turns.... Mr. Pacino and Mr. Liotta amble through their paces, but the screenplay works against them. *The Son of No One* self-destructs in a ludicrous, ineptly directed anticlimactic rooftop showdown in which bodies pile up, and nothing makes a shred of sense."

Lou Leminick of the *New York Post* delivered the final blow: " ... Pacino's character returns ... so the star can deliver the latest hammy turn of this paycheck phase of his career.... Ineptly written and directed, the nihilistic *The Son of No One* flaunts an attitude best summed up by a cynical Pacino—'A man has to live with s–t.' Maybe so, Al, but audiences have the option of skipping this bomb."

Wilde Salomé

SNEAKY PETE PRODUCTIONS, 2011

Executive producer, Beni Atoori; director, Al Pacino; screenplay, Al Pacino from the play by Oscar Wilde; cinematography, Benoît Delhomme, Robert Leacock, Denis Maloney and Jeremy Weiss; music, Jeff Beal; editing, Pasquale Buba, David Leonard, Stan Salfas and Roberto Silvi. Running time: 95 min.

Cast

Al Pacino (*King Herod/Himself*); Jessica Chastain (*Salome*); Kevin Anderson (*John the Baptist/Himself*); Estelle Parsons (*Herself*); Roxanne Hart (*Herodias*).

While Pacino was performing as King Herod in Oscar Wilde's *Salome* in Los Angeles in 2006—he had performed it twice before on Broadway—and making a film of the movie as well (which was released two years later), he also wrote and directed this documentary, which was not released in the U.S. until 2014. "It's not a movie about a play," he said in his documentary, "it's a movie about inspiration." Pacino used the documentary to express his fascination with Oscar Wilde as well as his love for his work, much as he did for Shakespeare in *Looking for Richard*. With the cameras following him, Pacino explores the life and art of Wilde, traveling to the Irish writer's London home and other places that were associated with him. There is a trip to the Oscar Wilde LGBT bookshop in New York, and Pacino appears as Wilde himself in a staged scene when his lover "Bosie," a.k.a. Lord Alfred Douglas (Jack Huston), and his friend Robert Ross (Richard Cox) are importuning him to flee London so he doesn't have to go to jail; Pacino appears only for a few seconds and has no dialogue.

There is much discussion of Wilde's marriage, his affair with Lord Douglas, the suit filed against Bosie's father, Wilde's subsequent arrest and imprisonment, and his exile and death at age forty-six. Wilde's grandson insists that Oscar must have loved his wife because there was no need to use her as a "smokescreen" as the oppressive anti-homosexual laws were still in the future at the time of their marriage. Wilde may indeed have loved, in some fashion, his wife and certainly his children, but his true overwhelming passion was clearly for *men*.

Pacino also travels to the actual location of King Herod's palace in the Judean desert; this is so striking that despite it being in ruins one wishes the later adaptation of *Salome* could have been filmed there. The documentary shows a bit of conflict between Pacino and Estelle Parsons, the director of the stage version of *Salome*. "You should have scheduled the movie after the run of the play," she tells him. Producers argue about whether Pacino is only doing the play because of the film version, or the other way around. Some theater patrons are annoyed that this is a staged modern dress reading of the play. As noted, Pacino did his film adaptation of *Salome* during the run of the stage production, using the same actors, and is seen in the documentary showing a group of people a rough cut of that film. When the lights go up, it looks as if the people in the audience have been attending a funeral instead of a screening, and the look on Estelle Parson's face is priceless.

Interspersed throughout the film are comments about Wilde from the likes of Gore Vidal and even Bono of U2, who pronounces Salome with the emphasis on the middle syllable! At one point a journalist asks Pacino, "Where did you get that voice you use as Herod? Is he fey at all? Is he bisexual? Does he have that kind of power?" To which a somewhat annoyed and distracted Pacino replies, "Of course." (Of course, suggesting that Pacino's interpretation makes Herod gay or bisexual because of the higher pitch of his voice is ridiculous.) Much of the footage in the movie is not about Wilde at all but shows lengthy scenes from the stage production and from the movie, including the entire climax.

Wilde Salomé is not as effective as *Looking for Richard*, especially as Pacino's performance as Herod is on record in its entirety, thanks to *Salome*. Some saw *Wilde Salomé* almost as a vanity production, and essentially an ad for the film adaptation that was even longer than the movie it was promoting. As an in-depth biography of Wilde it failed because anyone with an interest in the author already knew all of his history. Jay Weissberg of *Variety* was unimpressed: "Pacino as both helmer and star fails to make clear the source of this obsession; nor does he demonstrate a particularly focused understanding of the play or Oscar Wilde." However, Geoffrey McNab of the *Independent* found it to be "an eccentric, quixotic but highly enjoyable affair."

Jack and Jill

COLUMBIA, 2011

Executive producer, Steve Koren; director, Dennis Dugan; screenplay, Adam Sandler and Steve Koren; cinematography, Dean Cundey; music, Rupert Gregson-Williams and Waddy Wachtel; editing, Tom Costain. Running time: 91 min.

CAST

Al Pacino (*Al Pacino*); Adam Sandler (*Jack/Jill*); Katie Holmes (*Erin*); Elodie Tougne (*Sofia*); Rohan Chand (*Gary*); David Spade (*Monica*); Eugenio Derbez (*Felipe*); Nick Swardson (*Todd*); Tim Meadows (*Ted*); Allen Covert (*Otto*).

Quite a few people wondered how on earth *Al Pacino* wound up in a movie starring Adam Sandler—who plays two roles no less. The answer is simple. Pacino relished the opportunity to spoof himself playing "Al Pacino" in a comedy with a not-bad premise and a fairly funny script—although many critics would by no means agree.

Jack (Adam Sandler) is an advertising man who lives in Los Angeles. His twin sister, Jill (Adam Sandler), who lives in New York, is coming out for a holiday visit, which he dreads. Jill has a good heart but she can be overly needy, loud, crude, neurotic, abrasive, highly gauche, and borderline obnoxious. Another problem Jack has is that one of his clients, Duncan Donuts, wants Al Pacino for a commercial—Pacino will be spokesperson for their new "Dunkachino"—which he is certain the actor will refuse to do, and he has only one month to get him to sign. Jack and Jill run into Pacino at a basketball game—Pacino remembers Jack and calls him "Popcorn" because at a movie theater the latter was kind enough to replace Pacino's kid's spilled popcorn with his own, but he is more fascinated with Jill. Jack hopes that the actor's attraction to his sister will play to his advantage but when she finds out what he has in mind she's insulted and Jack, in drag, has to take her place. Jack eventually shows Jill that he loves her and she is definitely a part of the family. Jill is more interested in Felipe (Eugenio Derbez), her brother's gardener, than she is in Pacino, but at the end of the film we see Pacino rapping and dancing—quite adroitly—as he does a commercial for the new ""Dunkachino."

Like most Adam Sandler films, *Jack and Jill* got a terrible critical drubbing but made a great deal of money. Strangely some fans thought the picture would destroy Sandler's career even though he's probably made much worse. The basic idea is a good one, but as in every "Adam Sandler" movie there are certain conventions it must follow, such as there has to be more than one flatulence joke, and people must behave stupidly for no other apparent reason than that it's in the script. Some jokes are dragged on beyond any point where they can still be funny and the whole tone is sophomoric, to say the least. Sandler's performance is not bad as either Jack or his sister, but Jill can be awfully hard to take at times, annoying the audience even more than she does her brother. "The good news is that Sandler is marginally better in drag than he is playing himself," said Graham Young in the *Birmingham Mail*. Elodie Tougne and Rohan Chand are adorable as Jack's children, and Eugenio Derbez makes an impression playing not only the gardener but his rather weird grandmother; Katie Holmes is cute and okay as Jack's wife. In a scene where Jill runs home to New York for her first New Year's Eve alone since the death of her mother, she is taunted by an old rival named Monica (David Spade, who probably looks better in drag than he does normally).

Then there's Pacino, who gives the best performance and is the main reason to see the movie. He seems to be having a ball good-naturedly making fun of his image, whether he is hiding behind a beard and shades at a game, eyeing the not-so-lovely Jill as if she were some succulent morsel, trying to slap the make on Jack-in-disguise-as-Jill in his Hollywood love pit, doing a rap song for coffee while boogie-ing audaciously across the Duncan Donuts set, or telling

Sandler, with a no-nonsense directness, "Get me the girl" in exchange for his services. When Pacino first appears at the game, the movie star hopes not to be recognized—just as they flash a huge picture of him on the giant screen.

Pacino is attracted to Jill because she comes from the Bronx like he does, and he thinks she has a certain raw—if invisible to others—appeal. Later, Pacino is so anxious to hear from Jill that he answers his cell phone in the middle of a stage performance. When Jack takes Jill's place and goes on the date with Pacino in her stead, Al tells Jill-Jack, "I think you're more feminine," once they are ensconced in his living room. When a boisterous "Jill" accidentally breaks Pacino's Oscar, she says, "I'm sure you have others."

"You'd think it," Pacino tells her, "but oddly enough, no."

Yet some critics didn't even think Pacino saved the movie, which is really not *that* awful. "So unforgivably, soul-destroying[ly] bad it'll have you wishing Pacino had made *Righteous Kill* 2 instead," wrote Shaun Munro of *What Culture*. And he was not alone in the sheer hatred the film engendered in critics and pop-culture observers. *Jack and Jill* won a number of "Razzie" awards, with Pacino "winning" as "Worst Supporting Actor." Fun's fun, but Pacino actually gives an excellent comic performance in the film—the critical lambasting almost always reserved for critic's non-darling Adam Sandler swept poor Al up in its wake.

Some might feel the funniest thing about *Jack and Jill* is the publicity, which claimed that Adam Sandler played "identical" twins in the movie—for twins to be identical they actually have to be of the same sex!

Stand Up Guys

LIONSGATE, 2012

Executive producer, Matt Berenson; director, Fisher Stevens; screenplay, Noah Haidle; cinematography, Michael Grady; music, Lyle Workman; editing, Mark Livolsi. Running time: 95 min.

CAST

Al Pacino (*Val*); Christopher Walken (*Doc*); Alan Arkin (*Hirsch*); Julianna Margulies (*Nina*); Mark Margolis (*Claphands*); Lucy Punch (*Wendy*); Addison Timlin (*Alex*); Bill Burr (*Larry*); Vanessa Ferlito (*Sylvia*); Craig Sheffer (*Jargoniew*).

Val (Al Pacino) has spent twenty-eight years in jail after a robbery gone awry. During the crossfire with cops, Val accidentally shot and killed the only son of the master planner, a man named Claphands. During his lengthy stay in jail Val was a "stand up guy" and refused to name his confederates. That doesn't stop Claphands from hating him, and telling another man, Val's best friend, "Doc" (Christopher Walken), that he expects him to kill Val once he gets out or his own life is forfeit. Val, who is picked up by Doc just as he leaves prison, is certain of what Doc intends to do, but also learns that Doc was given his orders twenty-eight years ago. Claphands wanted him to suffer all those years in jail, only to be killed on his very first day of freedom. Val seems philosophical about his fate, while Doc seems conflicted. Much of the film's strength is derived from the fact that you're never quite certain what these two fellows are going to do in regards to each other or anything else.

Most of the film deals with the misadventures of the two men—eventually joined by a third—during Val's (presumably) last night of life. Val has trouble performing with a hooker, so as they rob a drug store he pops so many Viagra pills that he can not only perform for hours but winds up in the emergency room with a case of priapism. There they meet a doctor, Nina (Julianna Margulies), who they knew in childhood, and who tells them that their old friend-in-larceny, her father, Hirsh (Alan Arkin), is in a retirement home. Stealing a car that is owned by the vicious Jorgoniew brothers, they drive to the home and take Hirsh out for a spin. Hirsh fulfills his fantasy of having a ménage a trois with two women, and the boys discover that another woman has been tied up in the trunk of the stolen car.

Freeing Sylvia (Vanessa Ferlito), said woman, the men learn that she got a lift from the Jorgoniew brothers, who gang-raped her and stuffed her in the trunk, probably to rape her again or dispose of her later. Outraged by this—apparently these are lowlifes who still have some standards—the three aging criminals storm the HQ of the brothers, tie them up, hand Sylvia a baseball bat, and walk out the door as she tells her former abductors: "You guys like the ballet? The nutcracker was my favorite." BAM! (It should be mentioned that joviality and feistiness is not the normal attitude of a rape victim.)

As the movie proceeds, Val keeps asking Doc how many hours he has left before he does the deed. He bears Doc no ill will. "If it were the other way around, I'd do it," he says. But Doc, who has probably killed many a man in his life, has a soft spot for his old friend. He pleads with Claphands to let him spare Val's life but the embittered gangster tells him that if he doesn't kill Val then his granddaughter, Alex, who works as a waitress in a coffee shop, will have a fatal "accident." Still, the two men come up with a possible solution, and guns ablaze, storm Claphand's headquarters ... maybe they'll survive, maybe not.

The tone of this entertaining black comedy is set early on, when the two old friends meet outside the prison for the first time in twenty-eight years.

"You look like shit," Doc tells Val.

"You look worse," Val rejoinders.

In truth, both men *do* look pretty bad—no soft focus, heavy make-up "prettying" for these fellows—but their performances are excellent. Pacino is in his sleazy, scuzzy, yet lovable mode throughout the movie, walking the fine line between comedy and pathos without ever falling off. Alan Arkin also offers a fine performance as Hirsh, and the smaller roles are also well cast. Walken and Pacino work very well together, like clockwork. Pacino displays his natural charm in a scene when he successfully importunes a very pretty young lady, Lisa, to give him just one dance in a bar.

Stand Up Guys is unusual and hard not to like, although it's fairly minor. In trying to bust some stereotypes regarding senior citizens—that they have no sex lives, and the like—it goes a little overboard at times, almost turning into a silly old-men-are-studs flick. The movie is not a farce, which is why some sequences—such as when the two pals and Hirsh's daughter bury the latter in the cemetery at night *sans* funeral and embalming shortly after his natural death—make no sense and just don't work. Still, the movie at least attempts to look at the lives of, and compromises made by, men on social security, who may feel their age at times but still feel vital and virile and useful; ironic that it's aging *crooks* whose world the film explores. But then, if *Stand Up Guys* were about, say, aging dentists or sanitation men nobody would go to see it.

Mark Kermode in the *Observer* (UK) observed that "Walken wears his trousers high and does the soft-shoe shuffle, Pacino keeps his shoulders low and dusts off the seductive old-fart-wows-young-lady dance from *Scent of a Woman*.... Viagra is consumed, erections wrestled, old scores settled—blah blah blah." Drew Hunt of the *Chicago Reader* criticized the actors and wrote: "Pacino is the worst offender, sleepwalking through the trite material (a drawn-out Viagra joke lasts 20 arduous minutes), though Walken and Arkin deliver little more than self-parody."

According to Graham Young in the *Birmingham Mail*, "... it's great to see these two veterans willing to tease us along. They'll leave you guessing as to how much of what we're seeing on screen is down to genuine old age. And how much is down to acting, make-up and an ability to hunch their shoulders?"

Phil Spector

HBO, 2013

Executive producers, Barry Levinson and David Mamet; writer/director, David Mamet; cinematography, Juan Ruiz Anchia; music, Marcelo Zarvos; editing, Barbara Tulliver. Running time: 92 min.

Cast

Al Pacino (*Phil Spector*); Helen Mirren (*Linda Kenney Baden*); Jeffrey Tambor (*Bruce Cutler*); Meghan Marx (Lana Clarkson); Linda Miller (Ronnie Spector); Matt Malloy (*Dr. Spitz*); David Aaron Baker (*Alan Jackson*); James Tolkan (*Judge Fidler*); Rebecca Pidgeon (*Dr. Fallon*); John Pirruccello (*Nick Stavros*).

Record producer Phil Spector was arrested in 2003 after actress Lana Clarkson was found shot to death in his home in Alhambra, California. Spector claimed that the death was a suicide, that Lana put the gun in her mouth and pulled the trigger, but prosecutors heard that the old and ugly, if wealthy, man often pulled a gun on visiting young women on whom he made unwelcome advances. Spector had several attorneys, and more than one trial, but was finally convicted and sentenced to nineteen years to life. *Phil Spector*, a made-for-cable film that was written and directed by David Mamet, presented a fictionalized version of the real-life events. The credits read: "This is a work of fiction. It's not 'based on a true story.' It is a drama inspired by actual persons in a trial, but it is neither an attempt to depict the actual persons, nor to comment upon the trial or its outcome." Therefore the filmmakers could pretty much say and do as they wanted.

Phil Spector (Pacino), accused of murdering Lana Clarkson (Meghan Marx), has hired attorney Bruce Cutler (Jeffrey Tambor), who wants to bring in Linda Kenney Baden (Helen Mirren) to help with the defense. Baden is not much interested at first, but she talks to Spector, who is difficult to deal with—he claims he's "a punching bag for being the most successful music producer in the world"—and comes to the conclusion that he may be innocent. Supposedly, blood-spatter evidence indicates that he had to be at least ten feet away when the shot that killed Lana was fired. Baden's theory is that the gun went off accidentally after Spector shouted at Lana to take the weapon out of her mouth. The jury rejects this theory, as well as the likelihood that Clarkson would have suddenly committed suicide in Spector's home, and he is convicted.

While Pacino should perhaps be congratulated for choosing such a strange and risky character part, his performance in *Phil Spector* isn't entirely successful. He allows himself to look like crap, but can't do much with his voice and accent. As Spector did, he wears a variety of wigs throughout the movie, including one ridiculous and huge blond "afro" at trial, which is just what happened in real life. In fact, the real Phil Spector is even weirder looking than Pacino in the movie. Pacino is quite successful at seeming small, frail, diminished, but can't quite disguise his obvious charisma and vitality. Pacino's performance, however, while sometimes bordering on parody, is otherwise quite good, and he gets excellent support from Jeffrey Tambor and the wonderful Helen Mirren. Pacino is given a chance to give out with a patented blast during a scene when they are rehearsing his testimony and trying to prepare him for what might happen in court. When a tape recording of ex-wife Ronnie Spector is played, he loses it, goes ballistic and screeches at everyone in the room.

But there's no disguising the fact that *Phil Spector* is a cynical project rushed out to take advantage of the publicity surrounding the Spector trial. Lana Clarkson gets very short shrift in the movie, as if she's being killed for the second time, and Spector's third wife, Rachelle, is not even depicted. (Spector actually met Rachelle Short after his arrest for the murder of Clarkson while he was out on bail; he married her in 2006.) Rachelle Spector objected to how the telefilm made her husband seem like a demented megalomaniac. However, the biggest objections came from Lana Clarkson's loved ones, the chief complaint being that too much credence and running time was given over to the suicide theory. "It's an insidious whitewash of a convicted killer and an infamous smear of his victim... a shame on all involved," charged Glenn Garvin of the *Miami Herald,* while Sara Smith of the *Kansas City Star* noted that the film was "another nonsensical, repetitive soliloquy about the victimization of a violent millionaire." While the majority of the critical reaction was unfavorable, Pacino did come in for a fair share of praise, with him being described as "dazzling" and Al Alexander of the *Patriot-Ledger* opining that "Pacino seldom fails to cut straight to the soul of a character who is both brilliant and pathetic."

In truth, neither Pacino's performance nor the film itself are especially memorable. What could have emerged as a powerful study of evil, ambition, and twisted psyches is instead just a slightly bizarre Movie-of-the-Week.

Salome

Salome Productions, 2013

Executive producer, Beni Atoori; director, Al Pacino; from the play by Oscar Wilde; cinematography, Benoit Delhomme; editing, Pasquale Buba, David Leonard, and Jeremy Weiss. Running time: 81 min.

Cast

Al Pacino (*King Herod*); Jessica Chastain (*Salome*); Kevin Anderson (*John the Baptist*); Roxanne Hart (*Herodias*); Joe Roseto (*Narraboth*); Anselm Clinard (*Tigellinus*); Brian Delate (soldier); Tim Dvorak (*soldier*).

At his birthday party King Herod (Pacino) irritates his wife, Queen Herodias (Roxanne Hart), with his continual fascination with his stepdaughter, Salome (Jessica Chastian). Salome is herself fascinated with the prisoner whom she hears crying out continuously, John the Baptist or Jokanaan (Kevin Anderson). Jokanaan has angered Herod by proclaiming against his marriage to the wife of his brother, and finds the queen immoral, a charge he levels against her daughter when Salome descends into the dank cistern to see him. Salome insists that Jokanaan let her kiss him on the mouth, but he is disgusted by her and refuses to let her touch him. Narraboth, the captain of the guard (Joe Roseto), who adores Salome, is so appalled by her actions that he immediately commits suicide. Herod is disturbed by this, but he promises Salome whatever she wishes—half of his kingdom, for instance—if she will dance for him. Salome insists that the only thing she wants is Jokanaan's head on a silver platter. Herod, who feels that the Baptist may be a messenger of God, and that his own death may follow if he kills him, pleads with Salome to ask for something else. He offers her priceless sapphires, beautiful peacocks, magnificent opals, anything and everything, but all she wants is Jokanaan's head. She dances the dance of the seven veils, then Herod reluctantly complies with her wishes. The severed head is brought to Salome, who finally kisses its mouth, disgusting all but Herodias, who hated the dead man. When Salome declares her undying love for Jokannan, Herod orders his soldiers to kill her.

As noted in the documentary *Wilde Salomé*, the Los Angeles stage production of Wilde's deliciously perverse drama in more or less modern dress was directed by Estelle Parsons. Pacino then took his cameras and filmed the play on the existing stage set, adapting both stage directions and cast performances. However, *Salome* is more than just a filmed play, as Pacino's inventive camera angles bring out the heightened tension and dramatic thrust of the piece. Although Pacino has always claimed that he can't direct and doesn't work well with actors, the excellent filming of *Salome* seems to belie this assertion.

Pacino's performance as Herod is good if definitely an acquired taste. Pacino is a strong enough actor to deliver in theater pieces à la Wilde and Shakespeare, but despite his appearing on stage and continuing to return to the theater periodically (unlike many another movie star), it could be argued that Pacino cut his teeth in modern theater, but is not necessarily a *classically* trained actor. Therefore his approach is more naturalistic and contemporary than that of other stage performers, whatever the approach's strengths or weaknesses. It could also be said that Pacino's approach appeals more to his movie fans than to devoted theater patrons. King Herod's is an interesting performance if not an entirely successful one. He may be miscast but at least he has the courage to *try*, and if that's not a serious actor than nobody is.

One problem is Pacino's somewhat strained voice, which does not always serve the play well, the voice being more shrill and tinny than theatrically rich; this may be less of a choice in interpretation than a matter of his own vocal limitations as he ages. His sing-song delivery is a choice, however, and if nothing else exhibits Herod's sense of humor. Herod never seems especially drunk but he definitely has a buzz. Pacino lacks the authority of many of the other actors, but this, too, may be indicative more of a risky interpretation than anything else. It's hardly Pacino's fault if Herod never comes off like the corpulent, hedonistic, gross Charles Laughton–type of Herod.

As Salome, Jessica Chastain eventually delivers a powerful performance, especially at the climax as she waxes over the severed head of Jokanaan. In earlier scenes she is like a college drama student struggling to find the character. Roxanne Hart is excellent as the haughty queen, and Joe Roseto makes a sensitive Narraboth, who dies for love. Kevin Anderson is acceptable as Jokanaan. Anselm Clinard as Tigellinus, and Brian Delate and Tim Dvorak as soldiers are also notable. Pacino ensures that *Salome* moves at a brisk page and has nary a dull moment, even if the ending—the death of Salome at the swords of the soldiers—is kind of muffed and occurs offstage.

The Humbling

AMBI PICTURES, 2014

Producers, Al Pacino and Barry Levinson; director, Barry Levinson; screenplay, Buck Henry and Michal Zebede; cinematography, Adam Jandrup; music, Marcelo Zarvos; editing, Aaron Yanes. Running time: 112 min.

CAST

Al Pacino (*Simon Axler*); Greta Gerwig (*Pegeen*); Kyra Sedgwick (*Louise*): Dianne Wiest (*Carol*); Charles Grodin (*Jerry*); Dylan Baker (*Dr. Farr*); Nina Arianda (*Sybil*); Billy Porter (*Prince*); Li Jun Li (*Tracy*); Dan Hedaya (*Asa*).

An aging actor named Simon Axler (Pacino) has a nervous breakdown on the stage, attempts suicide, and is committed to an institution. Sybil (Nina Arianda), another inmate, keeps trying to get Simon to murder her husband, which he refuses to do. Back home Simon gets a visit from the much younger Pegeen (Greta Gerwig), his goddaughter, who claims that she has had a crush on him for years and begins an affair with Simon, giving him a major ego boost. Still, Simon's agent, Jerry (Charles Grodin), fears that Simon is pretty much washed up as an actor. Pegeen has had a long relationship with a woman named Priscilla, who switched her gender and is now known as Prince (Billy Porter). Pegeen has no interest in continuing the relationship with Prince, even though she is now sleeping with men. Pegeen's parents (Dianne Weist; Dan Hedaya) are outraged by the age difference and even Simon feels it's pretty certain that

Pegeen won't stick around, especially when she admits to having casual sex with women behind his back. Simon manages to get a good part in King Lear, but has a bitter breakup with Pegeen, finding him stifling and old-fashioned. At the end of the performance, Simon stabs himself and presumably dies with the audience's applause ringing in his ears.

Pacino gives a superb serio-comic performance in *The Humbling*, another instance of the actor being brilliant in a movie that doesn't deserve his talents. Based on a novel by Philip Roth, *The Humbling* tries hard to be theater of the absurd, a crazy black comedy, but it lacks true humor and wit and its old-fashioned aspects make it, in many ways, terribly dated. *The Humbling* is another instance of a movie in which the filmmakers try to be "hip" by inserting LGBT (Lesbian Gay Bisexual Transgender) characters into the mix, but are too unknowing and backward in their thinking to make it work. Pegeen's character—who seems less bisexual than an on-again, off-again lesbian, contradicting both her sexuality and science—is more a "type" than a fully dimensional human being.

As in the even worse *Gigli*, it almost seems that Pegeen just needs to "meet the right man"—the let's-turn-a-lesbian-straight cliché—although she keeps sleeping with women despite her relationship with Simon. More offensive is the antiquated notion that Pegeen is somehow not a "real" woman, that she has trouble being sexy and feminine. "Did you want her to become a woman or just look like one?" asks Simon's shrink. Admittedly, Simon is angry when he says, "I turned you into something that is close to being a woman"—Pegeen at least tells him, "Fuck you!"—but Pegeen is never stereotypically "butch," so comments like these make no sense at all. Pegeen's lesbian lover (as opposed to the transgendered man) and her pain over the breakup, is treated like a joke, with her making impulsive and hysterical threats. It's probably all meant to be cute and amusing—having an affair with a lesbian is just one more indication of how Simon's life is a complete mess—but isn't.

A potentially interesting situation develops between Pegeen and Prince, her transgendered ex-lover. "Now that you're sleeping with men, why not me?" asks the hurt and baffled Prince. The immature Pegeen seems angry that Prince had a sex change despite the fact that it was emotionally imperative for her to do so. That she no longer finds his body attractive is one thing, but she seems to begin the affair with the much, much older Simon just to hurt Prince. Meanwhile, Simon has an attractive "lesbian" (the term bisexual is never used, another dated aspect to the movie, although Pegeen does seem to be essentially gay) to sleep with, so he's satisfied, if fairly certain, that this relationship can't last—"She's bound to leave me," says Simon.

Instead of finding some genuine and sympathetic humor in LGBT relationships, *The Humbling* only makes a mockery of them. Although Prince has clearly become a man, Simon asks him "which one?" when he asks to use the bathroom. Prince is treated more as a freak than a person. It's as if the "old men" who made the movie are thinking, along with Simon, how mystified they are by all these strange, sometimes ambiguous sexual minorities, the very thing that makes the movie so, ultimately, conventional at its core. (It should be said that dated attitudes should not be excused due to seniority, especially when there are elderly people who are very up to date in their thinking.)

Many of Simon's thoughts and feelings are strictly in his head, such as a sequence when he imagines that he and Pegeen are going to have a baby. "This officially marks the end of a sixteen-year mistake," Pegeen supposedly says, but the shrink wonders if that was only what Simon wanted to hear; he finds many inconsistencies in his stories. Is this a real, if weird, relationship or just a "flirtation" with a famous actor as Pegeen mends her wounds over her most recent breakup. Like a fantasy figure, Pegeen just shows up out of nowhere at Simon's house. One could almost imagine she was a complete fiction in his head. Simon also has a fantasy in which Pegeen's mother tells him that she had an affair with Simon and is actually her father.

There are other good performances in *The Humbling,* such as Greta Gerwig's, who tries as hard as possible not to come off like a stereotype despite the flannel shirts she's forced to wear. Nina Arianda is very effective as the neurotic and murderous Sybil, and Dianne Wiest has a good moment or two as Pegeen's mother. Billy Porter scores as Prince, and there is good work from Charles Grodin as Simon's agent and Dylan Baker as his shrink. Most critics felt that Pacino did a fine job in *The Humbling,* although many were not carried away with the movie itself. According to Peter Travers in *Rolling Stone,* "This is Pacino's best film performance in years. In playing an actor who has lost the art of fooling himself, he reveals with mordant wit the terrors of diminished capacity. To watch him do it is a master class." Simi Horwitz of the *Film Journal International* opined: "Al Pacino's superb performance as an aging, psychologically unraveling actor cannot save this pretentious and flat-footed film."

Rex Reed so hated the movie that he subjected its star to one of his most vituperative attacks: "At 5-foot-7 and wrinkled as a dried prune.... Al Pacino doesn't even try [to act] with any reasonable degree of craft or stature.... Self-indulgently allowed to mug by director Mr. Levinson, he's more unconvincing than ever.... They should have called this mess *The Mumbling.*"

A funny review, if not entirely accurate, as Pacino gives a sterling account of himself despite the mediocre quality of the movie. One should also address the nasty remarks about Pacino's appearance—"wrinkled like a dry prune" for instance—made by critics of varying ages who seem to be guilty of simple age discrimination. Pacino in his seventies still looks damn good—do they expect him to look twenty-five just because he's a movie star? It's bad enough when younger critics do it, but the big joke in this instance is that Rex Reed is two years older than Pacino!

Manglehorn (2014)

IFC, 2014

Producer/director, David Gordon Green; screenplay, Paul Logan; cinematography, Tim Orr; music, David Wingo; editing, Colin Patton. Running time: 97 min.

Cast

Al Pacino (*Manglehorn*); Holly Hunter (*Dawn*); Chris Messina (*Jacob*); Harmony Korine (*Gary*); Natalie Wilomon (*Clara*).

Although made in 2014, *Manglehorn* will not receive a theatrical release in the United States until June 2015 (before this book went to press). Peter Debruge in *Variety* headlined his review of the film thusly: "*Working with Indie-minded David Gordon Green, Al Pacino's Larger-Than-Life Persona Is Wrong Fit for What Could be a Spiritual Sequel to* Scarecrow." According to Debruge, "When you want subtle and nuanced, Al Pacino isn't the guy you call. Pacino does big and larger-than-life better than any thesp working today. But *Manglehorn* is a fragile, smaller-than-life portrait, focused on the kind of eccentric rural Southern character you might expect to encounter in one of Errol Morris's early documentaries."

Pacino plays a Texas locksmith named A.J. Manglehorn . After twenty years A.J. is still pining for a woman named Clara Massey, and continues to write to her. At the same time A.J. is emotionally distant from his son Jacob (Chris Messina) and a bank teller (Holly Hunter) that he sees on weekends. "If *Manglehorn* is a mystery," wrote *Variety*, "which seems to be [director] Green and screenwriter Paul Logan's intent, then the film hasn't been structured in a way to invite curiosity ... something about [the director] working with Pacino forces what could have been a breaks-the-mold character portrait into factory-made territory." Robbie Collin in the *Daily Telegraph* found the film "slight to the point of translucence," while Xan Brooks in the *Guardian* said of its star that it was "the finest performance Pacino has delivered in years."

Danny Collins

BLEECKER STREET MEDIA, 2015

Executive producer, Declan Baldwin; director/writer, Dan Fogelman; cinematography, Steve Yedlin; music, Ryan Adams and Theodore Shapiro; editing, Julie Monroe. Running time: 106 min.

CAST

Al Pacino (*Danny Collins*); Bobby Cannavale (*Tom Donnelly*); Jennifer Garner (*Samantha*); Annette Bening (*Mary Sinclair*); Christopher Plummer (*Frank Grubman*); Josh Peck (*Nicky*); Giselle Eisenberg (*Hope*); Melissa Benoist (*Jamie*); Scott Lawrence (*Dr. Kurtz*); Eric Lange (*Dr. Silverman*).

Danny Collins (Al Pacino) is a senior citizen who is also a long-time, very famous, and very rich rock star—along the lines of Mick Jagger. His manager, Frank (Christopher Plummer), gives Danny a birthday gift—a letter that had been sent to Danny years ago by John Lennon, in essence telling him to keep his head on straight, and telling him to call him. Danny never got the letter, but it wound up on eBay decades later. Danny wonders if his rather dissipated life might have been different if he had actually spoken to Lennon when he was younger. Reviewing his life, Danny decides to make contact with the son he never knew, Tom Donnelly (Bobby Cannavale), who is married with a child and lives in New Jersey. After checking into the local Hilton, Danny first meets his daughter-in-law, Samantha (Jennifer Garner), and his precocious granddaughter, Hope (Giselle Eisenberg), but Samantha warns him that her husband wants nothing to do with him. Danny is encouraged to keep trying with Tom by Mary Sinclair (Annette Bening), the hotel's manager, with whom Danny is having a very odd "romance." Encouraged, Danny slowly but surely insinuates himself into the lives of his son and his family only to learn that Tom may be dying of leukemia. As Danny's relationship with Tom hits a few bumps and nearly crumbles, Danny decides to be there with his boy when they have to find out from the doctor if Tom has a chance to recover or has only a few months to live. As the two men bond, the implication is that the doctor will give him good news.

Despite some awkward moments and the occasional soap-opera–like ambiance, *Danny Collins* is an excellent picture that boasts one of Pacino's finest performances. Pacino could in some ways identify with the famous, charismatic man he was playing, someone who is immediately recognized by everyone no matter where he goes. He also knows what it's like to have family issues and estrangements, as well as recognizing the difficulty of balancing a high-profile busy career with the demands of lovers and offspring. Then there's the much younger lover that Danny has and Pacino had for a time in real life.

"I look absurd with her," Danny tells Frank.

"Yes you do," Frank replies.

(It later develops that this fiancée, Sophie, played by Katarina Cas, turns out to be carrying on with Collins' security guard, Judd, played by Brian Smith.)

Danny Collins has an additional problem in that he's a coke head. But, as Frank tells Tom, the man has a good heart. "He just keeps it up his ass half the time." Pacino is charming when he talks to little Hope, and especially fine in the final scene with an equally good Bobby Cannavale as they sit together tensely in the office waiting for the doctor to deliver his news, Danny's desperate love for his son all too obvious.

It may not have been a wise decision to have Pacino do his own singing, which is raspy, unpleasant, and off-key, but it could be argued that Danny might sound that way after decades of drug and alcohol abuse. Pacino has two numbers: Collins' catchy signature tune, "Baby Doll," and Danny's first new composition in many years, the ballad "Don't Look Back," a pretty number that isn't served well by Pacino's "singing."

The other cast members are excellent support for Pacino, with Cannavale etching a strong portrait of a struggling working-class man whose lifestyle has been entirely different from his father's. Jennifer Garner is wonderful as the warm and sympathetic Samantha, and Annette Bening makes her sometimes awkwardly-written character work. Giselle Eisenberg makes an adorable Hope and there are nice bits from Josh Peck and Melissa Benoist as, respectively, Hilton staff members Nicky and Jamie. After Pacino, the best work in the film is done by Christopher Plummer, who is brilliant as the grizzled American Frank.

Some scenes may seem a touch unrealistic but most of these can be attributed to the humor of the piece. One might wonder how a man Danny Collins's age (although he's playing younger than Pacino) might get the beautiful young groupies to screech at the front of the stage—especially when in one scene in a lounge the audience seems comprised mostly of seniors—but Collins is still a big name, he's still performing, and he still has that incredible energy and chutzpah. Would Collins, who has just been told he has financial troubles, really give away a red Mercedes to a bellboy he barely knows? Would the hotel manager tactlessly tell Collins, a guest (who is clearly buzzed but not that inebriated), he was a "drunk?" Would Danny tell Tom while waiting for the doctor that the news about his health all depends on whether the oncologist addresses him by his first name or as "Mr. Donnelly"? Does the film explore the realities of leukemia, or is it just a plot point?

Ultimately, the film works so well and is so well acted that it doesn't make a difference. *Danny Collins* is at its heart an old-fashioned comedy-drama that either works for the viewer or doesn't. The movie is clearly winking at the audience throughout when Danny tells Mary that he was once married to Dawn Wells, "Mary Ann on *Gilligan's Island*."

Danny Collins and Pacino received mostly positive notices even if some critics felt the picture was slight. "Legendary as Al Pacino's skills are, he wouldn't be the first actor I'd cast to play a 70ish pop star who still fills mid-sized arenas some 40 years after he last charted a hit single. Yet Al Pacino sells the heck out of his performance as Danny Collins," opined Richard Roeper of the *Chicago Sun-Times*. "Like its hero, the movie is flawed but hard to resist," wrote Moira MacDonald in the *Seattle Times*. However, Marjorie Baumgarten in the *Austin Chronicle* felt, "You might be forgiven for mistaking the film for an extended Holiday Inn commercial."

Actually it was the Hilton.

Part Three

Pacino on Stage

Al Pacino's dedication to the art of acting is proven by his continued interest in a variety of theatrical ventures, all of which pay far less than his movie roles and many of which could be considered highly "risky." But it was in the theatrical circles of New York, where he was born, that he first made his mark. And he goes back to his "roots" on a periodic basis.

Pacino's earliest roles were in children's theater pieces at such places as the Cafe Bizarre and Theater East in New York. Later on, he was associated with Cafe La Mama—where he tried stand-up comedy—and the Living Theater, where he worked as a stagehand with Martin Sheen. Pacino had to do other kinds of part-time work to survive during this period. His acting coach at Herbert Berghof's studios, Charlie Laughton, had his class do a reading of William Saroyan's *Hello, Out There*. Laughton was acquainted with Joe Cino of the Caffe Cino and asked him to sit in on one of the readings. Cino was impressed enough to offer to stage the show at his cafe, leading to Pacino's Off Broadway debut. For the first time he was acting in front of a paying audience.

Hello, Out There was followed by Strindberg's *Creditors*, which Charlie Laughton mounted for a song in Lower Manhattan. Sometimes the actors onstage outnumbered the customers in the audience. Despite the lack of attendance—or maybe because of it—Pacino was able to overcome his jitters and a feeling of inadequacy and emerged as top contender for acting honors in the production.

By 1966 he was in the full bloom of confidence, bolstered by encouragement from Laughton and his peers, and proved particularly impressive in Fred Vassi's *Why Is a Crooked Letter*. Although performed in yet another of New York's seemingly inexhaustible supply of shoestring Off Broadway companies—Alec Rubin's Theater of Encounter on West Seventy-second Street—the play did garner Pacino a lot of attention *and* a nomination for an Obie, the awards given for Off and Off Off Broadway productions.

In the 1960s he also appeared with James Earl Jones in a production of

John Wolfson's *Peace Creeps* at the New Theater Workshop. By this time he had been accepted at the prestigious Actors Studio and been befriended by the studio's head and top acting coach, Lee Strasberg, who gave his new student both tea and sympathy and a great deal of encouragement. Pacino made up his mind that he would only accept worthy parts and not just take an assignment for the money. While his integrity could not be questioned, this often meant he went hungry when he didn't have to.

For instance, in 1966 he traveled to Massachusetts to meet with David Wheeler, head of the prestigious Theater Company of Boston, whose company he wished to join. According to Pacino's biographer Andrew Yule, Wheeler offered Pacino fifty dollars a week (no mean sum for an actor in those days), but the part in the company's first production was too "small" to suit Pacino, and he turned Wheeler down despite the fact that later productions might have garnered him more substantial roles. Pacino had to borrow money from Wheeler to get a bus back to New York.

A year later, Pacino did temporarily join the company, appearing in two productions at the Charles Playhouse: Clifford Odets's *Awake and Sing!* and Jean-Claude Van Itallie's *America, Hurrah*. It was in the latter production that Pacino worked with Jill Clayburgh, who became his live-in lover for several years before marrying playwright David Rabe and becoming a (limited) star (of *An Unmarried Woman* and other films) in her own right. In the latter play, Pacino had to go on stage right after reading a terrible review of his performance.

Pacino really began to "make it" with his next role, that of street punk and sociopath Murph in Israel Horovitz's *The Indian Wants the Bronx*. He had appeared in a workshop production of the play in Connecticut in 1966, but this new production was fully mounted for New York's Astor Place Theater. Pacino co-starred with Matthew Cowles and John Cazale, with whom he had a close friendship until Cazale's death from cancer. *The Indian Wants the Bronx* deals with two tough guys who come across an elderly Indian gentleman while wandering about Manhattan one night. They tease and torment the man, who only wants to get out to the Bronx to visit a relative. The Indian man is eventually beaten and finally stabbed. Much of the action revolves around a phone booth, which almost functions as a fourth character, a would-be lifeline for the abused Indian man. During the play Pacino strutted about in a menacing manner, shouting out, "Hey, pussyface!" to a woman in a window, using his swagger to disguise the basic insecurity of Murph the malicious. It won him a Best Actor Obie and established him as an actor to be reckoned with from that day forward. John Cazale and Israel Horovitz also won Obies. A disturbing play in the '60s, Horovitz's study of xenophobia and restless youth undoubtedly would seem quaint and dated in these days of metal protectors in grade schools, its Murph an all-too-typical nihilistic, marauding moron.

Pacino followed up this triumph with Don Petersen's *Does a Tiger Wear a Necktie?* in 1969, his Broadway debut at the Belasco Theatre. This study of the inner workings of a drug halfway house garnered Pacino even more attention—he made his film debut in *Me, Natalie* that same year—but it had a short run, and many felt Pacino's role of sadistic whacko "Bickham," as well as other roles to come, was too similar to his Murph. One critic praised Pacino's "ceaseless soft treadmill stance, sniffing nose and blinking eyes, the fingers that constantly scrabble at the air as if scratching the invisible monkey on his back." Pacino was awarded a Best Supporting Actor Tony for his performance. That fine actor Hal Holbrook was also in the cast.

Pacino was sorely disappointed with the results when he next appeared in a production of Heathcote Williams's *The Local Stigmatic* at the Actors Playhouse in 1969. On the same bill were several Harold Pinter plays, but these weren't enough to bring in the paying customers. *The Local Stigmatic* would have closed on opening night, except that Jon Voight, who wasn't even in the cast, used his own funds to keep it running a week longer.

Many dismissed *The Local Stigmatic* as a clone of *The Indian Wants the Bronx*. Again, Pacino was cast as a sociopathic loser who terrorizes an elderly man with the help of a buddy. Pacino has always been intrigued by the play, for in it the victim is a famous actor and the two punks destroy him out of jealousy of his achievements. Pacino was just getting a taste of fame in 1969 but was a major movie star by 1976 when Joseph Papp restaged *The Local Stigmatic* for a "by invitation only" audience at his Public Theater. By this time Pacino knew firsthand about fame and people who were jealous of your achievements, who hated you because of your press clippings. So fascinated was he by *The Local Stigmatic* that he put his own money in a short film version of Williams's unsuccessful play (see movie section).

Pacino's next theatrical venture was a revival of Tennessee Williams's *Camino Real* for the Lincoln Center Repertory Theater. A lesser but still interesting play by the author of *Cat on a Hot Tin Roof*, *Vieux Carre*, and other masterpieces, *Camino Real* has more than its share of heart-wrenching, powerful sequences, most of which were undermined by Milton Katselas's direction, which tried to turn the play into a campy comedy. Pacino, who made his entrance swinging over the audience and dropping onto the stage, survived this version unscathed, however, and even the great playwright was happily purring at "Kilroy's" energy onstage. Pacino got mostly good notices, but some felt there was a numbing sameness to his performances that he had better snap out of, or else.

Also in 1970, Pacino returned to David Wheeler's company in Boston, this time to *direct* a new Israel Horovitz play entitled *Rats*. The play never amounted to much, and Pacino didn't direct again for quite awhile, but he did strike up a long-term association with Wheeler's artistic troupe. For the next ten years, during which his film career flourished, all of his major theatrical appearances were with Wheeler's company.

First there was David Rabe's *Basic Training of Paolo Hummel*, which had already played at Joseph Papp's Public Theater without Pacino. Part of Rabe's Vietnam trilogy, which included *Streamers* and *Sticks and Bones*, the play dealt with draftees and how they coped with being stuck in the army during an unpopular war. Pacino's title character was a goofball who slowly matures during the stage play's running time. Many of the actors Pacino worked with in this revival would later turn up in supporting roles in his movies when *The Godfather* turned him into a star that same year. This wasn't just kindness on Pacino's part; rarely did he work with untalented people.

Wheeler took the revival of *The Basic Training of Pavlo Hummel* to Broadway five years later, when Pacino was famous. It had a more than respectful run at the Longacre Theatre, and Pacino won a Best Actor Tony for his performance. Notices were mixed, but generally favorable, in no small part due to the fact that critics, through his movies, could see how wide a range Pacino had. One critic noted that Pacino could essay the smooth, urbane Michael Corleone and the misfit-nitwit Pavlo Hummel with equal skill and veracity.

Another Wheeler production that moved from Boston to Broadway was *Richard III*, in which Pacino's portrayal of the title role was, to put it mildly, controversial. From the first he was lambasted for his audacity as much as he was coddled for his courage. How *dare* this Bronx-by-way-of-Manhattan boy with his appalling New Yorkese enact the Bard as if he'd come direct from Stratford-on-Avon, naysayers seemed to crow. Others felt that Pacino should be given credit for choosing such a noncommercial play and challenging role. The reviews were mostly brutal, but in the din a few encouraging voices were heard. (The same thing happened when Pacino attempted a period piece for the movies, *Revolution*).

The general consensus was that Pacino was using his Hollywood clout to muscle in on territory better left to Shakespearean specialists and the British and that he tried to win the audience to his side by making the bloody story of *Richard III* seem little different from the saga of the Corleone family. The UPI lively-arts editor was merciless: "He is a Richard who winks and leers at the audience and addresses his soliloquies to it, who spits out every word as if he hated the English language, who gives no indication what makes him tick, who plays for cheap laughs, and whose manner would never fool his royal brother or anyone else into believing a word he says.... All I can imagine is that movie star Pacino, who claims a cult following in the 18-to-25 age bracket, is playing for that young audience, trying to recreate the first production back in about 1692, giving the 'groundlings' a few extra laughs."

On the other hand, *Time* magazine declared: "[Pacino's] Richard may be a monster, yet how heroic and finally touching a monster Pacino makes him." Indeed, many felt Pacino's performance was quite passionate, energetic, and thoroughly superior but that most critics couldn't see past the (admittedly inappropriate) New York accent, unfortunate pronunciations, and certain ill-advised aspects of the production, such as costumes that mixed "the medieval with the modern." His habit of frequently spitting as he unleashed his dialogue didn't endear him to the critics, either.

People magazine headlined a piece on the production: "Attempting 'Richard III' Has Made Al Pacino the Toast of Broadway—Burnt Toast, That Is." Mary Vespa reported in *People* on July 2, 1979, how Pacino was depressed and eating a box of donuts a day, but then pulled himself together. "Pacino took Napoleonic control of the production. He called in two extra directors, allowed two actors to be fired and spread the critics over four days to improve his odds and decrease the pressure." Pacino refused to allow reviews to be published until five weeks of the nine week run had passed, figuring that advance ticket sales would make the show "reviewer-proof."

The last word was left to Richard Eder in the *New York Times*: "Al Pacino's portrayal of Richard III contains some intelligent and exciting ideas for playing Shakespeare's exuberant villain ... [but] what at one moment is riveting, at the next moment ... becomes ludicrous...." Eder felt that the biggest problem was the direction, that if the pieces of Pacino's performance could be put together and "governed, he could give us one of the great Richards of his generation."

Richard III was followed by Bertolt Brecht's *Resistible Rise of Arturo Ui*, which Wheeler staged at the Charles Playhouse in Boston. Paralleling the events in Nazi Germany, the play presented its title gangster as a grotesque Hitlerian figure. Both Pacino and the production got mixed reviews. Joseph Papp had originally underwritten the production with an eye to bringing it to New York, but assorted strains with Pacino and a basic lack of faith in the overall product prevented it from happening. However, Pacino was to appear later in a production with Tony Randall's National Actors Theater.

Pacino's next project was David Mamet's *American Buffalo*, in 1980, which he took from New Haven to New York (a successful five-month run) to Washington, D.C., at the Kennedy Center, and finally to the Duke of York Theatre in London. The play had debuted five years earlier with a different cast at New York's Theater at St. Clement's Church, of which Pacino was an ardent supporter, then made its way to another Off Broadway theater and finally to Broadway. Pacino's revival began life in New Haven at the Long Wharf Theater.

In the play Pacino is once again cast as a psychotic, but this one spends his time plotting to steal a rare coin instead of pummeling elderly actors or Indians. By the time Pacino got ahold of it, *American Buffalo* had been transformed from a straight drama to a kind of burlesque, with playwright Mamet nodding his approval over both versions. Pacino's Off Broadway rendition at the Downtown Circle in the Square was a smash hit, necessitating a move uptown to the Booth Theatre on Broadway. Pacino was devastated when early in the run his young costar Jimmy Hayden died of a drug overdose; he had been playing a junkie. Although the play itself got mixed notices, Pacino's reviews were generally raves. A few critics suggested that Pacino was technically proficient but too "surfacy."

Pacino's next project came along almost accidentally. Pacino had just shown his film version of *The Local Stigmatic* to Joseph Papp, who had produced one version of the play at his Public Theater. Papp, who also produced the New York Shakespeare Festival, asked Pacino which role, above all others, he would like to essay. "We were in the elevator here," Papp told the *New York Post*'s Diana Maychick, "and without missing a beat, Al said, 'Marc Antony.' And I just said, 'You got the part.'" Stuart Vaughan directed the production of *Julius Caesar* for Papp's Public Theater in 1988. Pacino shared the stage with Edward Herrmann and old buddy and former roommate Martin Sheen. That same year Pacino appeared in a workshop production of Dennis McIntyre's *National Anthems* as the mysterious neighbor of a suburban Yuppie couple in Detroit. Kevin Spacey later played the role in New Haven.

In 1992, Pacino appeared in a double bill at the Circle in the Square in New York. In Oscar Wilde's *Salome*, he played Herod to Sheryl Lee's Salome. In Ira Lewis's *Chinese Coffee* he was one half of a photographer-writer team that was down on its luck. According to *Variety*, the double bill was "a season extra, added as a benefit with a $50 ticket. Pacino missed several performances and cut back the schedule to seven shows a week. So instead of benefiting, Circle in the Square barely broke even." Al Pacino appeared in the film version of *Chinese Coffee* some years later and was to play Herod on both stage and in a film a decade later. Ira Lewis later wrote a play about Pacino which the actor admitted he has never seen.

Pacino's next project was Eugene O'Neill's *Hughie* in 1996. According to Vincent Canby in the *New York Times*: "As much as is possible for an actor appearing before a paying audience, Al Pacino likes to protect his privacy in the workplace. He doesn't appreciate kibitzers. He also has the box office clout to sell tickets no matter what the professional opinion-mongers say. Thus it wasn't until Wednesday night that he invited critics to see his production of Eugene O'Neill's 'Hughie' at the Circle in the Square, where the two-character, one-act play has been in previews since July 25, following an engagement at the Long Wharf Theater in New Haven. It's now apparent that Mr. Pacino knew what he was doing. However long he took to do it, he got it right. The word this morning: bravo! Although *Hughie* is essentially a monologue that runs less than an hour, it's a full, richly eccentric and satisfying evening of theater. This is a star turn that serves America's most grandly obsessed playwright and allows us to see what Mr. Pacino can do, as both the director and an actor, when he disciplines his sometimes raging talents."

In *Hughie*, Pacino plays Erie Smith, who's been drunk for five days following the funeral of his friend, Hughie, the last night clerk in the run-down hotel in whose lobby the play takes place. Erie impressed his dead friend with his inflated sense of importance, even as his own self-esteem was bolstered by Hughie's admiration for him. The only other living character is the new night clerk (Paul Benedict). According to Canby in a piece for the *New York Times*, "Though Mr. Pacino seems to be all over the stage, his is not a busy performance. It's big, but it's one of controlled exhaustion. His body suggests the fragile, tentacled mass of some sea anemone ... twisting in the unseen current of his own panic. It's a performance you see in close-up, no matter where he stands in the Circle in the Square's usually awkward space."

Eileen Jacobson of *Newsday* wrote: "So, of course, we ask—particularly after we see Pacino's name double the size of O'Neill's in the program—whether reality lives up to expectation, to say nothing of whether the $55 regular ticket price is worth 55 minutes of play. And the answer is yes. Pacino's performance is a delicately nuanced, varied and mesmerizing turn...."

Then it was time for a new production of Brecht's *The Resistible Rise of Arturo Ui*, mounted by the National Actors Theater in 2002. According to Charles Isherwood in *Variety*: "... Arturo Ui ... may just be Pacino's sleaziest gangster yet. Stooped and hollow-eyed, skulking around the stage in a soiled tanktop and garish plaid pants as he brays out orders in a high-pitched whine, Pacino's Ui suggests a mangy hyena with mild mental retardation."

David Finkle of *TheaterMania* opined: "Brecht was saying that, taking Hitler's brilliant machinations into account, he nevertheless was a little man with a corrupt heart and mind. And that's how Pacino, face whitened and slouching, plays him. Speaking with a guttural Bronx accent, the actor makes Ui someone who's crawled out from under a rock." And Linda Winer in *Newsday* wrote: "Pacino is a hoot as Ui ... a little man in a big suit—a cross between Pacino's Big Boy Caprice from *Dick Tracy* and an adenoidal 'Richard III.'"

Then it was time for a new production of Oscar Wilde's *Salome*. Estelle

Parsons was the director of a reading in 2003 which co-starred Marisa Tomei, Dianne Wiest, David Strathairn and others. Wrote Howard Kissel in the *New York Daily News*: "That Pacino is a great actor is indisputable. That he is not suited to playing Herod may be equally true.... Pacino has a high-pitched, nasal tenor voice. Sometimes, when he has done Shakespeare, he has made it musical. But here it is deliberately grating and whiny, as if Herod was a Bronx janitor rather than a king." Linda Winer in *Newsday* called Pacino as King Herod "a truly weird, intense, goofy and mesmerizing performance."

The year 2006 brought another production of *Salome*, this time in Los Angeles. According to Charles McNulty in the *Times*: "... Pacino delivers a portrait that, scenery-chewing though it is, can't really be considered egomaniacal.... The performance (think *Scarface* crossed with *The Nutty Professor*) is unseemly more in its execution than in its intermittently insightful interpretation."

After already playing the part of Shylock in a film adaptation of Shakespeare's *The Merchant of Venice*, Pacino reprised the role on stage, first in Central Park during the summer, after which the production moved to the Broadhurst on Broadway. Of this production Ben Brantley of the *Times* wrote: "Taking on one of the juiciest and most unsavory roles in the canon, Mr. Pacino avoids the classic characterizations of Shylock as either devil or martyr ... we're always conscious ... of the turmoil beneath the mannerisms. Shylock has spent his life cataloging sneers of contempt and slurs against Jews; that he will explode is beyond doubt."

The *Hollywood Reporter* opined: "There's a slow-burning pathos to Shylock.... That Pacino conveys this by showing sneers first and scars second is what makes the performance so devastating." Joe Dziemianowicz of the *New York Daily News* wrote: "He's an actor known for big whoo-ha-sized portraits, but Pacino is a study in control on stage. He makes his shaggy Shylock dynamic and believable. He's slightly eccentric, always compelling, right down to ... a singsongy cadence that seems intended to irritate."

Pacino had already appeared in the film version of *Glengarry Glen Ross* when he opted to appear in the play on Broadway in 2012, although now he was playing the part essayed by Jack Lemmon in the movie. Some members of the press took Pacino to task for having difficulty remembering lines during previews, while others suggested he was giving the weakest performance of the cast. David Finkle of the *Huffington Post* felt that Pacino only needed time to get fully into his character. "... Shelly Levene is now an utterly complete and unforgettable character ... a piece of acting so astonishing it's unlikely anything comparable will be seen on Broadway.... Pacino does something rarely if ever observed on stage: He produces all the signs of a man having a stroke."

However Sarah Crompton of *New York* magazine saw things differently: "Pacino plays Shelly as a man so fidgety and tentative that it is hard to believe he was ever the firm's top salesman ... he gives us both anger and a dreadful pathos, but never convinces that he is the man he is portraying.... Never for a second is he believable."

Some critics noted star Pacino's drawing power on Broadway but were none too impressed with him or with the production. "It hardly matters that the revival is only second-rate," wrote *Los Angeles Times* critic Charles McNulty. "Al Pacino ... has turned this Mamet classic into a box-office juggernaut. If the character he's portraying [is just] Pacino making a grand doddering display ... who but the critics are going to complain? ... Pacino is giving audiences their money's worth."

David Rooney, of the *Hollywood Reporter*, added, "Al Pacino is the headliner and principal draw, even if he's the most questionable element in this sluggish revival of David Mamet's best-known play."

In truth the Pulitzer-winning play is problematic, with characters that are over-familiar and not as well-developed as they could be, and many of its observations superficial. The film version was reasonably fast-paced but the play, especially the long first act, is fairly tedious. Pacino gave a good performance in the play, but he had to compete with the memory of the superb and better-cast Jack Lemmon in the film version. The audience—many of whom were more interested in seeing the star of *Scarface* than they were serious theater fans—roared at every obscenity as if they were witty lines written by Neil Simon.

What's next? In October 2015 Pacino is set to star in a new two-character play by David Mamet, *China Doll*, in which Pacino will play the billionaire, Mickey Ross. Ross is preparing to go into semiretirement with his young fiancée and is about to leave the office after giving last-minute instructions to his assistant, Carson, when he receives a phone call. According to the *Hollywood Reporter*, the playwright said what happens next is "better than oral sex," and that Pacino called the part "one of the most daunting and challenging roles I've been given to explore onstage."

One play in which Pacino will definitely not be appearing is a stage adaption of "Hunger," based on the novel by Norwegian writer Knut Hamsun. Pacino pulled out of the play when he learned that Hamsun had been a supporter of Adolf Hitler and his Nazi regime.

List of Major Stage Appearances

1963: *Hello, Out There*, William Saroyan. Gaffe Cino, New York.
1965: *The Creditors*, August Strindberg. The Actors' Gallery, New York.

1966: *Why Is a Crooked Letter,* Fred Vassi. Theater of Encounter, New York (Obie nomination).

1966: *The Indian Wants the Bronx,* Israel Horovitz. Eugene O'Neill Memorial Theater, Connecticut.

1966: *The Peace Creeps,* John Wolfson. New Theater Workshop, New York.

1967: *Awake and Sing!,* Clifford Odets. Charles Playhouse, Boston.

1967: *America, Hurrah,* Jean-Claude Van Itallie. Charles Playhouse, Boston.

1968: *The Indian Wants the Bronx,* Israel Horovitz. Astor Place Theater, New York (Best Actor, Obie).

1969: *Does a Tiger Wear a Necktie?,* Don Petersen. Belasco Theatre. New York (Best Dramatic Supporting Actor, Tony).

1969: *The Local Stigmatic,* Heathcote Williams. Actors Playhouse, New York.

1970: *Camino Real,* Tennessee Williams. Lincoln Center Repertory Theater, New York.

1972: *The Basic Training of Pavlo Hummel,* David Rabe. Charles Theater, Boston.

1972: *Richard III,* William Shakespeare. Loeb Drama Center, Boston.

1975: *The Resistible Rise of Arturo Ui,* Bertolt Brecht. Charles Playhouse, Boston.

1976: *The Local Stigmatic,* Heathcote Williams. Public Theater, New York.

1977: *The Basic Training of Pavlo Hummel,* David Rabe. Longacre Theatre, New York (Best Dramatic Actor, Tony).

1979: *Richard III,* William Shakespeare. Cort Theatre, New York.

1980: *American Buffalo,* David Mamet. Long Wharf Theater Company, New Haven.

1982: *American Buffalo,* David Mamet. Downtown Circle in the Square, New York.

1983: *American Buffalo,* David Mamet. Booth Theatre, New York.

1988: *Julius Caesar,* William Shakespeare. New York Shakespeare Festival Theater, New York.

1992: *Salome,* Oscar Wilde. *Chinese Coffee,* Ira Lewis. Circle in the Square, New York.

1996: *Hughie,* Eugene O'Neill. (Pacino also directed.) Circle in the Square, New York.

2002: *Salome,* Oscar Wilde. Ethel Barrymore Theatre, New York.

2011: *The Merchant of Venice,* William Shakespeare. Broadhurst, New York (Tony nominee).

2012: *Glengarry Glen Ross,* David Mamet. Gerald Schoenfeld, New York.

Additional Workshops, Readings and Small Productions

The Adventures of High Jump and *Jack and the Beanstalk* (Children's Theater), 1962; *A Brick and a Rose* (Louis John Carlino), 1964; *Rats* (Israel Horovitz), 1970; *Hamlet* (Shakespeare), 1979; *The Jungle of the Cities* (Bertolt Brecht), 1979; *Othello* (Shakespeare), 1979; *The Hairy Ape* (O'Neill), 1982; *Crystal Clear* (improvisational; devised by Phil Young), 1987; *National Anthems* (Dennis McIntyre), 1988; *The Father* (August Strindberg/reading), early 1990s; *Oedipus Rex* (Sophocles), 2002; *Orphans* (Lyle Kessler), 2005. Commercial voiceovers for Jeep Grand Cherokee (2012); Sky Broadband (2013).

Notes

1. Glenn Paskin, *New York Daily News*, circa 1970s.
2. Andrew Yule, *Al Pacino: A Life on the Wire*, p. 14.
3. Heide to author.
4. *Ibid.*
5. Otis to author.
6. Yule, *A Life on the Wire*, pp. 66–67.
7. *Ibid.*, p. 88.
8. Heide to author.
9. Pacino's issues with alcohol were documented in *A Life on the Wire*, pp. 29, 115, 144–48.
10. *A Life on the Wire*, pp. 97–98; information also gleaned from Kael's reviews of Pacino films.
11. Pacino's relationship with Martin Bregman has been well documented in *A Life on the Wire* and in contemporary press reports.
12. Grobel, *Al Pacino: In Conversation with Lawrence Grobel*, p. 19.
13. Interview with Friedkin in *The Wrap*; April 12, 2013.
14. Grobel, *Al Pacino*, p. 183.
15. Contemporary press interview; n.d.
16. Grobel, *Al Pacino*, p. 211.
17. *Ibid.*, p. 210.
18. *New York Times*, April 22, 2010, n.p.
19. Grobel, *Al Pacino*, pp. 124–25.
20. *Ibid.*, p. 174.
21. *Hollywood Reporter*, September 3, 2011, n.p.
22. *Los Angeles Times*, April 23, 2006, n.p.
23. Yule, *A Life on the Wire*, p. 19.
24. *Ibid.*, pp. 28–29, 33–35.
25. *Ibid.*, pp. 80–81.
26. Diane Keaton's relationships with Beatty, Allen, and Pacino were well-documented in contemporary press reports. See also Yule, *A Life on the Wire*, pp. 53–54, 234–35, 308–09, 344–45, 354–55.
27. *Ibid.*, 148–149, 151–54, 158–61, 178–80.
28. *Ibid.*, 261–62.
29. Pacino's relationships with Jan Tarrant and Annie Praeger, as well as information about Pacino's child with Tarrant, were covered extensively in the press at the time and afterward. See also Schoell, *The Films of Al Pacino*.
30. Interview with Pacino. *New York Daily News*, circa 1970s.
31. Pacino's relationships with Hobbs, and the bad blood between Hobbs and Bregman were well documented in the press, with many columnists gleefully noting each development. See also Schoell, *The Films of Al Pacino*.
32. Penelope Ann Miller did not keep silent about her affair with Pacino; indeed, she all but called a press conference about it at the time. See also Schoell, *The Films of Al Pacino*.
33. *Detroit News*, October 17, 1997.
34. Schoell, *The Films of Al Pacino*.
35. *EW.com* [*Entertainment Weekly*] May 23, 2003.
36. *Ibid.*
37. WENN (World Entertainment News Network) October 13, 2003.
38. There were numerous press reports about the relationship between Pacino and Sola.
39. *GQ*, November 2007.
40. *Los Angeles Times*, April 22, 2008.
41. *Slate*, August 9, 2007.
42. *New York Post*, circa February 1993.
43. *Atlantic City Weekly*, April 1, 2013.

Bibliography

Books

Bouzereau, Laurent. *The De Palma Cut.* New York: Dembner Books, 1988.
Grobel, Lawrence. *Al Pacino: In Conversation with Lawrence Grobel.* New York: Simon & Schuster/Gallery, 2008.
Quirk, Lawrence J. *The Films of Warren Beatty.* New York: Citadel Press, 1990.
_____. *The Great War Films: From* The Birth of a Nation *to Today.* New York: Citadel Press, 1994.
Schoell, William. *Stay Out of the Shower: 25 Years of Shocker Films Beginning with* Psycho. New York: Dembner Books, 1985.
Yule, Andrew. *Al Pacino: A Life on the Wire.* New York: Donald I. Fine, 1991.

Periodicals

Birmingham Mail
Chicago Reader
Film Journal International
GQ
Hollywood Reporter
Huffington Post
The Nation
New York Post
New York Daily News
New York Magazine
New York Post
New York Times
Newsday
The Observer (UK)
Philadelphia Inquirer
Quirk's Reviews
Salon
Seattle Times
Slate
Time
Toledo Blade
Variety

Websites

Al's Loft
efilmcritic
Great Old Movies
The Movie Report
Official Al Pacino website
Reel Film Reviews
Reelviews
Roger Ebert
TheaterMania
Time Out
What Culture

Index

Numbers in ***bold italics*** indicate pages with photographs.

www.ingramcontent.com/pod-product-compliance
Lightning Source LLC
LaVergne TN
LVHW091143080826
845145LV00008B/2244

* 9 7 8 0 7 8 6 4 7 1 9 6 6 *